James Ryan

IT'S HARD TO BELIEVE

To my beloved Barbara, a woman
of infinite resource and compassion to
whom nothing is impossible.

James Ryan

IT'S HARD TO BELIEVE

MEREO
Cirencester

Published by Mereo

Mereo is an imprint of Memoirs Publishing

25 Market Place, Cirencester, Gloucestershire, GL7 2NX
info@memoirsbooks.co.uk www.memoirspublishing.com

It's Hard to Believe

ISBN: 978-1-86151-054-9

CONTENTS

	Author's note	
Chapter 1	Early days	Page 1
Chapter 2	Evacuation	Page 33
Chapter 3	Learning the ropes	Page 63
Chapter 4	"This is the army, Mr Ryan!"	Page 83
Chapter 5	Sailing into the unknown	Page 137
Chapter 6	England my England	Page 190
Chapter 7	Homeward Bound	Page 226
Chapter 8	A slow boat to England	Page 257
Chapter 9	Hong Kong	Page 280
Chapter 10	Hong Kong – second innings	Page 331
Chapter 11	Family matters	Page 364
Chapter 12	Testing times	Page 397

AUTHOR'S NOTE

These memoirs were primarily intended for family and friends, but as they cover events spanning the last 85 years or so they may be of interest to others. They begin with my family's hard times before the Second World War, including life as a wartime evacuee, and continue with my time in Germany as a young soldier a few years later. My life as a War Office employee after my demobilization is followed by integration into GCCQ and how we were affected during our second tour in Cyprus by the EOKA campaign and the Suez crisis. The book goes on to deal with our tours of duty in Hong Kong, which began during the 1967 civil unrest and riots. I deal with our daughter Anne's involvement with a religious cult, which caused us great distress as a family.

I have called these memoirs "It's Hard to Believe" because the way things are in the world today it is indeed hard to believe in a loving God. Nevertheless my wife Barbara and I are ardent believers. We know from experience that everything which happens in our lives is part of God's purpose for us, although we may not realize it at the time.

CHAPTER 1

EARLY DAYS

I was born on the 15th July 1928, the first of five children of James and Kathleen Ryan, and weighed in at a massive twelve pounds five ounces. My father was a merchant seaman who had met my mother, Kathleen Hastie, in Hull in 1927. He was an Irishman from County Waterford, and his father was the captain of a small coaster which plied between Liverpool and the Irish ports. The family eventually came across and settled in Liverpool.

My father went to sea at a very early age and claimed to have sailed round the Horn in a windjammer at the age of thirteen; however he was a typical Irish romancer and many of his stories had to be taken with a pinch of salt.

He joined the British Army in 1914 and in the battle of the Somme he was a sergeant in the Royal Horse Artillery. He was blown up by German artillery fire and recovered some hours later by a stretcher party, by which time he had lost a lot of blood. His leg was shattered - in fact it was almost completely severed at the calf. He was evacuated to a base hospital and his parents were sent for, as he was not expected to live. His best chance was considered to be amputation, but his father refused to give permission for this. The surgeons then did what they could with his leg and inserted a metal plate. Miraculously he survived, but he spent the rest of the war in hospitals and convalescent homes. He was awarded a war pension but later opted for a lump sum of a few hundred pounds, which was soon dissipated in typical Irish fashion.

In 1920, with a pronounced limp but otherwise able bodied, he returned to the sea, where he was to remain for most of his working life.

I never met my paternal grandparents, but as far as I know my father had three brothers. I only know that one was called Peter and another was Michael and that one of them became a New York policeman. Tom and I met his two sisters, Kate and Bridie, in Salford in 1947 while I was on leave from the army and Tom was home from the Merchant Navy.

There is no doubt about my earliest recollection, since it remains vividly in my memory to this day. This was the death in very tragic circumstances of my cousins and playmates Georgie Johnson and Kathleen Woodhouse, who died as the result of a fire in their bedroom in the house in Scarborough Street where I was born. Georgie was just four years old and Kathleen less than two. They had been left alone while their mothers, who were mother and daughter, had gone out for the evening, one to the cinema and the other to Hull Fair. Not surprisingly there was a great outcry in the national press and they were both severely censured by the coroner, who commended the policeman who had tried to save them but decreed that the mother's punishment would be telling their husbands what had happened when they returned home from sea.

This memory became even more vivid for me on the day of the funeral. I remember I had been left in the charge of a teenager called Eric and it seemed to me that there were thousands of people thronging the street with lots of police in attendance. Eric lifted me on to his shoulders as the funeral cortege went by. I was completely overawed by this, the hearse with those two little white coffins and those huge magnificent black horses drawing the carriages. I glimpsed my mother in one of the carriages and noticed how everyone was dressed in black.

Years later, when I could rationalize all this, I couldn't help but wonder where the money had come from for the black outfits, because times were very hard in those days. I can clearly remember Christmas morning 1931, as I could see a stocking hanging over one of the brass knobs at the bottom of the bed where I was sleeping. My parents were still asleep at the top end of the bed, but I have no recollection of where my younger brother Tom was at this time. I do know that wedged in the top of the stocking was a toy aeroplane and I shouted excitedly to my parents that Santa had been.

At this time we were living with my maternal great-grandmother in a small two-bedroomed house at 64 Flinton Street which was quite close to Scarborough Street. Things must have been very difficult for my parents in those days with young children and no home of their own, but like lots of others at that time they managed somehow.

My great grandmother was a real character. She had been widowed twice and had borne thirteen children. I'm not sure how many of them survived, but she seemed to favour Irish husbands as her first was called Connor and her second Dillon. I don't know how they met their demise, but it was probably during the Great War. At the time I was living with my great-grandmother, and there was a boy across the street called Martin Pattison. He was at least a year older than me and was in the habit of bullying me. My great-grandmother remonstrated with the boy's mother, but to no avail and the bullying continued.

Shortly after this I can remember my great-grandmother taking me with her to draw her old age pension and then on to a shoe shop in Hessle Road to buy me a new pair of sturdy boots. When we returned home to Flinton Street she laced them up for me and I was instructed to go across to where Martin was playing and kick him on the shins several times. To my eternal shame this is exactly what I did. I must have really hurt him as he wept profusely, but strangely enough he never bothered me again!

I have quite a few memories our stay in Flinton Street, for it was there that I acquired my first ambition of what I wanted to be when I grew up. I used to watch fascinated as the lamplighter came around lighting up the street lights one after another with his long stick and thought what a wonderful job it must be. I dreamed of doing it myself one day. I also remember seeing my father draw up outside our house in a taxi from which he proceeded to unload what appeared to be a large cabinet which was laid across the back seat. The explanation was simple; his ship had just returned from a trip to the USA. (which was in the middle of the great depression following the Wall Street Crash), there he had purchased a large gramophone. The instrument came complete with a large supply of records and needles which he had bought for a ridiculously small sum in New York. I don't know if it was intended for us or if my father had intended to sell it, but it was soon transferred to my grandmother's house. Later on when I went to live with her, I had hours of enjoyment winding it up and listening to it.

While we lived in Flinton Street I have clear recollections of waking most mornings to the sound of fishworkers' clogs striking the pavement. These sounds were augmented by the noise of the horses and carts clattering past on their way to the nearby fish docks.

In September 1932 my sister Thora was born. At this time Grandmother Hastie was running a small general store in Welstead Street, also off Hessle Road, and this was where I saw my sister for the first time. Things must have been very awkward for my parents during this period living with three young children and my great grandmother in that small house, especially when my father was home from sea.

In July 1933, when I was five, it was decided that I would go and live with Grandma Hastie, who was by this time living at 66 Campbell Street, also off Hessle Road. This was to ease some of the congestion at Flinton Street and enable me to attend a nearby school in Villa Place. I had no objections to this and was for same reason very eager to start school. On our way to enrol me at Villa Place I recall running along in front of Mum and Dad, who were pushing a pram with Tom and Thora in it.

I went to live at Campbell Street after my first day at school. I took to school like a duck to water and thoroughly enjoyed it. I was very happy at my grandma's but used to go home to Flinton Street most weekends. In this modern age it is probably hard to believe that I used to travel unaccompanied on a tram along Hessle Road at five years of age, but I assure you, it is true!

Following the death of my grandad, my grandmother had taken in a lodger to help make ends meet. He was called Harry Stamford, and he became quite an important factor in my young life. He treated me as a grown up and never tired of answering my endless questions about anything and everything. As the second engineer on a coaster called the SS Gowrie he plied between Hull and Dundee, usually on a weekly basis. Most Sundays his ship would tie up at the same berth at Prince's Dock and I often walked down to meet him. This of course was dependent on the ship docking at a reasonable hour according to the tide times.

Sometimes I was allowed to go aboard and would walk home with Pop, as the family was calling him by this time. I really enjoyed these times and looked forward to the day when I could embark on a seafaring career. It was during this period that Grandma Hastie married Pop and thus became Grandma Stamford.

Shortly after this my Aunt Thora, who was one of my mother's younger sisters, met a ship's steward called Harry Clappison and within a few months they were married and living with us at 66 Campbell Street. A few months later their first baby, Barbara, was born. As was the custom in those days the mother was confined to bed for several days after the birth, indeed having a baby was known as a confinement.

One night a few nights after the baby was born I was left alone in the house with Aunt Thora and the baby while Grandma and Pop were a few hundred yards down the street at a public house called the Rising Sun. Our house was lit by gas, which was controlled by a coin meter. That evening the gas ran out and we were completely in the dark. Aunt Thora, who was in the front bedroom with the baby, gave me a coin to put in the metre, which I did; I then made a spill out of newspaper, lit it from the coal fire and climbed up the table to light the gas mantle. As I did so I touched the lace curtain and it went up in flames. I shouted up to Aunt Thora "I've set the house on fire and I'm running to bring Grandma and Pop!" I ran like a deer to the pub, burst into the room and told them what was happening. Grandma, Pop and several other people dashed back with us to see if they could help. We arrived back to find Aunt Thora with the baby under one arm, flinging water from a saucepan up at the curtains and the smouldering woodwork. It could so easily have been another tragedy, and at the tender age of six it taught me a lesson I have never forgotten.

I felt loved and well looked after at Grandma's, but I was not very well supervised and I often roamed the streets with my friends. I especially recall the General Election in 1934, when I went round the streets with crowds of other youngsters singing:

Vote, vote, vote for Mr Banham
You can't vote for a better man
Mr Banham is the man
And we'll have him if we can
And we'll throw all the others in the dock
At ten o'clock, without a shot [shirt].

This was to the tune of 'Tramp, tramp, tramp, the boys are marching'. I believe Mr Banham was elected, but I couldn't say which party he represented.

I used to attend Sunday School, but only on an

irregular basis, and my understanding of God was that he would repay out wrongdoings with a vengeance. There were quite a few crucifixes around the grandma's house, since their background was that of lapsed Catholics, who only attended church when some crisis or catastrophe hit their lives. In my bedroom opposite my bed was Christ on the cross and I used to lie in bed afraid to look at it, because I had been told that Jesus knew every wrong thing I had done. How foolish it seems no to have lain there with my head under the covers sweating profusely and expecting to be struck down for all the sins I had committed that day.

Apart from difficulties in getting to sleep at night, I was quite happy at my grandma's and used to look forward to my mother's sisters Lilian and Ethel coming home on their days off from the Wheatsheaf, a pub-cum-hotel at Kirkella where they lived and worked.

When my brother Terry was born he was an angelic-looking child with flaxen hair and rosy cheeks. His arrival made it well nigh impossible for Mum and Dad to continue living with my great grandma in Flinton Street. They decided to rent a small house in Pleasant Place, which was part of a group of terraced houses in Goodwin Street. It had two rooms and a kitchen downstairs and two bedrooms plus an attic upstairs. They then decided I could return home. Fortunately the other end of Goodwin Street went straight up to the back entrance of Villa Place School, where shortly afterwards my brother Tom began his studies.

In Pleasant Place our next-door neighbours were my mother's older sister Evelyn and her husband Ernie Davis. They had four daughters, Jean, Audrey, Eileen and Grace, though later they had a little boy who they called Ernie after his father. Uncle Ernie was a giant of a man at six foot four who worked as a 'bobber', unloading fish from trawlers. He earned the princely sum of eighteen shillings and sixpence a day for five or six days a week, so they were considered affluent.

During our time at Pleasant Place my father was often at sea for several months at a time and of course he was frequently between ships, so things were hard for my parents. We usually had enough to eat, but like all active, growing children we were always hungry. Our clothes and footwear were basic and well darned, but we always went to school clean and tidy. I was beginning to enjoy school immensely, and when I was eight years old I moved into a class with a teacher called Miss Boon. I soaked up knowledge like a sponge and couldn't get enough books to read, though I must admit I also enjoyed comics and weekly boys' adventure magazines like *Wizard* and *Hotspur*.

During this period my Aunt Thora had another baby, a boy called Harry after his father, who unfortunately had been out of a ship practically ever since they had been married. They now lived in Neptune Street, also off Hessle Road, and right next door to my grandma, who had moved from Campbell Street. Thora was now ill with TB, no doubt exacerbated by having to care for a husband and two young children with very little money and having to go hungry herself, as many women did in these circumstances. Funnily enough, even in these dire straits many families considered cigarettes for the man of the household to be essential!

Even to my young eyes it was obvious that my aunt was deteriorating rapidly. On at least two occasions I had to travel on the tram on her behalf to leave tiny parcels at Hull Royal Infirmary labelled as 'specimens for Dr Edy'. Tom and I would frequently come home from school to find that there was no one in, so we would help ourselves to bread and jam if there was any, and then go out to play until Mum returned with Tom and Terry in the pram. Needless to say we regularly got up to mischief and roamed the streets. We didn't realise that everyone knew Aunt Thora was dying and were trying to be with her as much as possible and to make things easy for her in her last months.

One of my friends was a lad called Joss Whitfield, who also lived in Goodwin Street. He was probably a couple of years older than me, very streetwise and possibly a bad influence. Tom was always tagging along with us, but we would give him the slip whenever we could and head across Anlaby Road into Park Street. If no one was watching us, we would climb up on to a three-foot wide parapet to watch the trains forty or fifty feet below. Passenger trains went in and out of Paragon Station and innumerable goods trains passed in both directions, as it was a very busy junction. Fortunately we never had an accident, although just thinking about it now gives me vertigo! From our vantage point we usually climbed down and carried on along Park Street to Corporation Field, a large outdoor marketplace.

During the summer of 1936 slogans and posters began to appear saying 'Down with the Fascists', 'Drive Mosley out of Hull' and the like. This led to a late summer evening confrontation which developed into a pitched battle between the Blackshirts, incited Sir Oswald Mosley, and a large anti-fascist crowd. Also in attendance was large contingent of police officers who were trying to restore law and order, and obviously had little sympathy for the Blackshirts. I wasn't there as Mum was home that evening, but I heard a first-hand account from my friend Joss and read every word in the next day's Hull Daily Mail about the 'Battle of Corporation Field'.

Several of us, including my brother Tom, used to meet in the cellar of a shop in the Porter Street area which was being demolished. We used to light candles or smoke-sticks of cinnamon and discuss our next exploit. These adventures came to an abrupt end when we accidentally set the cellar on fire. We tried unsuccessfully to put it out, but when it was out of control we ran off as fast as we could, returning half an hour later to watch the firemen put out the flames!

On the odd occasion in the summer would put us to bed early and go out, leaving me nominally in charge, although in bed. On one such evening Tom and I looked through the window to see some children playing. We dressed, grabs out whips and tops and went out to join them. We thoroughly enjoyed ourselves until darkness fell, when we went home, got undressed and got back into bed as fast as possible. We decided it was too risky to try again!

One day Mum came home looking very miserable and told us Aunt Thora had died. We were sad, but we had been expecting it. The funeral was held while I was at school, so I have no memory of the event.

By the time I was about nine years old I had an agreement with Grandma Stamford. I would run any errands she needed, and each week she would give me sixpence pocket money. I would use some of the money to treat my brother Tom to what we called the 'tuppenny rush' at the nearby Playhouse Cinema on Saturday mornings. It was usually a mixed programme of silent films and movies featuring such stars as Charlie Chaplin, Buster Keaton and Laurel and Hardy as well as the cowboy heroes Tom Mix, Gene Autry and Ken Maynard. The show usually incorporated an exciting episode of a serial such as *The Clutching Hand*, *Flash Gordon's Trip to Mars* or *Tailspin Tommy*, an air adventure.

Another Saturday morning errand was paying the rent, which was six shillings and threepence a week. It had to be taken to an officer in the old part of Hull, quaintly named 'Land of Green Ginger'.

Shortly before Aunt Thora died, Grandma Stamford

had moved yet again, to an address which was supposed to be kept secret from, us. After a few months we discovered that it was in Regent Street, which ran between Hessle Road and Anlaby Road. The house had a bathroom complete with toilet – a great luxury in your eyes, accustomed as we were to bathing in a tin bath in front of the fire once a week, plus the usual outside WC (water closet). I may be wrong but in retrospect, I can't help but believe that many of our moves, in particular my grandma's, were moonlight flits, carried out because they were unable to keep up with the rent.

My father was often at sea for several months at a time. When he landed and was paid off, there was usually plenty of money for a week or two, which meant there would be long sessions at whichever public house was in vogue at the time. There was never any question of saving for a rainy day. When my father signed on a new ship he followed the common practice of asking for an 'advance note' which was usually cashed by a friendly pub landlord. The cheque was a loan against any overtime a crew member would carry out on the coming voyage and it would be deducted from the total due to him at the end of the trip. This meant most of the crew were in debt before they even set sail.

Dad was an infrequent letter-writer, so while he was away Mum would often send me down to the relevant shipping company to ascertain the ship's last port of call and subsequent destination. We had a fright one evening when the headline in the evening paper read 'Hull ship's tragic voyage'. Four men had died on the SS Atlantic during a trip from North Africa to the UK. One of the dead sailors was called James Bryan, so there was some confusion until we learned that he was safe.

Generally speaking the pattern of our lives during the depression was this: whenever anyone, friend or family, was paid off at the end of a voyage, or as a fisherman had a good catch of fish, there would be a 'bit of a do'. Friends and family would embark on a session at their favourite public house, which usually lasted from opening time around 11 am until three in the afternoon. At the end of the session crates of bottled beer and a few bottles of mineral water would be carried to whichever house had been volunteered for the 'do'. As the revellers relaxed they nearly all took turns at performing their party pieces, usually a song or a recitation. Homes with pianos were favoured, and as Grandma Stanford had one, her house was often chosen. If my father was home he would recite 'The Face on the Bar-Room Floor' or 'Dangerous Dan McGrew'. Children were expected to contribute too, and I was often called upon to recite Rudyard Kipling's 'Big Steamers'. After such an occasion we children enjoyed a lucrative trade in returning empty bottles, which attracted a penny deposit.

I continued to do well at school and was told by Miss Boon that I had a good chance of obtaining a scholarship to one of the Hull Grammar schools. Even at that age I was realistic enough to know that a good education was an open sesame to a much better standard of living. It was about this time that I began saying my prayers to God every night, bargaining with him that if he allowed me to pass my scholarship I would be good, which I knew wouldn't be easy!

Our next move was from Pleasant Place to Staniforth Place, yet again off Hessle Road – in fact it was still quite close to Villa Place, so it still took only a few minutes to walk to school. This was another two up, two down with a tiny backyard, an outside toilet, but without the benefit of an attic. The rent was I believe at least a shilling a week cheaper, and a shilling was a lot of money to people in our circumstances.

Not long after we had moved into Staniforth Place my father signed on a ship in Hull and sailed off. About a fortnight later he walked through the door looking terrible, with several days' growth of beard. Along with another shipmate, he had jumped ship in London as a protest against bad food and appalling conditions and they had walked most of the way from London to Hull, as his worn-out shoes testified.

This put my parents in a terrible dilemma. My father had already received an advance against any overtime he might have earned on the voyage and the allocation of about thirty shillings which was paid to his wife on a weekly basis while he was away was not going to be forthcoming. In fact he owed the shipping company money. With four children to support, the only option they had was to go 'on the parish' which meant being subject to a means test in order to qualify for a weekly handout of a selection of essential groceries, and, I believe, enough money to pay the rent.

I'm not sure how many weeks this lasted, but times were hard and we were often hungry. Dad was eventually reinstated on the dole, but was blacklisted for leaving his ship and consequently found it difficult to find another.

A few months after we moved into Staniforth Place my Great Aunt Ada and her husband George moved into a house only a couple of doors away. This was the mother of my cousin Georgie, who had perished so tragically about seven years

previously. They now had another son called Joey, who was about five years old. The move had obviously been due for financial reasons, because Uncle George was a merchant seaman like my father but had been out of a ship for a couple of years. They had moved from a larger house in Day Street, which ran parallel to Campbell Street.

While we were living there both Terry and Thora caught whooping cough, and as it was highly contagious Tom and I were not allowed to attend school for six weeks. It was extremely distressing to watch Terry and Thora during their paroxysms of coughing. Sometimes they lost their breath and went blue in the face. One way to make them breathe again was to throw them up in the air and catch them - this usually worked!

Twice during this period Tom and I were accosted

in the street by the School Board man, who wanted to know which school we attended and why we were not there. He rode a bike and wore a black suit and a bowler hat, and to us he was quite a forbidding figure.

Another recollection I have is of the airship the Hindenburg sailing slowly and majestically over Hull in the middle of the afternoon en route from Germany to the USA. Shortly afterwards it exploded and caught fire while coming into land in New Jersey. It does not require much imagination to believe that the Hindenburg was also taking photographs of the extensive docks and oil storage installations in the area, which could be invaluable in the event of the war which was appearing more and more likely.

I can also vividly recall a biplane which flew over and around Hull for about a week at regular intervals towing a large advertising windsock, which read, 'Mine's a Minor, De Reske of course, a ten minute smoke at ten for sixpence". I don't think that particular brand long survived the war.

Eventually my father managed to get a job on one of the 'O' boats, so called because their names all ended with the letter 'o'. They were part of Ellerman's Wilson line and made a regular ten-day round voyage between Hull and the Scandinavian ports. This made things a little easier financially. One of our favourite meals at this time was corned beef hash, which my mother could produce for sixpence - two pence for a quarter of a stone of potatoes, two pence for about six ounces of sliced corned beef and two pence for a few carrots and an onion. We all adored it.

Our diet mainly consisted of bread and jam, bread and dripping or bread and margarine. A sheep's head or a few bones from the butcher were converted into a nourishing stew with the aid of a few vegetables. Rabbit pie or rabbit stew was considered a great delicacy. I'm sure that most children in our circumstances ate all that was put before them.

It is difficult to imagine, but even in the hard times of the 1930s there was class distinction among the unemployed. The overwhelming majority of unemployed manual workers wore a flat cap and a white silk scarf. Unemployed fishermen occasionally wore this garb, but unemployed merchant seamen never did - it was beneath their dignity. Despite all the unemployment and deprivation, the public houses always seemed to be prospering and even out of a meagre dole allowance the men always seemed to manage to have enough money for their pint of beer and the inevitable cigarettes, which could be Woodbines or hand-rolled with tobacco and papers.

My father was a qualified bosun, but he often had to sign on a ship as an AB (able bodied seaman). Wages were at rock bottom. As a bosun my father earned

£10 per month, out of which he allotted £8 per month to my mother. As an AB he earned £8 per month and gave £6 to my mother. In money terms he was better off on the dole, but while he was at sea his food was provided and he had the chance to earn overtime.

One Saturday evening in Staniforth Place, we children were in bed and Aunt Ada was in our house talking to my mother. Suddenly there was a loud hammering at our front door. They opened it to be confronted by the man from the house opposite, who was obviously drunk. He was raving and ranting about his wife and children being ostracised by the rest of the terrace. He grabbed hold of my aunt by the hair and proceeded to swing her round and round. My father and Uncle George were both at sea, so there was no one to help. My mother shouted to me to run down the road as fast as I could and bring a policeman, but I didn't see one until I approached West Dock Avenue. I blurted out my tale and tried to persuade him to run back with me. He walked fast, but it just wasn't quick enough for me as I was sure that lives were in danger. The policeman arrested the man and thanks to the timely intervention of a couple of young men who lived nearby, my mother and aunt were not too badly hurt.

A few weeks after this the headlines in the *Hull Daily Mail* announced "Notorious Cat Burglar sentenced to three years imprisonment for a string of robberies going back several years' and this, believe it or not, was the same man who had assaulted my mother and aunt only a couple of months previously.

While we were in Staniforth Place the day arrived for me to sit for my scholarship exam. I had to attend a school in Osborne Street for a day - the regular pupils had been given the day off. I considered I had done quite well in the exam, but wasn't really sure I had passed.

That night when I went to bed I commenced an all-out bargaining session with God and promised to be good for the rest of my life as long as he would let me pass my scholarship. I kept up this incessant barrage every night for the next six months.

One day my Great Uncle Jim and Aunt Annie appeared at our house in Staniforth Place, both looking very upset. Uncle Jim was Grandma Dillon's youngest son and Keith was the youngest of thirteen children and was still a baby. They had been visiting Keith in hospital, and told us he had scarlet fever and was not expected to survive. A couple of days later they called again to tell us that Keith had just died.

In the autumn of 1938 war clouds were gathering and no one seemed convinced by Mr Chamberlain's piece of paper when he returned from his Munich meeting with Hitler and declared that he had secured "peace in our time". Despite this declaration Britain had awoken to the fact that she needed to rearm, and as quickly as possible.

Our next house move must I think have been a moonlight flit because of accumulated rent arrears, and it is printed indelibly on my mind for several reasons. We moved on November 5th 1938 into a terraced house in St Paul's street, which was off Beverly Road and a long way from home as far as I was concerned. The house was only two doors away from my Great Uncle George Dillon, who was Grandma Dillon's second youngest living son. Thus the pattern of living close to relatives was maintained. Dad hired a handcart which cost a shilling and had to be returned before five in the evening. We proceeded to load it with as many household possessions as we could, and Dad and I set off pushing the now very heavy handcart a distance of at least two miles. On arrival we unloaded it in an almost identical terraced house with the same amenities as Staniforth Place.

We returned for a second load and cleared the rest of the house. That was the sum total of our possessions in those days – two handcart loads!

Dad then had to return the handcart, and I think I waited at the new house while the rest of the family made the journey with the pram.

I now had the problem of a long walk to school in all weathers, but I had no intention of leaving Villa Place until the scholarship result was known; it was due to be announced some time in May 1939.

Tom and Thora started at new schools nearby, but I was happy at Villa Place and was determined to stay there because I had some good friends in my class. One of them was a boy called Albert Weatherill, who lived only a minute from the school. Albert's sister was married to a fisherman and lived next door. His parents kindly let me eat my lunchtime sandwiches at his house and always gave me a cup of tea or something to drink with them. They seemed to be a loving and close-knit family, but I was shocked by the stream of foul language which came from them all, including the sister, who I think was called Vi. My parents swore, but only mildly, and for some reason I hated swearing.

Friends in my class included Robert Anderson, Robert Hudson, Johnny Flocton and Philip Chester, whose parents owned a nearby public house but had been interned on the Isle of Man at the outbreak of the war. Girls I can remember include Moira Atkinson, Joan Oakes and Doreen Pinder, who was considered to have a good chance of passing her scholarship.

Schools in the Hull area always had their summer holidays foreshortened by a week to allow for the week off they always had in early October to attend Hull Fair. The fair was held on a large playing field off Walton Street, which was on Anlaby Road. To us children it was a wondrous affair and we looked forward to it almost as eagerly as Christmas, since it incorporated every imaginable thing you can associate with fairs. It rivalled Nottingham Goose Fair as the biggest in the country. There were not one but several circuses, all on the same site; the Wall of Death; the Helter Skelter; the Bearded Lady; the world's largest rat; the smallest woman alongside the largest man, and freaks and sideshows galore. Even if you had no money, you had to go and look around. I never tired of walking around it.

I remember Christmas 1938 as being one when we had very little of value in our stockings. This was not really surprising in our circumstances. Although I was ten years old and no longer a believer in Father Christmas, I was still a little disgruntled at the contents of my stocking. I didn't take into consideration the fact that there were three other stockings to fill.

Slowly the time approached for the scholarship results and I was as diligent as ever in my dialogue with God. I always dealt with God, as I considered Jesus to be subordinate to him. I was also worried that because we had moved house the notification might go astray and not reach our new address, but my teacher Miss Boon assured me that it would.

One day in early May the fateful letter arrived before I left for school. Needless to say I was overjoyed, but very aware of how difficult it might become to keep my promises and keep to the straight and narrow. I had been awarded a place at Kingston High School, a recently completed and prestigious school on the outskirts of Hull. Though my parents congratulated me I sensed that there was something not quite right. I soon realised what the problem was; no money to provide for school uniform, satchel, PE kit etc. Every pupil was expected to have all the requisite items and unlike an ordinary school, you couldn't make do. There were grants and allowances to help pupils whose parents were unable to afford things, but this help had to be applied for. To my parents it was like going on the parish again, and though I continued to ask what was happening about my school uniform I always received evasive replies.

Two other people in my class, Robert Hudson and Doreen Pinder, had also been awarded places and we naturally enjoyed talking about our new schools and what we knew and had heard about them. The anticipation was wonderful.

One evening in early June I had just walked home from school when I saw a man getting into a car at the end of our terrace. It turned out to be a doctor who had just visited our house. My father was in the scullery running water over bloodstained sheets. My brothers and sister were being looked after by neighbours. My mother had suffered a massive haemorrhage as a result of a stomach ulcer which had plagued her for several years. She was very ill and they were trying to find her a place in hospital. My father gave me a sealed envelope containing a note he had written, and he told me I had to take it to my mother's youngest sister, Aunt Ethel, who (following yet another flit by her mother) was living with Grandma Stamford in Perry Street off Anlaby Road, opposite the main gates to West Park.

This was three miles away, so I was pretty tired by the time I arrived. From outside the house I could hear piano playing and singing; there was clearly a "do" in full swing. It appeared that Ted Thomas, a young merchant seaman who was sweet on Aunt Ethel, had just returned from a long voyage, and was celebrating in accordance with the custom described previously. No one took much notice of me, but when Aunt Ethel read Dad's note she immediately grabbed her coat and told me to come with her. When we reached the park she went into the telephone kiosk and rang for a taxi. One arrived within a few minutes, and I must admit it was most welcome to me as I was really tired.

Aunt Ethel helped my father to sort things out and put the younger ones to bed. I looked in to say goodnight to Mum before I went to bed and she really did look terrible. The next day an ambulance came for her and she was taken into hospital, listed as seriously ill.

This began a period of limbo for me. I continued to make my daily trek to Villa Place, but I knew my future was no longer assured and began to wonder why. Had I done something wrong and not kept my bargain with God? I never mentioned Kingston High, because I knew Dad had enough on his plate looking after us and trying to see Mum as often as possible. She was still very poorly but had improved.

Early in July, not long before schools broke up for the summer holidays, my father at last managed to find a ship. If I remember rightly it was a coaster called the *Gurkha*. As she wasn't due to sail for two or three weeks, he began what was known as 'working by his ship', in other words undertaking jobs which needed doing before she was considered fit for a Board of Trade seaworthiness certificate. Thora and Terry went to stay with Grandma Stamford in Perry Street, but Tom and I stayed in St Paul's street. Dad nearly always came home in the evening to make us a meal before he went to visit Mum, but we were left to our own devices more and more, especially when we were no longer at school.

That seemed an endless summer to me, especially since I had little or no supervision. I would go fishing with a big jam jar and a bent pin tied to a piece of string attached to a stick. I got worms from any nearby piece of waste ground or garden and would callously break them in half before putting one half on the hook. The place we fished was a small river-cum-drain which was only about ten minutes walk away. I caught dozens and dozens of sticklebacks, put them in my jar and wondered why they died. I certainly wasn't keeping my side of the bargain, because at a time when I should have been responsible and looking after Tom I was always trying to give him the slip and go off on my own whenever possible.

One evening Dad came in late, and he had obviously been drinking. He came upstairs and made Tom and me get out of bed and kneel down with him. Then he insisted that we repeat after him a whole litany of Catholic prayers that Mum would recover. Even though it was Mum we were praying for, I hated it and felt humiliated.

While fishing during those seemingly endless days of August I used to sit and muse about what was going to happen to us all. I knew we had given our support to Poland and stated that if Hitler attacked her it would be the same as if he had attacked us and we would come to Poland's assistance. There was a strong belief that Germany would commence a war against us with all-out bombing attacks on all our major cities and ports.

Plans for the evacuation of women and children from these places had long since been drawn up.

Everyone was amazed when on the 23rd of August the Germans signed a pact with Russia when they were thought to be sworn enemies. Britain then called up all her reservists and the ARP services were warned to stand ready. In the early hours of September 1st German troops moved into Poland, and by six o'clock that morning Warsaw was being bombed. On that same day the official evacuation of mothers, children and disabled people from London and other major towns began.

That evening Dad, who was still 'working by' his ship, came home and told Tom and me to pack a few things and go round to Grandma Stamford's as quickly as possible, as his ship was ready for sea and expected to sail at any time. When we arrived at Grandma's house we were overjoyed to see Mum there. She wasn't really well, but she looked much better and we hadn't seen her for several weeks. All hospitals throughout the country had been ordered to discharge all patients other than the terminally ill.

There had been several family discussions as to what we would do if war was declared, and it had been unanimously agreed that we would all go across the river to Grimsby and stay with Aunt Minnie and Uncle Charlie Wilding, who had a reasonably large house in Hainton Avenue.

When we heard Mr Chamberlain's momentous words on the Sunday morning, we all felt a deep sense of foreboding and made our last-minute preparations to catch the ferry and train to Grimsby. About half an hour after the declaration of war the air raid warning sirens sounded and we thought our worst fears were going to be realised. Fortunately it was a false alarm and we continued with our preparations.

A telegram was sent to Aunt Minnie telling her what time we would be arriving and we locked the house and headed for the ferry at Corporation Pier. It was called the *Wingfield Castle*, and it was crowded, as was the train at New Holland, but to us children it was an adventure and we didn't mind standing.

When we arrived at Grimsby Docks Station Aunt Minnie was there waiting to meet us and we proceeded to catch a wonderful-looking trolley bus which deposited us right outside 337 Hainton Avenue, tired but thankful.

Thus began the period which was called the "Phoney War" because for several months very little happened. In no time Hitler and Stalin had gobbled up Poland between them, but on the potential battlefields of France and in the air very little was happening; the expected wholesale bombing had not materialised and here we were with seventeen people in one house. Our sleeping arrangements inevitably meant children had to sleep sometimes five or six to a bed utilising top and bottom, and food preparation and washing up was a never-ending task. Aunt Minnie was one of Grandma Stamford's sisters and Uncle Charlie, who had been a merchant seaman, was now chief engineer on a trawler fishing out of Grimsby.

The first thing he did when he came home from sea was to start digging out the garden for an Anderson air raid shelter. These shelters had been delivered to all the houses in the area with enough space to erect one. After about three days' hard work it was duly assembled, but I couldn't help wondering how seventeen of us were going to fit into it. 1 can remember going with Mum to a church hall in Welsby Road to get our ration books and National Registration numbers for our identity cards, and I can still recall that my number commenced with TKCJ 219... 13 which indicated that I was the thirteenth in age order of the people registered in our household.

For the first couple of weeks of the war all schools were closed, but one day there was a knock at the door and a couple of men explained that they were teachers from the nearby Welholme School. They were looking for people with reasonable-sized front rooms who were willing to let them start lessons again for anyone who was interested. Aunt Minnie was very altruistic and agreed straight away, so I started having home tuition, along with several other boys. This only lasted for a couple of weeks until the schools reopened and I was enrolled as a pupil at Welholme Avenue.

About a week later a letter arrived from Hull Education Authority saying that if I didn't take up my place at Kingston High within the next four weeks my place would be awarded to someone else. I knew it was a waste of time and didn't even ask my parents. Ironically, after about six weeks we all returned to Hull, to a terraced house in Laurel Grove, off Perry Street and very close to Grandma Stamford's house.

Dad was still at sea somewhere. Ships' movements were now secret in line with the posters plastered on the billboards which read "Careless Talk Costs Lives", and "Be Like Dad, Keep Mum".

My next school was The Boulevard, which was in a large tree-lined street which bridged Anlaby Road and Hessle Road. Strangely enough it was the forerunner of Kingston High and its pupils had transferred there, but it was now a senior school for boys. I soon settled in and began to enjoy my schoolwork once again.

The war was continuing with very little happening when a bombshell of another kind hit me. Mum told me she was expecting another baby and would be relying on me to give her all the help I could with the other children. I don't think I was very pleased, but I adored my mother and would do anything for her. I knew there had been many times in the past when she had gone short of food herself so that we could have more. It was a minor miracle that she was still pregnant when you consider she had been at death's door with that massive haemorrhage at the earliest stage.

My sister Valerie was born on the 27th January 1940, at Aunt Minnie's in Grimsby. It was bitterly cold with large amounts of pack ice floating around in the

Humber and crashing against the sides of the ferry. I made the trip to Grimsby several times to carry out errands for Mum or Grandma Stamford as it was cheaper for me.

CHAPTER 2

EVACUATION

Pop Stamford was still making his weekly trip between Hull and Dundee when the Phoney War for him came to a sudden end. The *Gowrie* was bombed and machine-gunned in the North Sea just off Newcastle. The boilers burst and they had to abandon ship. Several of the crew, including Pop, were thrown into the icy sea; they were all rescued, but Pop was never fit enough to go back to sea.

At about this time the Hull area began to be the target of minor sorties by the Luftwaffe. We didn't have a garden shelter in Laurel Grove, so whenever the warnings sounded we would make our way as quickly as possible to the large communal shelters near the entrance to West Park a couple of hundred yards away. I believe the rule was that if there was an air raid warning and the all-clear didn't sound until after three in the morning, we didn't have to attend school the next day. If it sounded before three we didn't attend until the afternoon. This was quite a novelty at first, but when there were several alerts in one night, trekking backwards and forwards to the shelters began to pall.

There was a real community spirit in those times. and people often shared food, drinks or sweets, even though the latter were becoming very scarce, despite not having yet been officially rationed. We knew London was now beginning to be bombed and fresh evacuation plans for schoolchildren were being discussed. Eventually Mum reluctantly agreed that we children should be evacuated while she and baby Valerie would stay behind in Hull. I had heard and read all about the German's speedy advance through France and the Low Countries but considered the evacuation of our routed forces from Dunkirk as a major victory.

In August 1940 we were told to be ready at 24 hours' notice, and a few days later we queued up to board buses to take us to Paragon Station to catch trains to unknown destinations. In a way it was quite exciting, but we must have looked a bewildered and motley crowd with the few clothes we possessed in small cases or more often in carrier bags. Everyone carried a gas mask in a cardboard box with string loops from the corners. We also had identity tags round our necks.

Aunt Ethel came to see Tom and me off on our bus, as Mum had gone to another place to see Thora and Terry safely away. When I think about this now I can't help but think how traumatic it must have been for them. Thora was not quite eight and Terry just six years old. We had a few teachers and grown-up volunteers with our parties. After what seemed an age our train puffed away and we all tried to imagine just where we were going to end up.

After hours of travelling we pulled into a station. All the names of stations had been removed throughout the country so that any German paratroops would not know where they had landed. We alighted from our train to be met by more buses waiting to take us to what turned out to be our final destination, which was the village of Middleton on the Wolds. Our train had brought us to Driffield Station and we had travelled eight miles by bus to Middleton. We had been travelling most of the day yet the actual distance from Hull to Middleton was about eighteen miles and we could have been transported direct in our original buses in about an hour. I suppose the plan was to keep the enemy guessing about our movements.

We all filed into the village school, where we were given sandwiches and lemonade, and then we had to go to a desk to be checked and documented. I kept a close watch on Tom, as Mum had instructed me that we had to stay together no matter what happened.

Shortly after this, local people began to arrive and began to look us over, checking our clothes and seeing how presentable we looked. Any notions Tom and I had nurtured of going to live on a farm soon came to naught, because the farmers selected only the big strapping lads and we were quite small. A process of selection continued for at least a couple of hours, until there were just ten of us left. This included two other sets of brothers, the policy being not to separate brothers or sisters if possible.

There was still one teacher left with us, Mr Dakin from our school, who was accompanied by his wife, a volunteer helper. The Billeting Officer turned out to be Mr Hogarth, the headmaster of the village school. With him in the lead we all followed in twos, carrying our carrier bags and gas masks, while Mr and Mrs Dakin brought up the rear. We turned right at the village pond and continued for the best part of a mile, the last quarter of which had an eight-foot high brick wall to our right. This was the outer boundary of a mature wooded area. The road continued at a gentle slope until we came to an entrance set in the wall. The metal gates which should have been there, like gates ands railings all over the country, had been removed to be melted down to make weapons for the war effort.

By the time we followed Mr Hogarth round to the left through an arched stone gate into a courtyard of shingle-type stones our feet were dragging a little. We congregated around the back door of what appeared to be an enormous house. Mr Hogarth rang the bell and a lady came to the door. She stared at us and said to Mr Hogarth, "Hoo many have ye got here?"

This was our introduction to the formidable Miss McKellar, the housekeeper at Middleton Hall. We followed two uniformed maids through the servants' quarters to a large room with a sign saying 'BILLIARD

ROOM' on the door. The billiard table had been removed and replaced with an exceptionally large dining table, and there were many chairs dotted around the perimeter. This was to be our dining and living room. It contained a large French window which looked out on to a magnificent lawn. We asked the maids, Nancy and Dorothy, if we could go out on to the lawn. They said we could and opened the French window, and we all ran excitedly out on to the grass.

The lawn extended out from the house to a deep, grassy ditch, at the top of which stretched a single strand of barbed wire supported by posts at strategic intervals. Beyond the ditch was a vast expanse of green field surrounded by woods, and we could see lots of black and white cows grazing in the distance. We didn't venture into the field, partly because we thought the wire might be electrified to stop the cows coming on the lawns.

The lawn stretched from the front of the house for about a quarter of a mile towards another lawn with trees and a large fishpond. This in turn led to a gate which opened into the adjoining woods. We were all beginning to think how marvellous it seemed when we were called in to wash our hands and sit down for something to eat. This proved to be sandwiches of some kind, and we sat down at the enormous table and devoured them with gusto.

After we had eaten, Miss McKellar came through with Mr and Mrs Dakin and began to explain the dos and don'ts and where we could and couldn't go. She told us that Middleton Hall was one of the country residences of Sir William and Lady Prince-Smith and that they had another residence at Southburn, about eight miles away. They normally lived at Keighley in West Yorkshire, where they had manufacturing interests. We were to address them as 'Sir William' and 'Milady'. They had a 12-year-old son whom we should address as 'Master Richard' and a daughter of ten who was to be 'Miss Claire'. They explained further that for the time being we would be looked after by Miss McKellar and the maids with assistance from Mr and Mrs Dakin until another housekeeper or foster mother arrived.

We were then shown our sleeping quarters on the top floor. There was quite a large bathroom where we all had baths, several of us at the same time, then cleaned our teeth and flopped thankfully into bed.

I don't think any of us had trouble sleeping that first night. That night I prayed that Thora and Terry had been allowed to stay together and had found a good billet, that Mum and Valerie were safe and that Dad would come home safe and sound.

That first week we generally ate plain fare, but occasionally there were rather more exotic dishes on offer such as jugged hare or pheasant. I quite liked these dishes, but funnily enough not many of the other boys did.

During the second week Mr Lodge, the Area Billeting Officer, turned up in his car accompanied by a Mrs Crawford, who was going to be employed to look after us. The next day a young girl from the village called

Iris Bell arrived - she was to be Mrs Crawford's assistant. And so a new régime commenced. We were allocated the boiler room which provided the hot water and central heating as our kitchen. It included a large sink and cooking stove, so it was quite adequate for the purpose. Mrs Crawford soon drew up rosters for setting the table and peeling the potatoes every evening. We didn't mind peeling them, but scraping the new ones when it was such a huge pan seemed to take forever.

The original contingent of evacuees consisted of three sets of brothers, Tom and me, Jack and Frank Mould (Frank was known as 'Squeak'), and Maurice and Alan Batty; Alan was known as Sugar Plum because we overheard his mum calling him that as she bade him a fond farewell. The solo boys were Geoffrey Laurence, Charlie Aldred, Stanley Carter and Trevor Lunnon. Later we were joined by George and Jack Kent, Norman Deering, Alan Bradley and Frank Russell.

In no time at all it was school, and Mr Dakin rounded us up and walked us down to the village school, where we were assigned to classes. The headmaster, Mr Hogarth, did not have a very high opinion of the academic standards of his
evacuees and as a rule of thumb always downgraded them at least one class. I was thus placed in Miss Walmsley's class, which consisted of ten and eleven year olds. This was a bit of an affront to my dignity, as I had just had my twelfth birthday.

I found the arithmetic very easy, but when a few

days later I was asked to do an essay on "My New Home", I decided I would rise to the challenge. My opening paragraph read thus: "My home is the bijou part-time residence of Sir William and Lady Prince-Smith, the upper storeys of which provide panoramic views of a picturesque landscape". This was followed by much more in the same vein. When Miss Walmsley marked it she told me she thought it was very good and wanted to show it to the headmaster. Mr Hogarth said he thought it was the best essay he had seen for a long time and gave me a shilling out of his own pocket, which was a good sum in those days. I'm afraid I became the victim of my own success, for he then took me into the top class, stood me in front of them all and told me to read it out. I wanted the ground to open and swallow me up, but went ahead and read it all aloud. When I had finished Mr Hogarth said "That is the standard 1 would like from you all in future".

I cringed inwardly and wondered how many enemies I had made that day. The very next day I was moved up to the top class with Miss Thomas, and I stayed there until I left the school two years later.

When we arrived in Middleton there were quite a few evacuees there already. They came from Sunderland and had been there since the beginning of the war. Some of them had their mothers with them arid were either billeted on locals or had managed to rent accommodation. Because of the influx of evacuees the school was crowded, and it had been decided that the infants would be taught in the Methodist chapel, which was about a hundred yards lower down the High street. I think the, teacher was a local lady called Mrs Appleby. The rest of us were split into three classes, Mr Dakin taking the youngest ones, Miss Walmsley the next youngest and Miss Thomas the oldest. Incidentally Miss Walmsley and Miss Thomas had come from Sunderland with the first evacuees. Mr Hogarth often stepped in and took lessons in any subject

On Sundays everyone had to go to church or chapel at least once, and those who were listed as Church of England had to attend the village church, so dressed in our Sunday best, such as it was, we sallied forth accompanied by the two maids, Dorothy and Nancy. When we arrived we were ushered into a large pew at the very front which was reserved for the Prince-Smith family and their retainers - I wasn't quite sure how we fitted in to this category.

Initially we didn't mind going to church once on a Sunday, but when the Prince-Smiths were in residence and attending church it was difficult sitting through long sermons without wanting to fidget or giggle at anything at all, especially the antics of the choirboys during the sermon.

Shortly afterwards, the vicar, the Reverend Silian Evans, asked me if I would like to join the choir. I agreed, mainly because a new friend of mine, a Sunderland evacuee called Ronnie Thompson, was already a choirboy and had told me about the lucrative payments if you were asked to sing at a funeral or wedding. In the two years I was in the choir we never participated in either.

Mr Dakin, or 'David Martin' as we called him when he wasn't within earshot, was very likeable and soon won our respect because he was very fair-minded. It had been arranged that any serious misdemeanours would be punished by an appropriate number of blows on the bottom with his slipper, but this was a very rare occurrence. Mr Dakin was a conscientious objector and while he was at Oxford had become a member of the Peace Pledge Union. He was an absolute mine of information on practically everything other than things concerned with war. Every night before we went to bed we would gather in the room next to the billiard room while he read to us from Conan Doyle, Agatha Christie, G K Chesterton and P G Wodehouse, to name but a few, introducing us to Sherlock Holmes, Hercule Poirot, Father Brown and Jeeves. They became living entities as he read to us night after night.

The shingled courtyard which faced the back of the house was roughly square with a pigeon cote set at the top of a pole in the centre of the square. On the two sides from the back of the house were a series of outhouses which were used for storage of garden equipment, hanging game and storing vegetables from the large kitchen garden. A huge greenhouse produced magnificent black and white grapes and other exotic fruits such as nectarines and peaches. The head gardener was a pleasant man called Mr George and his assistant and general handyman was called Walter Ellerington. We boys liked his friendly manner, but after a few months he was called up into the Royal Air Force, though we did see him again once when he came home on leave.

The other side of the courtyard facing the house was known as the stables, a two-storey building with accommodation comprising several rooms, while the so-called stables down below housed a magnificent-looking Triumph car which was in pristine condition and was out of action for the duration. At the side of the entrance arch into the courtyard was an espaliered pear tree which produced delicious fruit - in fact the whole of the grounds abounded with various fruit trees and we often succumbed to temptation when no one was looking.

The back of the stable building had a verandah which accessed a pigeon loft. This housed quite a few trophies and photographs, since they were fancy pigeons, and one I recall in particular was called Nobby. He was an Oriental Frill and had won many prizes.

Next to Middleton Hall was a dairy farm which was owned by Frank Fitzgeorge Hepworth. Mr Hepworth had a large herd of pedigree Ayrshire cows which grazed in the parkland in front of the hall. The business was thriving and prosperous and bottled its own milk. Mr Aylott was the head stockman and he was assisted by his sons Bill and Henry, the latter doubling as the driver of a Singer milk van. There were two other drivers, one called Trevor Kettley and the other Shell Moore.

We were all very impressed the first time we saw the Price-Smiths, as they rode majestically into the courtyard in a magnificent Rolls Royce. A couple of weeks later they made an equally impressive appearance in a Daimler. I think we half expected Sir William to have a chauffeur, but on both times he was driving himself. They were always pleasant to us and we did our best to be respectful when we spoke to them. On the odd occasion when their offspring accompanied them, Claire tended to hang around us, probably out of curiosity and to see what we were playing. Richard, however, usually strode purposefully away, quite possibly under orders not to fraternise.

I wrote to Mum most weeks, but rarely received a prompt reply, although both Tom and I were eager for letters or parcels, especially when we needed clothes. While we had been away Mum had given up the house in Laurel Grove and with Grandma Stamford, Pop and Aunt Ethel she had moved into a lovely modern house in Springfield Road, off Anlaby Road near the Carlton Cinema.

Christmas was fast approaching, and as the raids on Hull so far had been relatively light, Tom and I were to be allowed home for a few days. Dad was going to be home for Christmas, and we went by train to Driffield, where we had to meet them at about two o'clock in Woolworth's, as they would already have been to Langtoft to pick up Thora and Terry. We waited all afternoon, but there was no sign of them, and as we didn't want to be caught in the blackout, we went to the station and caught the next train back to Middleton. Fortunately we had just enough money for this, though we felt utterly miserable and wondered what on earth could have happened.

Next morning there was a phone call from Mum asking Mrs Crawford if she could loan us the bus fare to Hull, where they would meet us at the bus station. When we met them they explained that when they had seen the conditions Thora was living in they had been appalled and had decided that she couldn't possibly remain there. They had had to see the billeting officer and state why they were removing her. Apparently she had been dressed virtually in rags, her beautiful long hair had been cropped and looked thoroughly miserable. It transpired that the woman she was billeted with had her own children in the care of the local authority because she had neglected them and had been unable to look after them properly. They thought it might be a good idea to see how she managed with just one evacuee!

In retrospect you would have thought that in the circumstances someone should have been monitoring the situation closely, but of course there was a war on. I wonder how many other children suffered similar or even worse fates than my sister Thora.

We had a very enjoyable Christmas together as a family, especially with Dad at home with us. We were very impressed with the Springfield Road house, which was a cut above any of our previous homes. But all too soon it was time to return to Middleton. The decision was made that Thora would stay in Hull with Mum and Valerie, but that they would try to arrange for Terry to be transferred from Langtoft to Middleton Hall as soon as possible. We really felt sorry for him going back on his own.

A few weeks later the Area Billeting Officer turned up with Terry in his car and he was duly installed with us, so we now had three brothers together.

Apart from the fact that we were away from home, most of us quite enjoyed life as evacuees. There were always plenty of things to interest us in our spare time, and I was still enjoying school and basking in my ability to be top dog in practically every subject.

At Easter Mr Dakin called on my mother in Hull to try and persuade her that I should enter for another scholarship, for Riley High School, which later became Hull Technical College. Dad was away at sea, but Mum was quite agreeable to my having another chance, so about two months later I took the exam. I sat in my normal classroom, but alone in the centre of a row of desks under the watchful eye of Mr Hogarth. None of the questions caused me any problems and as usual I thought I had done well.

Tom was a bit harum-scarum and had an unfortunate habit of picking fights with some of the bigger village schoolboys. Of course when he became involved in a fight I was duty bound to stand and fight with him and no matter how big the opposition was it was two to one, so we always came out on top. Consequently we were feared as a terrible twosome and no one ever bothered us after a few initial fights. I still can't understand why a couple of them didn't join forces and take us on at our own game.

One Saturday morning when Terry had not been with us many weeks, he was playing in the game outhouse, which contained a large triangular wooden rack which went up towards the roof like a wide staircase, with a series of hooks set out along each stair. I heard yells and dashed in to find Terry halfway down, firmly impaled by a hook through his thigh and bleeding profusely. I lifted him up as best I could, squeezed the flesh of his impaled thigh together and eased it off the hook, which had gone in one side and out the other. This particular weekend the Prince-Smiths were not in residence, so there was no transport available. Mrs Crawford bandaged his leg as best she could. I borrowed one of the maid's bikes and with Terry sitting on the saddle holding on to my back, I pedalled as fast as I could down to the doctor in the village. He put a couple of stitches in each gash and I pedalled him back to Middleton Hall. Incidentally the doctor was Dr Clements, the brother of the Dr Clements who murdered several wealthy widows a few years later.

I now spent a considerable amount of my spare time travelling around in that Singer milk van delivering Hepworth's famous TT milk and covered most of the area between Driffield and Bridlington. On the odd occasion when the big dairy in Bridlington needed it, we would take several churns to help them out. One Saturday morning Henry had dropped me off carrying half a dozen bottles of milk for some regular customers in an enclosed row of terraced cottages just outside Driffield. As I turned the corner I literally bumped into a Hampden bomber which had miraculously pancaked into a small area of green in front of the cottages without damaging a single one of them. It had happened in the early hours of the morning and there was a single policeman guarding it. There were lots of what I took to be shrapnel or bullet holes in it, and I wondered how the crew had fared. Since then I have often scanned books about the RAF during the war to find out what the story was, but without success.

A German invasion was still considered a strong possibility; a small unit of the British army had commandeered the so-called stable area and the quarters up above and began intensive training of the local Home Guard. The unit commander was a Captain Hollis, who only looked about eighteen. A couple of other men I remember were Harry Hutchinson and Edgar Helliwell. I'm sure they took an interest in us because they were away from their own families.

The Home Guard training had to take place at weekends or in the evenings as long as daylight lasted. The main training ground was a field we called our picnic field, which contained quite a steep hill and

where we had on occasions picnicked with Mrs Crawford and Iris. There was considerable rivalry between the Home Guard platoons, which the regular army encouraged, and most weekends there
would be shooting matches between the rival platoons. We boys often used to watch from what we considered a safe distance, but there were lots of ricochets and really it was quite dangerous. We knew that Hull was now beginning to be bombed much more by the Luftwaffe, and some nights you could see the glow in the sky. Sometimes we would be told by telephone that there were enemy aircraft close by and we would go down into the cellar. I got into the habit of running back to the Hall every day at dinner time. In the two years I was there no one ever reached home before me and I'm convinced that this was the foundation of my cross-country running successes in later life.

One dinner time I arrived home to find a letter from Mum with the good news that I had passed my exam and won a place at Riley High. Then came the crunch. She went on to say that if I accepted the place I would have to transfer to the evacuated section of the school, which was somewhere outside Doncaster, because it was out of the question for me to attend in Hull. It was up to me to decide. I didn't know that Hull had just experienced its heaviest air attacks since the beginning of the war, with several nights of sustained blitz bringing heavy loss of life and many injuries. To add to this our house in Springfield Road had been devastated by a blast from a landmine which had landed at the top of Stirling Street, less than a hundred yards away. We didn't know that arrangements had already been made for us to go back to Grimsby, which seemed now to be a much safer haven. Unaware of all this, I made the stupid on-the-spot decision that I was not going to Doncaster in September. If I'm honest I think it was because I was scared of going off on my own to a new school and being billeted with people I might not like.

Mr Dakin and Mr Hogarth both tried to make me change my mind, but I refused to budge. A few weeks later we had another letter from Mum postmarked Grimsby telling us that they had been bombed out and intended staying in Grimsby. There was not a word about my decision about Doncaster.

A little while after this another incident occurred which is burnt in my memory. It was a school day and we were all sitting round the table eating our dinner. Mrs Crawford sat at one end of the table and Iris at the other and I was sitting in my usual place next to Mrs Crawford when she suddenly began, "We've got two dirty little devils sitting here at this table right now, they've both wet the bed and never said a word, and those dirty little devils are the Ryans".

I felt a seething red rage come over me. I took my dinner and threw it all over her, then ran from the room. Tom and I slept together in a single bed and I was aware that he had wet the bed that night, something he had very occasionally done before. I had just kept as far as possible to my own side of the bed and gone back to sleep, expecting that Tom would see Iris in the morning and say "Sorry, I wet my bed last night".

Still seething, I ran off into the woods, knowing I had gone beyond the pale and thoroughly blotted my copybook, but I did consider that my indignation was righteous. When I heard them shouting that it was time for school, I ignored it and went deeper into the woods.

After a couple of hours of my own company I began to get bored and waited at a vantage point on top of the perimeter wall to see who was going to be first home from school. When the first-comers arrived I told them to tell Mrs Crawford that I would never again eat any food she prepared and that I was going on hunger strike. I had eaten nothing since breakfast except for a couple of unripe apples I had taken from a tree and I was famished. It was beginning to get dark and I had begun to see the error of my ways when Mr Dakin came along and found me - not that I was trying to hide any more. I explained to him exactly what had happened. He said that though Mrs Crawford had been wrong to publicly humiliate us in that way, I should not have resorted to swearing at her and throwing the dinner over her! It was a kindly admonishment. I was ordered to apologise to Mrs Crawford and receive four hard whacks with Mr Dakin's slipper. Funnily enough I have no recollection of swearing at her. I found apologising very difficult because I really thought she should have been apologising to me, but under Mr Dakin's watchful eye I did it with as much grace as I could muster.

Things soon settled down into our usual routine and life didn't seem too bad, but I found it difficult to be in the same room as Mrs Crawford and no longer trusted her.

When the summer holidays began we enjoyed ourselves immensely playing day after day in the woods. One day we made a den or shelter just on the edge of the woods, using yew branches, which were in abundant supply. We used part of the inner perimeter metal fence as one side and played Robin Hood games from our new den for several days.

One morning at breakfast the news came that six of Mr Hepworth's pedigree Ayrshires had been found dead in the park. I knew instinctively what had happened but hoped I was wrong. Straight after breakfast several of us ran as fast as we could to our den where our worst fears were confirmed. The den had collapsed and the outer part had vanished. We hastily demolished the rest of the structure and spread the offending yew branches around a wide area, fervently hoping that no more cows would die and that we wouldn't be found out. We had been warned about the danger of cattle eating yew when we first arrived, but had completely forgotten. Fortunately there were no more casualties, no one in authority found out and we had well and truly learned our lesson.

When the brambles began to ripen we would often go out all day round the hedgerows, gathering large amounts of blackberries which Mrs Crawford made into pies for us all. One day Miss McKellar saw us returning with the blackberries and said that if we would like to get some for her, we would be rewarded. The next day about six of us set off, and we came across hedgerows with prolific amounts of big juicy fruits. We filled every container we had with us, including a large basket, and there were probably ten pounds of blackberries. Miss McKellar was overjoyed and said her ladyship would be pleased. Later that evening she came to our dining room, gave us sixpence to share between six of us and promised "Ye'll have another if ye go again". As you may have guessed, we didn't, not for her anyway!

There were many army vehicles coming and going into the courtyard and round the back of the stable building, and there were usually two or three army lorries parked round the back. One day Tom fell from the back verandah and caught his tongue on the iron frame over which the canvas stretched. He looked terrible, and the end of his tongue was practically severed. Once again there were no adults with transport present, so again we borrowed a bike, me pedalling like fury down to the village while Tom hung on. We were fortunate for a second time, as Dr Clements was again at home. He examined Tom carefully and said that he hadn't broken anything and would be all right. When I said "What about his tongue?" he replied, "Don't worry about that, just leave it'. How right he was, because the next morning, the tongue was completely healed with no trace of the cut his teeth had inflicted! I often wonder what the doctor would have done if he had severed it completely.

At about this time we were joined by another evacuee called Eric. I can't remember his surname, but we called him "Eric Ooslem" and he didn't seem to mind. A few weeks previously, his house in Hull had suffered a direct hit and Eric had been the only survivor. His father was not at home at the time. Eric told us that his parents' marriage had been over for quite a while, and his father now had another woman in his life, so perhaps things had turned out for the best. He seemed quite a resilient lad for an eleven-year-old who had just gone through such a trauma and his father and Lynne, his girlfriend, visited Eric on a regular basis. She seemed a very nice lady, but looking back, I can't help but feel that Eric was emotionally scarred - he always seemed very flippant.

We were told to be considerate and make him feel at home because of all that had happened to him. When we introduced him to our Robin Hood games, he grabbed a stout yew stick and said to the person next to him "Can you quarterstaff?" He brought his staff over and gave him a crack on the skull which almost knocked him out! I had to explain that we didn't extend our make-believes to those extremes. He didn't seem to think that he had done anything particularly wrong, so we decided we would need to watch him carefully!

We now had another couple of lads join us. One was Frank Russell, who became a firm friend of my brother

Tom, and the other was Alan Bradley, who was about six months younger than me. Alan was quite a smoothie and all the girls in the class vied for his attention.

It was about this time that Iris Bell, who we all loved, left us to join the ATS. Her sweetheart Wally was in the army somewhere near the south coast, and Iris was hoping to be posted somewhere near him; I believe she was eventually successful. To replace Iris we had another village girl called Joyce Cutler. We soon got to like her, but we missed Iris.

Mr Dakin had been making enquiries on my behalf about further advanced education, and he had discovered that as the son of a merchant seaman I was entitled to sit the entrance exam for Trinity House College at Hull, which trained cadets to become navigators and seamen. There would be few if any expenses for my parents to pay as in their circumstances I was eligible for board, tuition and uniform grants.

It seemed heaven sent. My parents were all for it, and I realised that this really was my last chance and I was not going to throw it away. Though I felt quite confident, I agreed to take some extra tuition with Mr Dakin. He really was a gifted teacher with a huge store of general knowledge. In 1954 he proved just how good he was by winning the BBC's 'Brain of Britain' contest on the radio with a tremendous score. He went on to be a TV personality for several years. I was quite proud to have known him.

About this time I and a couple of other boys

developed mumps, so the billeting officer (a lady whose name escapes me) took us in her car to a large country house at Stamford Bridge, near York. I wasn't very ill, and this turned out to be a fascinating three weeks. The matron was called Mrs Madge and her husband was a doctor in the Royal Army Medical Corps. In the First World War he had been Pilot Officer Madge of the Royal Flying Corps and he had been shot down by the Red Baron, Manfred bon Richthofen. I was hoping he would visit while we were there, but it wasn't to be. Matron, however, had practically every book and article ever written about the Red Baron, so I learned an awful lot about him during those three weeks.

When we returned to Middleton, rumour was rife that Mrs Crawford was leaving us, and this turned out to be true. We were amazed by her replacement, a young woman in her late twenties called Anne. She immediately instituted a new, more liberal regime which we took to like ducks to water, but it was too good to be true – it didn't last a month. We were allowed to go to bed late, and there was a seemingly endless procession of soldiers calling to see, one of whom always seemed to be in her arms. She told us he was her brother, but not surprisingly she left very suddenly and for a couple of days we all helped as best we could while Joyce managed on her own.

The next incumbent was Mrs Smith from Sunderland, an evacuee herself. She had a boy and a girl, Enid, who was in my class at school but had just had her fourteenth birthday and was due to leave. The Prince-Smiths had just lost a maid to the services and Enid was taken in as a replacement. With Mrs Smith and her young son coming to work with us, it seemed a neat arrangement. We soon took to Mrs Smith, who was kind and motherly and above all very fair. We felt we could trust her, but that we wouldn't be able to take advantage of her, so things began to run smoothly once more.

That October we found that several of us had scabies. Our treatment consisted of getting up at half past six in the morning, coming downstairs and gathering round the large central heating stove in the kitchen. As we stood there shivering away in the nude, we were liberally painted with a tepid solution of derris powder, which we had to allow to dry to a crust. This went on for about a week, until we were pronounced cured.

In the park were two large walnut trees, and as they were getting ripe we often made sorties to collect the nuts, as did some of the village boys. One day Mr Hogarth said "I want to see every boy in the top two classes". Then he lined us all up in the schoolyard and made us hold out our hands. Anyone with stained hands went into another line to receive four strokes of the cane on the offending hand – no excuses were accepted. That was the only time I got the cane at that school, but I'm sure it did me good. Of course the purloining of walnuts ceased forthwith, as stain from the outer case of the walnut took ages to fade away.

A few weeks later Alan Bradley was in the classroom

sitting his exam for entrance to Riley High, and once again the whole of the row was vacated except for Alan. I was sitting in the row parallel to his. This time it was Miss Thomas who was overseeing the exam, but she tended to leave the room from time to time and whenever she did, Alan would lean across and ask me any questions he couldn't answer, and there were quite a few. I felt rather annoyed about this, but at the same time flattered that he should be asking me and also admiring his nerve. A few months later it was announced that he had passed and would be going to Riley High the following September.

A couple of months after this I took my Nautical College exam. As usual I thought I had done well, but because I knew it was my last chance, I went back to bargaining with God. A couple of weeks before we broke up for Christmas there were several huge cardboard boxes delivered at the school; they had come from America and were addressed to all evacuees, wishing us a Happy Christmas from friends in the USA. We had some marvellous toys and games, which really made our Christmas, as very few now went home because of the war situation. Some of the village children were understandably quite envious of us.

That January and February we had tremendous snowfalls with drifts piling up to the top parts of some telegraph poles. At one point we were cut off for five days before the snowploughs broke through. Some of the boys didn't want to go out in the cold, but a few of us borrowed wellington boots from those who wouldn't venture out and we thoroughly enjoyed ourselves trekking here, there and everywhere in the deep snow, examining footprints left by birds, rabbits and hares as they foraged for food during the bitter weather. We made sledges and as there was no traffic we had great fun tobogganing up and down the hill on the main road outside Middleton Hall.

The following weekend the road was cleared and the Prince-Smiths managed to get up for the weekend, but we blotted our copybook once more because we snowballed Master Richard and caused him to beat a hasty retreat while we were out in the woods.

Those long winter evenings were made very enjoyable, thanks to Mr Dakin reading to us sometimes; if there was no school next morning, he would read for a solid hour, and we enjoyed every minute of it. Quite a few of us were into stamp collecting, and we never tired of swapping and learning about stamps.

I had received a football for Christmas, a very valuable possession in those days, and we used to spend endless hours playing in the fields.

I was by now beginning to feel a little anxious about my last exam. Suppose I hadn't done as well as I thought? If I hadn't made it I would have to go to Grimsby in a few months' time and look for a job. What sort of job could I get? What sort of job would suit me, or would I be suitable for? My mind dwelt quite a lot on such thoughts, but apart from that I was still happy and carefree, still enjoying life and school. One of the reasons I enjoyed school so much was a girl in my class called Betty Scott, a red-headed Sunderland evacuee who I thought beautiful. She had a friend named Flossie Farrow (another Sunderland girl) who happened to be billeted with Mrs Bell, Iris's mother. One day she agreed to go for a walk with me, provided Flossie could come too. I readily acquiesced. But the outing ended with a minor disaster because when Betty sat down on the grass she acquired a big green stain on the back of her lovely white dress. My offer to pay for it to be cleaned was turned down flat.

A few weeks after the Easter holidays, I had a letter from Mum enclosing a letter from Hull Education Authorities offering me a place at the Nautical College starting about the sixth of September. I was overjoyed. I thanked God that night in my prayers and began to visualise myself as the captain of a liner, or at least a large cargo ship. Life was beginning to look rosy again. July arrived all too quickly, and when the fifteenth dawned I was actually fourteen years of age. Even though there was a war in progress I had a lot to look forward to, or so I thought.

A few days later I said my goodbyes to my teachers and friends, including Mr Hogarth and Mr Dakin. They all wished me well, and off I set to catch the East Yorkshire bus which would take me on the first stage of my journey to Grimsby via Hull. As the bus travelled into Hull along Beverly Road I was appalled at the bomb damage I was witnessing on both sides of the road. I then had to catch a tram which took me quite close to Corporation Pier to catch the ferry to New Holland and then the train to Grimsby. The train stopped at every station en route to Grimsby. The first stop was a small station called Goxhill, where normally you might expect a couple of passengers either way. I was amazed to see what appeared to be a couple of hundred American Air Force men waiting to alight. As we pulled out of Goxhill, practically every seat on the train was occupied. I just sat back and took in their conversations, their different American dialects, their cigarette smoking and their gum chewing. I was very impressed. They all looked so smart.

As usual I left the train at Grimsby Docks station and caught a trolley bus to Tasburgh Street, where Mum and Thora now lived with Grandma Stamford and Pop. Also living in the house were Barbara and Harry Clappison, my late Aunt Thora's children, who had lived with Grandma for some time now. Aunt Lilian worked full time and lived at the County Hotel, Immingham, while Aunt Ethel worked as a barmaid at a large public house in Freeman Street, but I lived at home in Tasburgh street. Although it was a fairly large house, there wasn't much room to spare and the front room downstairs was utilised as a bedroom.

Tasburgh Street was a rented house and one of its previous occupants had left behind quite a large library of every type of book imaginable. I was fascinated and spent all my time reading them.

My appointment to be fitted for my uniforms in Hull was fast approaching. And then – disaster. In mid August, a few days before my appointment, another official letter arrived addressed to Mum and Dad which stated that as my parents were no longer ratepayers of Hull I was no longer entitled to take up my place the following month unless they were either willing to pay a substantial amount every year or to move back to Hull. I knew it was impossible for them to afford that kind of money. I also knew that though they were proud of what I had achieved at school so far, education for their children was not a high priority.

CHAPTER 3

LEARNING THE ROPES

I spent the next week after receiving that letter in black despair, but I managed to rally at the beginning of September and on the first Monday of the month I started work at the Great Grimsby Coal, Salt and Tanning Works in the Ropewalk as a winder for the magnificent sum of nineteen shillings per week.

How the mighty had fallen! My hours were eight till five, with an hour for lunch Monday to Friday and eight till twelve on a Saturday. Thus began my contribution to the war effort.

We were informed that our work in transforming old ropes into new was of vital importance to our navies. The ropewalk was about one hundred yards in length and at one end it had a long wooden bench on which were set a dozen foot-operated turntables. Behind this bench was the machine area, where new ropes of various thicknesses were manufactured. The first step in the process was to collect a length of old rope and apply one end of it to a machine which reverse-turned it and separated the three or four main strands. One end of a main strand was attached to a hook at the side of a turntable. The next step was to walk back to the end of the strand and proceed to shake it out and allow the individual strands to separate. A weight was then placed on the far end of the strands and one at a time they were reeled on to a metal bobbin. As one strand ended another was selected and tied with a neat reef knot. This process continued until the bobbin was full, when it was replaced with an empty one. Every few minutes someone came with a collection trolley and empty bobbins were returned and full ones transferred to the rope-making machines.

I soon got the hang of the procedure, but by the end of the first day the palm of my right hand was sore and blistered by the strands crossing my palm as I played the strand up and down to make the bobbin even. At the end of the day I went home exhausted. As long as I worked there I rarely went to bed later than eight o'clock. It was also a dirty job, because the ropes were old and tarry and produced a lot of dust when shaken out. The work became more and more monotonous and after a few months I was longing for a change.

The plum jobs were considered to be those done by the machine operators, which were graded in importance according to the thickness of the rope they produced. On the thickest rope it took two men to unload the completed coil. The foreman's name was

Mark, and everyone behaved impeccably when he was in the area. One day he asked me if I thought I could run a machine. I said yes, as I had watched the procedure many time, and he gave me a trial. Though there was no extra money involved, I felt as if I had been promoted, and it wasn't half as dirty and dusty in the machine area.

For the next few months I really began to enjoy my work and take pride in keeping my machine clean and well lubricated. My machine was twinned with an identical one operated by a lad called Ginger, and produced rope of an identical thickness. The bobbins were set on a number of steel pins set in three rows at staggered heights on a metal framework. The strands from the bobbins fed into the machine via a flat circular piece of steel covered with small round colander-like holes. Whenever Ginger or I were called away briefly for a call of nature the other had to watch 96 bobbins to make sure they didn't snag or snap. If a strand snapped it could twist around several other strands and turn the whole operation into an unholy mess. If this happened it you had to cut the strand and tie it up with a reef knot. The more experienced you became the less the risk of having to hold up production.

Grimsby was now becoming a target for the Luftwaffe and we often had to resort to our shelter. My little sister Valerie was never very happy at being disturbed and once we were settled in the shelter she always said through her tears "I wornta winka worta", which meant "I want a drink of water".

One morning, after a fairly heavy raid, I walked to work and could see shattered windows in all directions. At the factory we were warned to be careful as we released the blackout covers in the flat roof overhead. Practically every roof window was broken, and no matter how carefully the rope of the blind was released the glass showered down. I managed to get a splinter of glass in my eye and had to go to hospital to have it removed.

A few months after this I asked my friend Ginger to keep an eye on my machine for a moment. On my return I found him yelling and holding his hand. Mark put a piece of rag around it and hurried him to the office, where an ambulance was called. It seemed there had been a double snap and snarl on my machine. As he tried to sort it out, a snapped end had fed itself into one of the colander holes and taken off the top half of his finger like a wire cutting through cheese. As I was clearing up later I spotted something beneath the machine and picked it up to realise to my horror that it was the end of Ginger's finger. I handed it in, but it was too late. I imagine that today it might have been possible to sew it back on. Ginger never came back to work, and my love affair with my machine was over. In those days health and safety at work was unheard of, and I began to look in earnest for a safer job.

I had just completed a year in that job when I applied for a job with Pool Petrol, a wartime amalgamation of all the petrol companies. I was taken on as a depot hand at what had been a National Benzole depot. My wages now rose to 25 shillings a week, so I thought I was doing really well. The work consisted mainly of keeping the depot clean, unloading railcars as they pulled into our siding and going to a house a few doors down the street to fetch cake and a jug of tea for any drivers and their mates who happened to be in the depot. I found unloading railcars heavy going, as I was small in stature at that time. You had to put a ladder at the side of the railcar, open the top, check the amount inside with a long metal dipstick, then climb down for a heavy metal standpipe which was dropped through the top and connected to a large, flexible hose. Then you had to ensure all the right valves were open to the storage tank in the depot, check the level of the receiving tank and switch on the extraction pump. It could take up to two hours to unload, after which the railcar had to be checked to make sure it was completely unloaded and the recipient tank examined to make sure it had received the appropriate number of gallons. Heady stuff, I hear you saying! But for the first few months I really enjoyed it and was quite wrapped up in my work.

We dealt with gas oil (diesel) and vaporising oil (paraffin), which were used for tractors, generators and similar types of engines. We delivered to the whole of North Lincolnshire. Sometimes the driver had to be accompanied by a mate, depending on the destination, which could be anywhere from a lonely farm to a remote airfield.

One day I was delighted to be told I had to accompany a driver as his mate. His name was Ferdy Persson, a Swede who had lived in Grimsby for many years. He spoke a delightful broken English and was a kind and generous man. As time went on I spent more and more time working as Ferdy's mate and less time in the depot. We delivered to nearly all the airfields in the area, including Scampton, the base of Guy Gibson and the Dambusters. One day we had the excitement of watching a badly shot-up Flying Fortress making an emergency landing.

Another day we were driving through Louth when we were stopped by a Military Police Jeep. We were ordered to drive up as far as we could on to the pavement and stay until we were told to move. Ferdy was fuming, but it was wartime and he knew we had do as we were told. About five minutes later a huge convoy of US Army vehicles began thundering past. One of them hit the side of our tanker so hard we thought it had been ruptured. Fortunately it wasn't, but Ferdy jumped out of his cab and went dancing like a dervish after the offending vehicle.

The last vehicle in the convoy was another MP Jeep and I managed to flag him down and showed him the damage just as Ferdy returned from his fruitless chase panting and spluttering. The military policeman said he couldn't give any information about the unit the driver belonged to or who we could contact. I jotted down the markings on his vehicle as he pulled away and volunteered to complete the report for Ferdy. Fortunately all the equipment was still working. When we finally returned to the depot Ferdy meticulously copied out my little essay. He was congratulated on his report and thanked me over and over again.

At the end of my first year, it was decided by a higher authority that our depot no longer merited a depot hand. By a strange coincidence the depot hand at headquarters about a mile away had just joined up, and they had been unable to find a replacement, so I was transferred there. There were two depots at headquarters, one belonging to Shell Mex and the other to Esso. They supplied aviation, fuel, which was conveyed in large articulated tankers; a particular brand of 73 octane fuel for the high-speed rescue launches based at Grimsby and the normal gas and vaporising oil. The depot also provided ordinary pool petrol for our own vehicles and for naval staff cars. This meant that the Shell depot hand usually had plenty to do keeping the depot clean, serving naval customers and unloading from railcars.

Another job was to prepare samples from every railcar delivery to send to Liverpool for analysis. I tried hard to arrange a transfer to working as a mate again, but I had no success except on the very odd occasion when they were desperate. I did fall from grace once when I unloaded 10,000 gallons of 73 octane into a tank containing 30,000 gallons of vaporising oil normally used for tractors. I had failed to check every valve on every tank top. There were a myriad of them and the valve on the vaporising tank had been left open. Since it preceded the 73, it had pumped through to the line of least resistance and I was sure I was for the high jump. Fortunately my foreman, Cyril Sheardown, said it had been his fault as he should have checked all the valves first thing in the morning. The whole tankful was sold and delivered as vaporising oil, and lots of farmers commented on how well their tractors were running!

Once I had turned sixteen I was eligible for firewatching duties on a rota basis covering the two headquarters depots, and I was expected to do them. It wasn't a particularly onerous job, but it entailed sleeping on the premises, and always hoping that the air raid sirens would not sound. If they did, regular patrols had to be made around the installations to deal with any incendiary bombs before they could do any real damage. I was often called upon to substitute for other staff who didn't like to turn out at night, and as I received seven shillings and sixpence for each night and didn't have to report for duty until eleven in the morning, I was always pleased to carry out extra firewatching duties! There were quite a few alerts while I was on these duties, but there were never any bombs in our area.

I have mentioned my Aunt Lilian, who worked at the County Hotel at Immingham about eight miles from Grimsby. She lived in and only came home on her day off. While she worked there, Lord Louis Mountbatten and his entourage lived at the hotel for six months after his ship, the *Kelly*, was almost sunk in action in the North Sea. While he was in residence scores of VIPs visited, but because of the need for secrecy and that well-known wartime slogan, "Careless Talk Costs Lives', she wasn't able to reveal any of this until after the war.

After working there for two years she was drafted into munitions in the Midlands. Only about six months later she came home to Tasburgh Street a ghastly yellow colour and was invalided out of munitions work.

It was during this period that I began to keep rabbits as a hobby. The idea was to breed them and fatten them up for the table. We had a battery of hutches stacked against the dividing wall and at one time we had about 120 rabbits. Meat was hard to come by in those days and rabbit meat was very popular. Unfortunately our relatives seemed to think that when they ordered a rabbit for the weekend, it was unnecessary to pay for it, so our little enterprise gradually evaporated and we just kept a few rabbits for our own use. I hated killing them for the table and usually passed the job on to Pop.

Aunt Ethel was still at home and working as a barmaid at a pub called the Wheatsheaf in Freeman Street. She had not been drafted into war work because of an injury to her hand sustained when working at the Broadway Hotel in Hull just before the war.

The house in Tasburgh Street was becoming quite congested and it was obvious that someone would have to move out now that Aunt Lilian was back at home.

Mum, Thora, Valerie and I moved in with my mother's cousin Gladys, who had a fairly large house in Park Street, Cleethorpes. Park Street was and still is the dividing line between the two boroughs, one side Grimsby and the other Cleethorpes. Aunt Gladys was married to Kay Neilson, a Danish Seine net fisherman who continued to fish out of Grimsby throughout the war. He was a very pleasant and likeable man and didn't make us feel we were intruding.

After about six months in Park Street Mum decided we needed a place of our own once again, as Dad was expected home shortly and Tom, now almost fourteen, would be leaving Middleton and coming home to look for a job. We found a house in a street off Park Street, no. 56 Tunnard Street, with two rooms, a kitchen, an outside toilet and a small garden. It was in a row of identical terraced houses, but no doubt the reasonable rent was an important factor in the move!

It was difficult at this time knowing just where Dad was. We knew he had been involved in the invasion of Madagascar (which had been occupied by the Vichy French) but next thing we knew, a telegram arrived saying he would be home the next day. He was in Scotland and had just been repatriated from Cape Town on the *Queen Mary*, which was used as a troop carrier during the war. Her great speed allowed her to travel without an escort. He had only a couple of weeks at home and then he was off again, to heaven knows where as far as we were concerned.

When Tom came home he found a job as an errand boy and store assistant at Burt's, an old-world quality provisions store on Cleethorpes Road. He used to deliver orders on an old-fashioned delivery bicycle and I think he stayed with them for about a year before moving on to Bromley's lemonade factory.

Grimsby and the area around it was still experiencing the odd air raid at night. There was a tremendous barrage from the anti-aircraft guns and how any of the German planes survived escapes me. The noise was quite frightening, though I can't recall any enemy planes being shot down.

One bright moonlit night when there was an alert on, I saw three flying bombs (Doodlebugs as they were called) fly over with their bright flaming exhaust trails visible. Apparently they had been launched from German aircraft over the North Sea and had been targeted at the Manchester area. I believe one reached there but didn't do much damage. This was almost the end of the flying bomb phase and London and the South of England had borne the brunt of these attacks.

Thanks to double British Summer Time there was usually enough daylight for me to go to the Hardy Recreation ground after I had finished work to play football, which I adored. It was usually just a kickabout between lads, often with as many as twenty in each team if we had only one football! Of course, the owner of the ball was in a kingpin position and when teams were selected he always chose first. Because I often came down to play straight from work and was wearing my Pool overalls, I was known as "Poolie" and some people remember me as that to this day.

I then joined a local youth club called Hardy Rangers, adjoining Old Clee Church, which ran several youth football teams which were highly successful. They had a nice club room with a full-size snooker table. The vicar of Old Clee was the Rev C K Clay, who was our president, but the youth club and teams were managed by a man called Charlie Shaw. I tried without success to get into one of the regular Hardy Ranger teams, but though I used to go down and practise with them I could never even make it to the third team. I was also a member of the Sea Cadets, who decided to enter a team in the local leagues. We had one or two useful players, including a boy called Newell who was an excellent player and a former Hardy Ranger. We soon began to win a few matches and I was scoring quite a few goals. Charlie Shaw immediately showed an interest, and shortly afterwards I began to get a regular game for Hardy Rangers, though never in the first team.

One day Dad rolled up out of the blue in a taxi (a difficult thing to obtain in those days) with his sea bag and a big heavily-laden suitcase which, when opened, revealed tins of every type of food and delicacy imaginable in those days. Against the background of wartime austerity, such food was magnificent. The next day he gave Tom and me two pounds each, a lot of money in those days, and asked us to look after things while he and Mum, accompanied by Valerie, went over to Hull for a few days. How we gorged ourselves, particularly on tinned fruit and cream, over the next few days. It's a wonder we weren't sick.

A few days later, Dad was off again. D-Day had arrived and he was on the first British ship into the French port of Caen. When the Allies landed in France everyone was in a state of elation and thought the war would soon be over, but after the initial successes it seemed the Germans had regrouped, brought in reinforcements and were regaining some lost ground. This was only temporary however, and in less than a year the war was over.

The last year of the war was quite a busy one for me. I was still obsessed with sport, football and cricket according to season, I also spent a lot of time on the snooker tables and was getting quite good. I till attended my weekly stint with the Sea Cadets as I knew that at eighteen I was liable to be called up, and I wanted to join the navy and not the army.

Most Saturday evenings I went to the Palace Theatre, which was one of the Moss Empires, and saw lots of what I then considered first-rate variety shows. I don't think I would rate them so highly now, but they included people like Dorothy Squires, Jane of *Daily Mirror* fame, Max Miller and Donald Peers, to name but a few.

My closest friend was a lad called Harry Delew, a Jew but not a very orthodox one. He lived in Oxford

Street, quite close to us in Tunnard Street, and worked for a baker. I don't think he was actually apprenticed, but he was learning the trade.

Every Sunday morning we would congregate on Hardy Recreation ground and play football or cricket for a couple of hours, then go home for Sunday dinner, after which we would go to another friend's house to play cards. Yes, to play cards on a Sunday, and for money too – we really were decadent! The friend whose house we used was called Bill Todd and he had a close friend called Bob Potterton. Although I have lost track of Harry and Bill, Bob became a firm friend and remains so to this day.

Harry and I both fancied ourselves as potential middle-distance runners and could outrun anyone else in the club. We trained whenever we had any spare time and would often finish a game of snooker and run from the club to Cleethorpes marketplace and back again, always trying to slice a few seconds off our previous best time. Strange as it seems, none of us seemed very interested in girls, probably because we just didn't have the time.

That spring, news was coming through every day of more and more prisoners of war being liberated. The Allies were advancing on Germany from all sides, primarily the British and US forces from the west and the Russians from the east. It had already been agreed that the Russians would be first into Berlin. When VE Day was announced there were lots of street parties to celebrate. Tables were loaded with good things to eat, and everyone seemed to bring out some special delicacy which was either in short supply or so scarce we had almost forgotten that it existed. Many streets were festooned with 'Welcome Home' banners, and it was amazing just how many people, including newly-released prisoners of war, managed to get home for the festivities.

In the midst of these celebrations came news of more and more prisoners being released as the victorious Allies pressed forward, meeting little or no resistance. Shortly after this, every newspaper in Britain, and probably most of the world, carried huge front-page pictures and stories about the dead and living skeletons which had been revealed when the Nazi concentration camps at Belsen and Dachau were liberated. It was horrific enough in the newspaper reports, but when we saw it a few weeks later on cinema newsreels it was truly blood-curdling, and a great wave of anti-German feeling swept the country.

The sweeping victory of the Labour Party in the rapidly-arranged General Election was seen as ushering in a period peace and prosperity, jobs for everyone and a new National Health Service to look after everyone from the cradle to the grave. Churchill was deposed, despite having led us to victory.

That August I was on a three-day biking holiday in the East Riding of Yorkshire with a couple of Hardy Ranger friends, Eric Wringe and Smudger Smith. As we rode through Beverly we saw placards announcing that atomic bombs had been dropped on Japan. We bought a newspaper and read the astonishing news that Japan had surrendered and the war really was over. There were more parties and parades and of course 'Welcome Home' banners for prisoners of wear returning from the Far East.

Back at work, we saw a trickle of arrivals as the first forces to be demobilised rejoined us. Their jobs had been guaranteed by the various petroleum companies and their service pay had been made up to what they would have earned had they been working for the company throughout the war. Now they had to be found jobs within Pool Petroleum until it was disbanded and reformed into the various component companies.

Sport was flourishing once again, and there had been a series of victory test matches arranged between England and Australia, with most of the players drawn from British and Australian forces. On top of this a new English League football season was about to start.

How had the war years affected me and my family? I suppose we had come through relatively unscathed compared with other families. Pop had become one of our first casualties when his ship the *Gowrie* had sunk and he had been disabled and thus unable to work. Freddie Woodhouse, the father of Kathleen, whose tragic death I related at the beginning of my narrative, was blown to smithereens by a landmine while firewatching during the blitz on Hull, along with his lifetime friend George Cannon. My cousin Charlie

Dillon was lost at sea without trace. No one knew what had happened to him. During the summer of 1942, Uncle George Bartley, soon to marry my Aunt Ethel, was on a Malta convoy which limped into Malta with only two other ships out of the original eleven. Between January and August of 1942 35 supply ships had sailed in four major convoys, and only ten of the ships arrived. The margin by which Malta survived was very narrow, and the siege was not lifted until the time of the Allied landings in North Africa in November 1942.

My father sailed on two winter convoys to Russia and on one of them he had actually arranged for me to accompany him on the ship as a galley boy. Praise the Lord, my mum put her foot down and I remained where I was at the Ropewalk. I used to think at the time that the war had robbed me of the better education I craved, but in the cold light of day almost sixty years later I realise that it was not really anyone's fault. My parents had been through hard times and they considered education of only secondary importance, mainly because they were uneducated themselves.

Though the war was over, things were far from normal. Practically everything you could think of was still rationed, just as it had been through the conflict. A great morale booster, however, was the return of street lights, illuminated signs, bright car headlights and the removal of all the blackout paraphernalia. Lights shone from house windows once again and that alone seemed to lift people's spirits. I remember that several of us went to a specially-arranged international match between England and Scotland in aid of the Bolton Disaster Fund. It was a wonderful match which England won, thanks to an outstanding performance from Stanley Matthews on the right wing. Once he received the ball no one else touched it until he decided to cross it. He was truly magical and the Shaw brothers, who were both playing fullback for Scotland that day, must have wondered what had hit them!

That night we went to a cinema in Manchester to see Laurence Olivier in Henry V, then caught the early morning milk train back to Grimsby. As the 1945 football season was about to begin, half a dozen Hardy Rangers, accompanied by Charlie Shaw, went to London for a conducted tour around the Arsenal Stadium. We were met by Tom Whittaker, who had taken over from George Allison as manager, and with him was Jack Crayston, a former Arsenal and England stalwart who was now the Arsenal trainer. We were introduced to several players including Leslie and Denis Compton. Denis had only just returned from service in India and had come for a massage prior to playing in a match that afternoon between an FA eleven and an Army Physical Training Corps eleven. We went to Wembley in the afternoon and saw a wonderful match. The skills of people like Tommy Lawton, Wilf Mannion, Len Shackleton, Neil Franklin and Stanley Matthews made it a great exhibition of football.

My younger brother Terry had come home from

Middleton a few months before the war ended, and he and my sister Thora were at a nearby school. Tom was now into weightlifting and boxing and was with a local club and making a name for himself. I was still diligently attending the Sea Cadets in preparation for what I hoped would be my call up in to the navy. A few days before my 18th birthday I received a letter asking me to present myself for a medical at Lincoln the following week. I duly presented myself and went through the usual routine and completed the questionnaires they placed before me. We were then handed out two papers of questions, basic maths, English and General Knowledge. We were also asked which service we would prefer if given the choice. Of course I said the navy.

About half an hour later I was called in before a naval Chief Petty Officer who said to me, “I'm afraid you didn't do quite well enough in those tests to be accepted in the navy as a conscript. If however you would be willing to sign on initially for seven years, we could find a place for you in most trades”.

I was dumbfounded at first. Then I began to wonder why I had wasted all that time in preparation in the Sea Cadets. Why had I not been asked any questions about my Sea Cadet training? It was like talking to a brick wall. I received no answers and was on the verge of asking to see my papers. If I had done so badly, I wanted to know why. Looking back, I'm sure my attitude was wrong and put his back up. Presumably his job was to try to recruit a certain quota of regulars for the navy and that was how he went about it.

Three weeks later I received my call-up papers. I was to report to the army barracks at Lincoln on the 6th of September.

CHAPTER 4

"THIS IS THE ARMY, MR RYAN!"

The 6th September 1946 was an unforgettable day for me. We were told so many things that it was imperative for us to remember, probably the most important being our names, ranks and numbers. I was Ryan, Private, 19063807 – a number which needless to say I have never forgotten. Once we had been allocated numbers we were divided into platoons of thirty men. Each had a regular army corporal in charge with a lance corporal to assist him. The training cadre at Lincoln was divided between the Royal Lincolnshire Regiment and the Sherwood Foresters. Our platoon commander was Corporal Crane of the Lincolnshire Regiment, assisted by Lance Corporal Jones of the Sherwood Foresters.

Our first port of call was the Quartermaster's stores, where we individually accumulated, in a very short period of time, a vast collection of army clothes and equipment. This included a Lee Enfield .303 rifle with a bayonet; two sets of battledress (one for best and one for everyday use); two pairs of socks; two pairs of underpants; two pairs of boots; one kitbag; and a set of field service marching order equipment including a haversack and the appropriate webbing, with the panniers for attaching to same. There was also a groundsheet which doubled as a waterproof when it was raining and of course the inevitable pair of gaiters. Just when we thought we were coming to the end we had to make a further visit to the stores to collect blankets and pillows. We had by then deposited all our other equipment in the Nissen hut which had been allocated to our "B" Troop. We were then instructed in the art of making the bed and how a soldier's bed should be arranged with all the appropriate articles laid out on it for inspection.

I remember during what was probably the busiest day of my life also finding time to draw a mess tin, knives, forks and spoons, along with an enamel mug.

I think everyone was a little bewildered and very tired by the end of the day, and when the bugler sounded lights out at ten o'clock most of us dropped into an exhausted sleep.

When reveille sounded at six thirty our hut became a hive of frantic activity with most of us trying to emulate the model of bedding and equipment set out on the NCOs' beds. There were big queues at the washhouse and latrines, as we had to be lined up outside our huts by seven for breakfast parade. Fortunately, during my first few weeks at Lincoln, I didn't yet need to shave, which saved me quite a few valuable minutes every morning. This however was too good to last.

I must have looked quite something during my first couple of weeks in the army, thanks to my size and weight. I was five feet two inches in height and weighed only seven stone five pounds, but army uniforms and equipment (including boots) catered for what they considered to be the "average" to the large and the smallest boots issued were size six. I took only a size four, but I had two pairs of size sixes for the whole of my army career. My uniform enveloped me and I spent a considerable time at the camp tailor's gradually getting my uniforms and my greatcoat altered until they were a reasonable fit.

Our first week of training consisted almost entirely of drill on the parade ground, with at least one period of physical training in the gym, clad in shorts, vests and plimsolls, further items which we had/to draw on that bewildering first day. The drawback with gym work was that the last one in the troop to be changed and ready for PT was singled out and given a dirty job later on, as was the last one to be back in uniform afterwards. this led to some unholy mad scrambles, I can tell you, but somehow I managed never to be last.

The second week began with more parade ground drill, but now a new element was introduced, the heavy Lee Enfield rifle. I found that week very hard going with my small hands and stature, but by the end of it I was managing reasonably well. I was still dropping into dreamless deep sleep every night at lights out. No one ever got into bed and went to sleep before ten, because there was always so much to do. Boots and brass had to be polished, equipment had to be blancoed, rifles had to be pulled through and cleaned.

At the end of our second week of training we were given 48-hour passes. We had all been confined to barracks for the first fortnight, so everyone was looking forward to that! I had made friends with Val Ebenezerson, who also came from Grimsby and was the son of an Icelandic trawler skipper. Val had reported to Lincoln on a beautiful brand new motor cycle and offered me a ride home, which I gladly accepted. There were no crash helmets in those days and it was my first time on a pillion, but we had an uneventful run home on the Friday evening and back again on the Sunday evening.

On the Monday of the third week we were introduced to the intricacies of the Bren gun, and believe it or not believe it or not at the end of that week most of us could assemble and strip down the gun blindfolded.

It was during that third week that I was told to report to the Medical Centre, and I wondered what on earth this could be for. When I arrived I was told to strip off completely and stand in front of three doctors who in turn examined, poked, sounded and prodded me in various places. Although I had learned to speak only when spoken to, I could keep quiet no longer and asked why I was being re- examined. I was told in a kindly way that I had been recommended for PDC at Chester. When I asked what PDC was, I was told it was a place where I would be given eight weeks of intensive physical training and a high-protein diet with extra rations to improve my stature and enable me to put on weight. The ignominy of this idea was appalling to me, so once again I spoke up saying that I didn't want to go to Chester, because was having no problems with any of the drill or physical training and would appreciate being allowed to complete my initial training. I don't know if it was my appeal to the doctors or because their minds were already made up, because I was told "Although you are apparently under weight you are reasonably well developed, so we have decided not to recommend you attend the Physical Development Centre and you can continue with your basic training". I felt a great burden had been lifted from me and reported back to my platoon with alacrity.

During the third week we began formation drill on the parade ground under the eagle eye of the Regimental Sergeant Major, Corky Mason, a name I will never forget. I was in the front row of our squad and when he came along and stood about a foot in front of me, gazed at me intently and then shouted out in that unmistakable sergeant major's bark, "Am I hurting you soldier?

"No sir" I replied.

"I bloody well ought to be man, I'm standing on your whiskers! When did you last shave?"

"But I don't shave sir" I replied, foolishly. He almost

had a seizure on the spot. When he regained his composure he screamed at me, "Well you bloody well do now! I shall be watching you closely from now on."

I took quite a bit of stick from the rest of the lads when we returned to our billet, but most of them thought it was a great joke. Corporal Crane wasn't unduly annoyed with me, but he advised me to nick myself with the razor now and again before I went on parade as added proof that I had shaved. This was something I often did, but inadvertently.

Our fourth week was another hectic round of activities, including sessions of the firing range with Bren guns and rifles and a never-to-be-forgotten session practising throwing live hand grenades. We each had to throw two. We were instructed in how to withdraw the pin, throw the grenade from the dugout overarm, then observe where the grenade had landed before taking cover by ducking our heads below the parapet. A young second lieutenant was in charge of instruction in our dugout. For my first grenade I simply pulled the pin, flung it as far as I could and threw myself to the ground. I was worried about the shrapnel and grenade base plates which had been whistling overhead when other people threw their grenades. As I hit the ground I heard the officer yelling to me to get up and observe where my grenade had landed. He shouted once again for me to stand up and once again I refused. He then flung himself down beside me as the base plate whistled over our heads. I half expected to be court martialled, but escaped with a few well-chosen oaths about my stupidity.

The fourth week of our training was supposedly concerned with deciding which regiment each individual would be most suited to at the end of his training. How this was decided I never quite knew, because we didn't take any aptitude tests. Presumably it was on the recommendations of the NCOs in charge of each platoon, but we had no inkling of where we might be heading. Anyone who had a School-leaving certificate was usually an automatic choice for one of the War Office Selection Boards which convened to decide which candidates had the attributes necessary for becoming an officer. A couple from our platoon were selected.

The parade ground drill was becoming more and more intense as we practised for our final passing-out parade, most of the time under the watchful eye of the RSM. We constantly vied with each other to be the smartest, the most efficient and best-drilled troop of the intake. There was actually a prize for the best troop and we knew that Corporal Crane had produced the prizewinners from the last two intakes. He was anxious to complete a hat trick, so as we respected and liked him, and buckled down to it with a will.

During our fifth week, when we were supposed to be honing up all we had learnt so far, we were amazed to be told that for the next three days we were all going potato picking. We were to report after breakfast in denims and ammunition boots to be transported to a farm a few miles away. Apparently there was a national emergency and troops all over the country were being drafted in to save the potato crop, as there was a great shortage of labour.

It proved to be three days of unforgettable and back-breaking work, but the farmer did pay us! I think we got about £2 each, and as we still received our army pay as well we didn't feel we had done too badly.

Another factor which counted towards the prize for the best troop was how well troop members fared in a six-mile cross-country race around Lincoln racecourse to take place on the Wednesday of our last week. I was anxious to participate because I thought I could do well. However on the Tuesday afternoon when everyone had to walk the course I was given the job of being a course marshal, to direct runners and to make sure no one was making short cuts. I was told I must be in position half an hour before the race commenced. With the blessing of Corporal Crane I soon managed to get someone who was only too willing to take my place as a marshal and I was in!

When the race started I was almost knocked over in a mad dash by about 600 bodies. I reflected that they obviously didn't know how far they had to go and knew most of them would never keep the pace up. Using my controlled breathing techniques (which I abandoned later in my running career) I gradually began to pick off and overtake the people in front of me. The main problem was that whenever there was a five-barred gate or a gap in the hedge to negotiate I lost minutes queuing up to go over or through, so I was getting very frustrated. Another disadvantage was that as I had been dropped off as a marshal the previous day I didn't know the rest of the course or just how far I had to go.

I would like to tell you that I gradually overhauled the rest of the field and won the race, but I actually finished fourth. However this was way ahead of anyone else in my troop, a success which whetted my appetite for competitive cross-country running.

Our last week was one frantic whirl of activity, preparing for final passing out parade cleaning and polishing equipment, boots, rifles etc, trying to find out where we had been assigned and awaiting the decision as to which one of us would be the billet orderly on the final passing out parade. This job was usually given to the person who was least able at parade ground drill or didn't quite conform to the symmetry of the rest of the squad. As was considerably smaller than everyone else, it was thought that I might be the unlucky one.

For a bunch of men who had been in the army less than six weeks there was fierce competition to participate. Fortunately I was included in the chosen squad, but we didn't win; we came second.

When the postings were announced I found I had been posted to the Royal Corps of Signals at Catterick to train as a radio operator. After such a short time together it was surprising how sad most of us were to be splitting up. That short period of intensive training had certainly bonded us together. On the Monday morning we lined up bright and early with full kit, rifles and kit bags to board a convoy of three tonners which would take us to Lincoln railway station. We changed at York before continuing to Catterick. We were met at Richmond station by a corporal and bundled into the back of another three-tonner. We had to stand up and hold on to the canvas-covered metal frame for the half-hour journey to Bourlon Lines. Here we congregated in a large mess hall to be allocated to various squads and receive an introductory talk from the Company Sergeant Major. I still remember his opening words: "You are now in Catterick, where a lance corporal is a little tin god and a sergeant major is Jesus Christ Almighty". That's certainly how it felt!

Bourlon Lines consisted of a large Sandhurst block with a huge parade ground in front of it surrounded by many training huts. The block was divided into three wings, each occupied by a different squadron. Our Commanding Officer was Lt. Col. T A R Scott, an ex-Japanese POW, whom we rarely saw. The Lance Corporal in charge of our troop was an old soldier who was also an ex POW and had served with the CO. We soon settled into our daily routine of training, which was mainly concerned with learning Morse code and sitting in training huts at desks with headphones on for hour after hour and day after day. There was usually one alternative period in both morning and afternoon when we did something else, which might be electricity and magnetism, radio procedure or even physical education. Whatever it was it was usually a welcome break from Morse training.

Wednesday afternoon was always a sports afternoon and everyone had to participate in some form of sport unless for some exceptional reason they had a note from the Medical Officer excusing participation.

Our regiment had a very fine football team which consisted mainly of NCOs who because of their footballing skills had been promoted and retained on the training staff. One of our physical training instructors was a corporal named Billy Dare who went on to be a professional with Brentford and for two years was among the league's leading goal scorers.

The food was not particularly good, but as we were always hungry our mess tins were nearly always scraped clean with the exception of one item on the menu, namely cheese and potato, which appeared at least twice a week. I had never tasted this before and initially disliked it intensely, but when I saw that there was always so much of it to spare I decided to cultivate a taste for it. I accomplished this in a very short time, so when this was on the menu I was always well satisfied.

About the beginning of December it was decreed on daily orders by the Colonel that the following Wednesday there would be a six-mile cross country run for the whole regiment, with no exemptions. It was amazing how many people found legitimate excuses for not competing. The race which took place in atrocious weather, which was just my cup of tea, and I romped home well ahead of anyone else and was showered and lying on my bunk before my troop returned. This win gave me quite a bit of status among my troop, but because of the weather during the rest of that winter there was no more cross country before we were posted.

We were all overjoyed when we were granted ten days' leave, which included Christmas and New Year. In January 1947 winter came with a vengeance. Everywhere around us was snowed up and it was the same in much of the country. There was a severe shortage of fuel, so we had no heating in our training huts, though heating was maintained in the main living block. Orders were then given that after every half hour of a Morse session we had to come outside in the snow, form into two teams and kick a football around for fifteen minutes. This went on for about six weeks. There were numerous fresh falls of snow during this period and our illustrious football team had progressed to the latter stages of the Army Cup. On several occasions the whole regiment turned out to clear the pitch of snow the day before a match, only for it to be covered thicker than ever the next day. Unfortunately we didn't manage to win the Army Cup later that year.

We were now in the final phase of our training and our immediate goal was to pass our B3 Trade Test. In order to pass we had to be able to read automatic Morse in plain language and in cypher at 20 and 18 words per minute respectively. The theory side of it was quite basic and consisted of a written paper on electricity and magnetism, for which an hour and a half was allowed.

There were quite a few characters in our squad. One was a lad called Hounslow, a Londoner who had made a living as a film extra and played bit parts in several films including *The Way To The Stars*, starring Michael Redgrave. Hounslow wore his hat at all times, even in bed. We all shared two tiered bunk beds and the lad I shared with was called Norman Ethel, a Geordie from East Bolden, which was only about twenty miles away from Catterick. He invited me to his home one weekend. His parents made me very welcome and we had a great time.

In our barrack room there was usually a card school going on when we were off duty. The main game was Three Card Brag. One Friday lunchtime I learned a lesson I have never forgotten. I was on Pay Parade at twelve thirty and by the time I went on parade at one o'clock I had lost every penny of my pay, all 21 shillings. I didn't gamble on Brag or anything else for the rest of my army career.

Another member of our squad was a lad called Parr, who had a beautiful voice and frequently entertained us with songs from opera to pop. I half expected him to make it big as a singer, but I guess he didn't. A Scot we all knew as wee Jock was only as tall as I was, if a little stockier, and came from the Gorbals. He was constantly in trouble for disciplinary matters, so he was always on fatigues or confined to barracks, or both. Confined to barracks, or CB, meant having to report to the Guard Room every night in FSMOA. This meant carrying most of your equipment, including haversacks and panniers, all freshly blancoed with brasses polished. The haversack and panniers had to contain the regulation contents. Any little detail which was not up to scratch meant more CB. Wee Jock stuck it out for about two months and then went AWOL; no one ever saw him again.

Most of us passed our trade test first time and those who didn't were back-squadded according to their degree of failure, with usually a month or two months' extra training before taking their test again. At the beginning of March 1947 we were all posted to Thirsk, near York, the Royal Signals transit camp. The atmosphere at Thirsk was entirely different from Lincoln or Catterick, much more relaxed and easy going. The routine was that you paraded in the morning after breakfast, when a few unlucky ones were selected for various fatigues and the rest dispersed back to their billets. To most of us after seven hectic months in the army doing most things at the double, it was very hard to comprehend and we wondered what was coming next. Card schools and gambling resumed in earnest, but I had no desire to be sucked into that circle again. Rumours were rife as to where we were going to be posted to, but somewhere in the Far East seemed to be the favourite.

On the Monday of our second week we all lined up for various inoculations and were presented with ration cards and pay and ration money for three weeks and sent home on leave that same afternoon. This was standard embarkation leave for a Far East posting, so we naturally thought that that was where we must be heading.

On the railway station at Thirsk a porter came up to me and said "Fancy seeing you!" It was a lad I had known at Middleton, a Sunderland evacuee called Alan Steel. He was a big lad who had been snapped up by a farmer to assist on the farm. His parents had now moved to Thirsk and he was now awaiting his call up into the RAF. It's a small world!

When I first returned home I had a few days when I didn't feel so good, most likely due to the inoculations I thought. I soon recovered and enjoyed the rest of my leave immensely. By this time my brother Tom had joined the Merchant Navy and was on a tanker en route to Curaçao.

The first day back at Thirsk we were all lined up for yet another batch of inoculations and informed that we were not going to the Far East after all but would leave for Germany the following Saturday. We travelled by rail from Thirsk to Hull, and there tied up alongside part of the Mulberry harbour which had been used in the D-Day landings was the troopship *Empire Halladale*. Our quarters on board were extremely cramped as you might expect but in no time at all it seemed, we had cast off and were heading towards the mouth of the Humber estuary, our destination Cuxhaven.

As soon as we were told it was all right for us to go

up on deck I was up there in a flash. The mass of bodies around me and the throb of the engines were already making me feel a little queasy. The fresh air on deck made me feel much better, but I declined to line up for food. I remained on deck as we left the estuary and headed out into the North Sea, and almost immediately the ship began to pitch and roll and within a very few minutes I had to push my way through a group of ATS girls and be violently sick. Fortunately I had chosen the lee side and it went straight into the sea.

Eventually I was ordered to go below and had to make lots of trips to the heads (toilets) during the night. The trouble was that lots of my companions were feeling the same way and you were lucky if there was a vacancy. I dragged myself up on deck next morning still feeling wretched and managed to find a small corner to prop myself up in with my greatcoat around me. Shortly after this the sun began to shine and either the ship wasn't rolling so much or I was getting used to it.

We were informed that the small island we were about to pass on our left was Heligoland, the famous German naval base. Only a few days previously it had been the scene of the largest explosion since the atomic bombs when thousands of tons of shells, mines and ammunition had been detonated in a huge controlled explosion organised by the Royal Engineers.

By late afternoon I was feeling much better. I actually went down to the mess deck and ate fish and chips, with no ill effects. After we disembarked at Cuxhaven we were transported to a German naval barracks to sleep. Next morning we boarded a troop train and were told that our destination was Bielefeld, an RFU (Reinforcement Holding Unit) in North Rhine Westphalia. Cuxhaven was a relatively small town on the estuary of the river Elbe and we headed in a south-easterly direction for about five hours until we reached Hanover.

So far we had seen very little bomb damage, but as we travelled the last mile or so into Hanover railway station we were amazed at the devastation. There was nothing on either side of us but completely flattened buildings. London, Coventry, Hull etc were as nothing compared with this. From Hanover it was another couple of hours to Bielefeld, where we boarded the usual three-tonners to take us to the RFU.

The next morning we were informed of our postings. Along with five others from my squad I was to be posted to 2 L of C Signals Regiment at Herford, which was only about 35 miles away. After only one night at Herford I was informed that we were to be posted yet again to 10 and 14 High Speed Wireless Troop, situated at Rhine Army Headquarters at Bad Oeynhausen about another ten miles away. This was however considered to be a detachment, and Herford remained our headquarters.

Arriving in 'Bad O' was quite an eye-opener for us. The whole of the population of this small spa town had been moved out and their homes and public buildings requisitioned. I don't know if they were offered other accommodation; I doubt it because houses were in extremely short supply. Our billet was at 18 Porterstrasse, a good-sized, pleasant-looking house which had probably been a guest house in happier times. The wireless station was half of a printing works less than two minutes from our house.

Our unit consisted of about 50 men, and our Commanding Officer was a Lieutenant Blackburn. We had an admin sergeant and a Lance Corporal in the office and three men at the transmitter site, which was a couple of miles outside town. The rest were divided into three watches with an NCO in charge. Most of the men were ex-Post Office or Cable and Wireless employees who had been specially recruited in 1943 to man the high-speed units which would accompany the invasion forces. They were equipped with large articulated vehicles known as Golden Arrows. These vehicles contained a powerful Swab 8 transmitter, a tall sectional aerial and a number of keyboards which produced Morse characters on a punched paper tape. One of the sections was a press section and transmitted all the newspaper correspondents' reports back to UK from D-Day to the surrender. The other one was concerned with normal army signals traffic. This section only moved when necessary, while the press section was usually much closer to the front line.

The idea behind the Golden Arrows was that they were a self-contained and if necessary mobile unit, capable of moving large volumes of traffic at high speed, which obviated the need for slow manual links. When we first arrived most of the old hands were very amused, because here we were, a bunch of newly-trained Operators Wireless and Line, a trade, sent to replace a bunch of élite experienced Operators Wireless and Keyboard. They were concerned too because the time for their demobilisation was fast approaching and they knew that if there were no trained replacements their demob could well be deferred. The chief problem was that none of us could type, so all we could do at first was to man the manual point-to-point links with the various units within Rhine Army.

Two weeks later it was decided that as there were no more OWKs due to finish training for another six months we would have to train and sit an “A” trade test and, provided we passed, remuster as OWKs. There followed six weeks of an intensive typing course, at the end of which you had to pass out at 40 words per minute on plain language and 35 words per minute on cipher and slip reading. Fortunately I had become very friendly with a couple of the old hands and they started me off on touch typing in my spare time a couple of weeks before the actual course began, so I didn't find the pass-out speeds too difficult to attain.

The course also included the erection of 70 foot aerial masts, which was quite an art, especially if it was windy. We all managed to pass the course and the would be demob candidates heaved sighs of relief. As a consequence of passing our trade tests, remustering as

A3s meant an extra three shillings a day, not to be sneezed at in those days.

One of the first things we noticed about our new unit was the relaxed discipline, which was very much in contrast to our training units. There were occasional guard duties and a compulsory church parade for off-duty personnel every month, but nothing too strenuous, and no fatigues at all.

My first compulsory church parade triggered off an attempt to start a new relationship with God by attending the Garrison church every Sunday morning when I wasn't on duty. If anything else cropped up, such as a football or cricket match, even a recreational transport trip, church had to take second place.

Field Marshal Montgomery was a regular attender at our church and always made a habit of chatting to other ranks after the service. I did speak to him on a couple of occasions, but I am sure some people attended just to rub shoulders with the great man (more about Monty later).

This was the dawn of a new era for the British Army, initiated by Montgomery himself. His new model army would have sheets on their beds, a drastic reduction in drills and parades and a continuation of the relaxed discipline we were already enjoying.

Some of us had a rude awakening when we were detailed to go out into the German countryside for a week to provide communications for a big combined services exercise. Lots of things went wrong during the exercise, but the experience was invaluable.

Shortly after this I made another big mistake when I informed our admin sergeant that I would prefer not to attend a Drill and Duties course at Herford. This course was a prerequisite for promotion and meant a lance corporal's stripe. Four members of our troop accepted with alacrity and within three months had a second stripe and were full corporals. This was the long hot glorious summer of 1947, when Compton and Edrich were rewriting the record books in English County cricket. As servicemen on active service abroad we had a free issue of 50 cigarettes per week, plus the opportunity to buy more from the NAAFI at duty-free prices. Cigarettes and coffee were the main currency of a thriving black market, and most of us saw nothing wrong in participating in it. As I was a non-smoker I was in a very good position and freely exchanged my cigarettes for German currency or other items in demand.

We were all made aware that black market dealing was illegal and could lead to prosecution. The black market was now part and parcel of the way of life in occupied Germany and at that time it was a tide which could not be stemmed. My first real involvement came about as a result of a trip with a couple of friends, Alec Grey and Derek Spence. We had spent Saturday afternoon in town at the YMCA, and as we left we were approached by a German whom we came to know as Karl-Heinz. He spoke quite good English and asked us if we had any cigarettes to barter for money, watches or cameras. We arranged to meet in Herford the following week, when he would take us to his home for an English tea! This turned out to be some rather dubious coffee and a plate of small fancy Continental-style cakes. Remember that this was immediate post-war Germany, which had not yet begun its recovery.

Karl was in his mid forties and a former major in the German army. He was an instrument and watchmaker by profession but had worked for most of the war years as a technical liaison officer with the Krupps organisation. He was small and lean, as was his wife Veda. Their home was a small and sparsely-furnished flat in a block on the outskirts of Herford. Despite the small flat they had a large and nondescript but very friendly dog; it must have been difficult for them to feed him in those days. This began a friendship which lasted for the best part of my stay in Germany and gave us some idea of the way we were looked upon by the Germans.

I can imagine the reader thinking that we were taking advantage of an acquaintanceship which was of mutual benefit to both sides. Initially this was true, but later we often visited with no exchange involved, always making sure that one of us took a small jar of coffee as a gift, which was always greeted with great joy as it was virtually unobtainable by the local population.

Karl and his wife had managed to escape from the Russian zone a few weeks after the war ended. They had some horrifying and almost unbelievable tales of atrocities by Russian troops. As the hostility between East and West began to intensify, they feared what might happen if the Red Army invaded Allied-occupied Germany.

I remember one night at Karl's we had a little party for a neighbour who had just returned home. He had been a prisoner of war in Russia since Stalingrad and here he was only just being repatriated nearly two and a half years after the war. Though obviously overjoyed to be home and reunited with his wife, he looked thin and emaciated. He was just thirty years old, but he looked at least fifty. I can imagine the reader wondering how I knew that Karl wasn't a war criminal who had fled to the west to escape prosecution. I don't, but my instincts told me that they were decent people and looking back over fifty years I still believe so. Germany was flooded with DPs (displaced persons), a real hotchpotch of humanity, most of whom had suffered greatly during the war years, chiefly at the hands of the Germans and Russians. These people, many of whom were Jews, were scattered throughout Germany in DP camps, surrounded once again by barbed wire. The Jews still lived in hope of the promised homeland in Palestine, while many of the others longed to return to their homes in Eastern Europe. The fate of these unfortunates was still the subject of countless debates by the United Nations.

In Nuremburg the trials of the Nazi war criminals ground slowly but inexorably on, accounts of the day's proceedings being published every day in the forces' daily newspaper.

Life in Germany for the occupying forces was good. We had plenty of recreational facilities and ten days local leave annually, which could be spent at leave centres such as Bad Hartzburg or Winterburg. We had 19 days' home leave in the UK every six months and were given excellent food and plenty of it, while the local people existed on a very austere diet. There was usually plenty of recreational transport. I made two trips to the Bielefeld Stadt Opera House to see La Bohème and later Carmen. This was my first introduction to opera, and though it was in German I thoroughly enjoyed it. The opera house always played to packed houses, mostly Germans, but we had free seats with the best view in the house.

Another perk was that as occupying forces we had free seats on all public transport. Civilian transport had to stop and offer lifts when flagged down. This meant that on a day off you could pay a visit to any place of interest in Westphalia. The Volkswagen was resuming production and the basic model was available to British servicemen on a unit allocation basis for the sum of just over £70 sterling.

The work in our wireless room was quite interesting. On the high speed side we had regular schedules with War Office and British Troops Berlin. Besides our manual Morse links with the surrounding units, we were the control for about eight outstations on Operation Woodpecker. This was an operation organised by the British in their own zone to fell and ship as much timber as possible to the areas where it was most needed for rebuilding and repairing bomb-damaged property. At the end of each day they sent us reports on the amount of work completed plus any requirements. When the morning watch came on duty the first thing that had to be done was to phone the details to the appropriate department in Rhine Army HQ.

The main Signals Office was situated only about fifty yards away from our wireless HQ room and they transmitted the bulk of the traffic from HQ, enciphered and by landline. About once a month we would have saturation exercises for a 24-hour period, when every message other than high-grade cipher had to be transmitted by radio. This was to prepare us for coping with an emergency. We had a weekly schedule every Sunday evening at eight o'clock with the British Forces Leave Centre at Ehrwald in the Austrian Tyrol.

One Sunday evening I was alone on duty and at five minutes to eight I sat down at the Ehrwald position. I sent a few v's on my key and the Ehrwald operator immediately came back to me. We exchanged callsigns and the appropriate signals confirming that neither of us had any traffic to send and terminated our schedule; the time was then four minutes to eight. Two minutes later the bell sounded; it was an ATS girl with a top priority message for Ehrwald concerning a sergeant who had to return home immediately because his father was dying!

I signed for the message and dashed back to the set and began to send the callsign. I expect I was praying, but I don't really remember. At first there was no response, but about two minutes later I heard the sweet sound of my callsign coming over the speaker from the Ehrwald operator. I rapidly sent the message, had it acknowledged and closed the link down. I thanked my lucky stars, though I know now it should have been God I thanked.

In the summer of 1947 I tried to visit as many places as possible in my off-duty time. I went to the Mohne See to view the site of the historic Dambusters' raid, and visited Bad Hartzberg and the Black Forest.

Bad Oeynhausen was very close to the River Weser of Pied Piper fame and it skirted our football pitches. After one hectic match both teams went straight into the river to cool off.

Bomb damage was still very much in evidence across Germany. In the worst-hit cities it was usual to observe the work of the Trummerfrauen or 'rubble women' as they cleared away the debris of bomb damage with their bare hands, usually forming human chains. I still don't know whether this was an organised effort with payment involved or if it was voluntary.

I proceeded on my first home leave with plenty of money, because I had needed to draw very little pay during my first six months in Germany. On the leave train travelling to the Hook of Holland I had my kit bag searched by a CCG official (Control Commission of Germany), an English civilian. He found only the permitted number of cigarettes and liquor, but homed in on a tin containing three pounds of butter which had been procured for me by Karl Heinz in exchange for cigarettes. He gave me a real dressing down in front of the other occupants of the carriage, but fortunately did not confiscate the butter, which was still rationed in the UK.

I returned to Germany after a very enjoyable leave, but not looking forward to my first winter there. To cheer myself up I applied for and was granted ten days' local leave in mid December, at the winter sports leave centre at Wintersberg. I was reliably informed that the first snows came in late November, but during the whole of my leave there was never more than a light dusting of snow on a couple of days. Learning to ski was impossible, but the accommodation was very good, the food excellent and it was a relaxing break.

In mid January there were some good falls of snow in our own area. Several of us went down to the HQ sports store and signed out the necessary skiing equipment. Over the next few days we virtually taught ourselves the basics of skiing on some gentle slopes outside the town. This included lots of hilarious episodes which ended with one or the other of us half-buried in snowdrifts with skis and legs at impossible angles.

Early in 1948 the British Navy intercepted a ship loaded with Jewish refugees en route to Palestine and escorted the ship into Hamburg. The Jews refused to disembark and there was lots of media attention. We were ordered to set up and maintain a radio link between the ship and HQ Rhine Army.

I was often unhappy at some of the reports and replies we were receiving and transmitting, all in plain language. The Cold War was beginning to intensify and the Russians had started occasionally cutting our landlines to Berlin. Usually this was only for an hour or so, but it was a great source of irritation and worry to our communications centre. It meant that we were the sole method of communication between HQ and Berlin, and we were inundated with work.

In March 1948 I went home on leave, which coincided with my brother Tom being home as he was now in the Merchant Navy and had just returned from a trip to Curaçao. We decided to visit Dad's sisters Kate and Bridie in Salford, and while there we met our cousins Agnes and May for the first time. They were similar ages to us. On the first evening we were asked if we would like to accompany the girls down to the Mission. When we looked puzzled, Aunt Kate said, "Holy Mary Mother of God, ye've not been brought up in the faith". They were obviously very disappointed.

In the last few years my father had often said he had finished with the sea for good, but for the past year he had been working in a small shipyard in Grimsby called Doig's. They were just completing a new missionary ship called the John Williams VI. She had been built for the London Missionary Society for service in the South Sea Islands of the Pacific. Dad had been involved in her sea trials and had agree to crew her first to Australia and then on to Suva. The ship was due to be dedicated in a ceremony at Tower Bridge in London by Princess Margaret. After a few more publicity stops at other ports she would set sail on her maiden voyage at the end of September. Knowing I was to leave the army then, Dad had secured a place in the crew for me. I don't know how he did it, but it seemed a better prospect than a wartime Russian convoy!

Back once again in Germany, I thought long and hard about my aunt's reaction when she had realised that we hadn't been brought up as Catholics. I had been impressed by them all, as they seemed much more sincere about their religion and actually seemed to enjoy it! I thought perhaps this was the religion for me, as I was never really spiritually moved by my occasional visits to my Garrison Anglican church. I contacted our Regimental Roman Catholic padre and we had a long chat. He gave me some booklets to read and arranged another meeting a couple of weeks later. After a short exchange he told me he thought I was only dabbling and wasn't really serious about converting. He advised me to read some more pamphlets and think about what converting to Roman Catholicism really meant, and if I still felt the same way in a month's time I should contact him again.

A month later I had other things on my mind and the idea was forgotten. The Soviets then began to make travel through their zone to Berlin as difficult as possible and would hold up Allied trains. It was decided that in future any important train would carry a mobile transmitter and a Royal Signals operator who instruction from the train commander would inform HQ immediately if a problem arose. Only a few days later the Soviets stopped a train in the middle of their zone. We maintained a constant watch on the pre-arranged frequencies, but never managed to contact the train. After five days of mounting tension it was allowed to continue to Berlin.

One day in early May we had just returned to our billet after morning tea break (a sacred institution) when we were told to assemble in the set room at twelve o'clock. We were told that because of a desperate shortage of manpower at Berlin Signals Unit, six of us would be going on a temporary posting to Berlin the next day. I was one of the six. I must admit that I quailed a little at the thought of this, because thing were becoming extremely tense. Before we left we were told that our posting should not last very long because replacements would be arriving from the UK within about three weeks.

Next day we boarded the train at Bad Oeynhausen station to take us on the first part of our journey to Berlin. It took about five hours to get to Helmstedt, but the train had an excellent dining car which provided superb meals, free to service personnel.

Waiting for us on the British side of the border were six large single-deck army buses, each one allocated to an NCO to be bus commander (not an officer, although we had quite a few in our party). The bus I was to travel on also carried the man who was the convoy commander, a QSMI (Quarter Master Sergeant Instructor) in the Physical Training Corps. He checked my rifle, gave me five rounds to put in my breast pocket and informed me that I was to be the guard on his bus until we arrived in Berlin. He emphasised that I must be constantly on the alert and that I should sit on the front seat of the bus next to him.

To my amazement he came back a few minutes later with one of the biggest Alsatian dogs I've ever seen and said, "Keep a tight hold of him when we go through the checkpoints, he hates Russians". The buses then rolled gently through the British side of the checkpoint and as we approached the Russian side a Soviet officer (whom I christened "Smiling Jack" after a cartoon character) stepped out in front of us. He was flanked either side by two scruffy-looking Mongolian types with automatic guns at the ready.

As he stepped on to the boarding platform of our bus our QSMI stepped forward. His dog went berserk and I heard the safety catches come off their automatic weapons. They were in deadly fear of this dog and I visualised World War Three commencing as a result of this incident. My rifle was knocked to the floor as I tried restrain the dog. I'm sure that if I hadn't managed to hold the dog he would not have survived.

Our bus door was slammed shut and our QSMI accompanied Smiling Jack and as our cohorts as they checked the other buses. At last they were satisfied and we were allowed to move off along the autobahn towards Berlin. We had an uneventful journey of several hours until we finally pulled up on the outskirts of Berlin at the infamous Checkpoint Charlie. As I reflect on this time, I can't help but think how typically British it all was. If things had gone awry there I was, a signalman, not even a trained infantryman, with a cumbersome rifle and five rounds in my breast pocket.

We were met in Berlin by our unit transport, which took us straight to our billets. Our unit had been allocated part of a large block of flats in what had been a very upmarket area of Berlin called New Westend. As we travelled through Berlin we were surprised to see how much bomb damage there was. It was worse than any place we had seen and there was no sign of any work being carried out by the Trummerfrauen, yet this was three years after the end of the war.

Early next morning, accompanied by two signalmen who were going on for their shift, we walked a couple of hundred yards from our billet and caught the U- Bahn (underground railway), alighting a couple of stops later. We were now at the Headquarters of British Troops Berlin, very close to the famous Kurfürstendamm, which had been a very prestigious thoroughfare. Our wireless room was part of the HQ building and we were ushered in front of the officer in charge for a briefing. He confirmed that our sojourn in Berlin would only be three or four weeks at the maximum. He advised us not to go into the Russian zone and to visit any sights we wanted to see in the next couple of days, because after this we would be starting a shift rota of eight hours on and eight hours off. He added that it had been decided that our transmitters should remain on at all times even if we had no traffic. The idea of this was that if the Russians cut our landlines to HQ Rhine Army and our transmitters went off the air as well, it would indicate that things were very serious.

We were then allocated shift rotas which permitted me and my friend Len Crapper to play football in a very important cup match the following Saturday. With the help of free transport on both the U-Bahn and the S-Bahn (overhead transport) we visited lots of the popular attractions. The following Saturday Len and I had a conducted tour around the Olympic Stadium complex before playing and winning a hard-fought cup match, Len scoring two great goals.

In a very short space of time the shift pattern of eight hours on and eight off began to pall. Sometimes things were slack, but often we were working flat out. After about a week we stopped returning to our billets and slept on a mattress in an adjoining room. We found that among the reasons for the chronic staff shortage was that one soldier was absent without leave and another had been shot and seriously wounded by the Russians as he left their zone after visiting a Fräulein he was keeping company with. The media made much of this incident and the soldier's wife was brought out to Berlin to visit him in hospital. Unfortunately, when she arrived, the German girlfriend was also at his bedside. Oh what a tangled web we weave!

Our colleagues back at Rhine Army were also short staffed because of our postings, and they too were working the deadly eight on, eight off shift system. After almost two weeks of this system the powers that be either had a change of heart or knew from intelligence reports that the situation had toned down, because all of a sudden we were ordered to revert to normal shift working. Off-duty times during the next few days were usually spent in bed trying to catch up on lost sleep, but then we were told our temporary posting was terminated and we would be returning to our unit as soon as there were bus seats available.

Our last couple of days were occupied with viewing various places of interest, including the Brandenburg Gate and the Unter Den Linden. We had a farewell party with a few of our new friends in the French Club, where good champagne was cheaper than beer. This club in the French Sector was frequented by all the occupying powers, including the Russians, and there were quite a few that night watching the cabaret. No one felt particularly bright the next morning as we boarded our transport to be taken to our bus.

This time none of us were called upon to be a guard and we had a trouble-free trip through the Russian zone to Helmstedt. Once again we boarded a semi-luxurious train for our trip back to HQ. There was almost a disaster when we arrived at Bad Oeynhausen station to find we had all forgotten our kitbags, and the train was about to pull out. I sprinted up the platform, opened the guard's van door and flung our bags out as the train started to move. As I flung the last one out and jumped the train was leaving the platform, and I actually landed on the slope at the end, to the accompaniment of loud cheers. Fortunately I didn't hurt myself.

During my first week back from Berlin I was informed that HQ Rhine Army Sports Day was in a couple of days' time and that I would be representing our unit in the 5000 metres event. I hadn't trained for a while and was keyed up and nervous prior to the race. I knew the Garrison numbered over 10,000 men, including infantry regiments where athletics received a high priority. It was a blistering hot day and there seemed to be thousands of spectators, mostly service personnel and their families.

At the end of my first lap I felt good and went into the lead. About a quarter of the track was in the shade, so every time I ran into the shaded area I slowed slightly, enjoying the shade, but accelerated in the sunny part of the track. Using this system I ran away from the rest of the competitors and came home alone almost a lap ahead and in record time. My friend Ian Harper finished a close second in the high jump, so for a small unit we had fared very well.

As a consequence of this our Regimental Sports Officer, a young lieutenant from Herford, told us that we would both be representing the regiment in the

Rhine Army sports event at Detmold in a couple of weeks' time. I did manage to train a few times, but I played football the day before and that same evening I consumed about four pints of beer and six large hot cream doughnuts!

Next morning I was aroused by the sound of a Jeep's horn below my billet. It was the Regimental Sports Officer with official transport to take me to Detmold. I grabbed my haversack and piled into the Jeep with my head pounding and feeling ghastly. The Lieutenant admonished me for not being ready and then informed me that I would be competing in both the 1500 and the 5000 metres, as they were well apart in the programme.

It was a nightmare of a journey, though it was a distance of less than twenty miles. When the 5000 started my head was no better and I felt sick, but managed to settle down with the bunch at the rear of the field. Every time I ran past the lieutenant he told me to move up and overtake the man in front. I did manage to move up another couple of positions, but was then content to complete the race at the rear of the field. He was furious with me and said I would have to do better in the 1500 metres.

My heart sank. I could hardly walk, as my calf muscles were like iron and I still had a terrible headache. However there was a German Olympic coach in attendance, and when he saw me staggering off he called me to come and lie down on his bench. He then began to pummel and massage my legs. It hurt so much that I couldn't help yelling out. However, after about ten minutes of this torture, my muscles began to relax and my headache was fast disappearing. I felt like a new man. A few minutes later I was drinking copious amounts of water and even managed to eat a couple of sandwiches. Two hours later I managed to finish a creditable third in the 1500 (which wasn't my distance anyway).

Soon after this we had yet another 24-hour saturation exercise which did not end until eight in the morning. I was on the midnight to eight shift. Unfortunately this was the day when Field Marshal Montgomery was scheduled to inspect our Wireless Room and our billet. Our sergeant told us not to worry and said we should get to bed and place a card on the door saying "Night Shift - Do Not Disturb". At about eleven in the morning we were all sleeping soundly when there was a series of sharp raps on our door. It opened to reveal Monty and his entourage. He gazed in at us and we stared back through bleary eyes. He then closed the door. Our sergeant later told us that Monty had insisted on seeing for himself despite being informed that we were all sleeping.

June 1948 was a very eventful month, as East-West tension continued to mount. On June 20th the West Germans changed their currency overnight, abolishing the Mark and introduced the new Deutschmark. All West German citizens were given forty new Deutschmarks, and all the old currency was declared invalid, whether you possessed thousands or millions.

This virtually brought dealings on the black market to an end, and with the assistance of the Marshall Aid plan, West Germany... began its economic recovery.

Things really hotted up on June 24th when Russia blocked all rail and road land routes into Berlin and precipitated the start of the Berlin Airlift. They did not cut our landlines, but we were on tenterhooks wondering if and when they would do so. As the situation intensified, all I could think of was how it might affect my demobilisation in September and prevent me from taking a trip on the *John Williams*, which was becoming more appealing every day. Not long after this my hopes were dashed when it was officially announced that demobilisation of certain trades were to be deferred for six months. This appeared on Regimental Orders with the letters DOV (Deferred, Operationally Vital) in brackets next to each of our names. What incensed most of us was that all the infantry regiments continued with their normal demobilisation process, yet if the balloon did go up they were just as vital as we were.

I wrote and told my father of the bad news, which he had already guessed, as he had contacted my cousin Bernie (Aunt Kate's son) to see if he was interested in taking my place. Of course he jumped at the opportunity and joined the ship when it sailed in September.

The next few months were very unsettling. Whereas previously I had enjoyed practically every phase of my army career, I now found it very difficult to concentrate on my job. There was however one bonus to being deferred, because I was entitled to another ten days' local leave, which I took in late August at a delightful leave centre called Altenau, a small German village surrounded by pine woods and mountain streams. I returned to my unit in a better frame of mind, determined to enjoy my last few months in the army. I resumed my running training, played quite a lot of tennis and travelled around locally as much as possible on days off.

The airlift appeared to be a great success, but no doubt the coming winter would be a testing time. Our unit continued on a high state of alert and we still had our monthly saturation exercise. As winter approached with lots of cold damp and foggy weather and we were all pleased that we were not in Berlin.

In the November I competed in the HQ Cross Country Championships over a distance of five and a half miles, but could only finish third. The race was won by a Major on the HQ staff and a corporal from the Royal Engineers was second. These were the men who had finished second and third to me in the HQ 5000 metres a few months previously. The cross-country race was memorable for me because after the race we went in for a shower caked in mud and there was no hot water. Letting a trickle run over you removed very little mud, but it did respond to a cold jet, which was absolute agony. I must confess though that I felt terrific afterwards.

Just before Christmas I was called into the office to see the Commanding Officer. He asked me what I intended to do when I left the army and I told him I didn't know. He then said that if I would consider making a career of the army he would guarantee to make me a sergeant within six months. I politely declined his kind offer and carried on looking forward to my release.

On January 8 1949 I was playing table tennis in the Kurhaus (the NAAFI) when our admin corporal dashed in and said he'd been looking all over for me. He told me I was due to be demobbed in York the next day and they had omitted to let me know. It was eleven in the morning and the Hook of Holland train left at two in the afternoon. I had nothing packed, and leaving your unit was a very complex process involving visiting various departments and handing in various pieces of equipment and clothing. I told the corporal it was impossible for me to be on that train, and he said his job was on the line if I didn't make it.

Somehow we accomplished it and our unit transport pulled up with me at the station with five minutes to spare. I had ideas about relaxing on the train, but my mind was racing after the hectic rush I had just completed. I had not expected to finish in the army until March at the earliest, and here I was heading home two months early.

I was demobilised on the 9th January 1949, and I have clear recollections of the York centre. I was issued with a blue pin-striped suit which actually fitted me, a mackintosh, a trilby and one each of what were considered to be clothing essentials. These items were all neatly packed into a large brown cardboard box. I was given a month's pay in advance, plus ration allowance and a railway warrant to Grimsby, plus ration coupons, as many things were still rationed. I was granted 77 days' leave, 56 of which were the normal demobilisation leave, added to which was another 21 days, one day per month for every day I had spent overseas.

Outside the centre were a number of men who were offering ten pounds for our outfit boxes. I was surprised to see quite a few did dispose of their boxes in this way. There was a bus which ran every hour to the railway station but I shared a taxi with a friend. After ascertaining the times of our trains a large number of us congregated in the licensed part of the station buffet and indulged in all kinds of intoxicating drinks while we waited. By the time my train arrived it was nearly midnight and I had drunk far too much and didn't find it easy boarding the train carrying that big cardboard box, kitbag and carrier several bags. I vaguely remember changing trains at Retford and sitting in a carriage with a couple of railway workers and having to make numerous trips to the toilet to be sick.

I arrived in Grimsby at six in the morning and had to knock on our door for about five minutes before Mum came down and let me in. After greeting everyone, I stumbled into bed and slept for most of the day.

So began a new phase of my life. For the first few weeks of my leave I relaxed and enjoyed myself meeting up with old friends and attending dances at various dance halls in the area, in particular at a place known as the Gaiety Ballroom. The big attraction of this venue was the constant stream of well-known bands. Among them were Cyril Stapleton with Bill McGuffie on the piano, Ted Heath and h s Band, featuring singers Lita Rosa and Dennis Lotis, the Squadronaires, Oscar Rabin and his Band, featuring a vocalist called Bernard Manning (I preferred him as a singer to his later role as a racist, foul mouthed comedian). This was a time when many of the big bands were struggling to keep afloat. The entrance fee was only two and sixpence (twelve and a half new pence) Monday to Thursday and three and six (seventeen and a half pence) on Fridays and Saturdays. When I attended dances I usually wore my uniform (for obvious reasons), as I was entitled to do so until my leave expired.

It was at one of these dances that I met a girl who was to become a major factor in my life. Our initial meeting was a couple of slow foxtrots to the music of Cyril Stapleton. She was a small, very pretty reddish-haired girl in a pink Angora jumper and she danced beautifully, but I didn't see her again for several weeks.

My leave was slipping away at a very fast rate and I knew I had to start looking for employment. My Uncle George, now a deep sea fisherman, took me around several company offices to see if anyone would sponsor me to train as a trawler's radio operator, but there seemed to be a surfeit and no one was interested.

I had already joined the Royal Signals Association for servicemen and ex-servicemen, and they sent me details of a number of employment vacancies. The first I applied for was at a watercress farm at Healing, about five miles from Grimsby. It was run by an ex-Royal Signals major and the job was mine if I was interested. The pay was six pounds and ten shillings a week, good pay in those days. The thought of wading around cleaning out and cutting watercress beds just wasn't for me, so I declined the offer.

In the list of vacancies there were two similar advertisements asking for men who had served as radio operators who could send and receive Morse at certain speeds. One of them had an additional requirement of being able to type and slip read. I thought this was the job for me, and applied to GCHQ Bletchley Park. This organisation and its address didn't mean a thing to me in those days and I just sat back and waited to see whether they were interested in me or not.

Less than a week later I received a large buff envelope which contained rates of pay, conditions of service and a railway warrant for an interview at Bletchley a couple of weeks hence. A few days later when I was rereading the conditions of service I noticed that the minimum age was 21. This was in the March and I wasn't going to be 21 until July. When I contacted them and pointed this out, they asked me to make a fresh application as soon as I reached my birthday. I applied to a subsequent advertisement, and within another couple of weeks I received another railway warrant and the offer of an interview and Morse test the following month with the War Office station at Beaumanor in Leicestershire.

A few days later we had a letter from Dad to say that he was on his way home from Australia, where he had been reunited with long-lost cousins of his, Aunt Ruby and Uncle Jack, and of that he had some momentous news for us all. A couple of weeks later Dad arrived home. He had brought a young shipmate to stay with us for a few days.

The momentous news was that going to we were all going to Australia. Uncle Jack ran a large building firm there, there would be a new house for us to move into and Terry, Tom and I were to be given jobs with him and learn the trade from top to bottom.

I must admit it sounded good to me. My cousin Bernie had eagerly accepted and had remained behind in Sydney. There was however one stumbling block, and it turned out to be an insurmountable one. My mother would have none of it, so it withered immediately and was not considered again.

The second night Dad was home there was the inevitable "do" and we all trooped down to a small pub opposite Ethel's house. Lots of drinks were consumed and afterwards we went across to Aunt Ethel's to continue the revelry. By a stroke of bad luck I had to catch a train early next the morning for job interview and morse test. I awoke feeling terrible and long past the time when I should have caught my train to Loughborough. I arrived with a nasty hangover and the feeling that I had no chance of passing either my morse test or interview. Somehow I must have done because I was told there and then that I was accepted and given a starting date.

When I arrived at Beaumanor the second time I was in a much more receptive state of mind. As I left the bus I noted the lodge house at the end of the drive with a small sign with the letters WOYG (War Office "Y" Group) on it. I walked down the drive to the manor house, a distance of about four hundred yards. At the main entrance I was booked in by a security man and signed for and received my site pass. After a brief guided tour I was then shown to the second floor and to a fairly large room containing six beds with adjacent steel lockers, very much army style. Two of the beds were already occupied by a couple of "Geordies", Sam Spencer and Frank Mackin, and I was told I could take my pick of the four remaining beds.

A few days later Frank Mackin moved next door into a smaller two-bed room and we had four newcomers introduced to our room. Their names were Frank Donnelly, Ep Jones and the Dowsett twins, Les and Gerald. Ep and the twins had recently been demobbed after service in Cyprus but Frank, who had landed on "D" Day as an eighteen year old, was unhappy back in his civilian job and wanted a change.

Everyone joining Beaumanor had to spend a period of time in the training class irrespective of previous experience. As I was completely new to this type of work it was quite an eye opener for me, but it captured my interest straight away. The person in charge of the training was Harry Dix and his assistant was Jim Collins, an ex sergeant major in the Royal Signals.

When we had completed almost three weeks intensive training aimed at improving all-round morse speeds I naively asked "When do we start to practice our morse sending"? There was a silence and then I was told "You don't! Interception is the name the of game". I was later informed the mention of morse sending in the advert was for security purposes.

Beaumanor at this time had a very high turnover rate, of a few months or even weeks. Quite a few did not even complete the training class, objecting to the service type discipline which pervaded the establishment. The Officer Commander in Charge was Lt Ellingworth RN and his second in command was Major Wort. Both were civilians but had retained their honorary wartime service titles. At the outbreak of war the station was sited at Chatham but because of the intensification of Luftwaffe activity it was decided to move to Beaumanor because it was a much safer place. It had belonged to the Perry-Herrick family. The contingent which moved from Chatham numbered seventy eight and ever since had been known as 'the gallant seventy eight'.

After another couple of weeks in the training class

most of us were allocated to various operational watches to start work. This was the introduction to one of the most iniquitous shift systems I have ever worked (not counting my eight on, eight off in Berlin). It was a seven-week cycle which started with seven consecutive nights from 2200-0700 starting on a Mondays. Then came the seven afternoons 1400-2230 ending on Monday at 2230. Tuesday was actually a day off, followed by seven mornings from 0700-1400 which ended at 1400 on the Tuesday, then Wednesday was a day off. Then the whole cycle commenced again on the Thursday at 2230. The only redeeming features were the one shift off during the first lot of nights, afternoons and mornings and the so-called long weekend which began on a Thursday at 1400 and finished at 2230 on a Monday, the start of another seven week cycle. I 'm sure this shift system also contributed to the rapid turnover of personnel.

We had only been on operational duties a few weeks when a notice was circulated asking for volunteers for a three-year tour of duty in Cyprus. Two parties of men were already scheduled to leave in June and July but the volunteer lists were not oversubscribed, probably because lots of people had already spent long periods abroad in the services and were now looking forward to a settled life. The Dowsetts' tales of the beautiful island of Cyprus persuaded me and several others to volunteer, but we didn't think we would have much chance of being accepted after so little time in the job.

When my first long weekend was due I combined it with a few days' annual leave and went home for a week. On the Saturday evening I went to a dance at Scartho, a pleasant village hall type venue which had a good band and was very popular with my friends. On this particular evening I danced quite a few times with a girl called Brenda, who was an excellent dancer and worked for the Inland Revenue. We had often danced together previously but this night was different and at the interval we went outside and exchanged quite a few kisses. We arranged to go to the cinema the following Tuesday, but fate intervened. On the Monday evening I had arranged to go to the Gaiety with my friends Bob Potter and Ray Craggs. It was not a name band that evening but the resident, Bob Walker, and his band.

I soon noticed the girl in the angora sweater I remembered from a few months previously. I subsequently discovered that her name was Barbara and after the interval I deserted my friends and spent the rest of the evening with her. I walked her home to her sister Janet's house, which was quite near where I lived. I arranged to meet her outside her sister's the following evening.

The next day I spent a considerable time trying to contact Brenda to let to her know that our date was off. I can't remember what excuse I offered, but I still feel rather ashamed fifty years on. When I did finally get through she said "I knew you were ringing me to call it off".

Barbara told me her mother wouldn't usually let her go out on successive nights but because I was going back to Beaumanor on the Friday she could stay at her sister's house until then. The family house was at North Cotes, a few miles outside Grimsby. We were dancing again on the Wednesday and Thursday evenings and by this time there was little doubt that we were both very attracted to each other. When we parted late on Thursday evening we promised to write to each other and I said I would be back as soon as I had two consecutive days off.

Back at Beaumanor off duty time was spent playing cricket or table tennis or writing promised letters. Sometimes on a day off we would take the opportunity to watch county cricket at Derby, Nottingham or Leicester depending on who was playing the most attractive fixture, as the grounds were virtually equidistant from us. Middlesex and Derbyshire were playing a benefit match for the Derby stalwart Bill Copson, which was to be followed by a dance at Derby Town Hall. After an excellent day's play I turned up early at the dance and when I went into the bar there were only two people sitting there - Leslie and Denis Compton. We had quite a conversation about Middlesex and Arsenal and Denis said he remembered meeting our Hardy Rangers party four years previously when he had just returned from India (I suspect Denis was just being kind!) It was a privilege to be chatting to two of the greatest all-rounders England possessed.

Another friend who joined Beaumanor a couple of months after me was Bill Fairhurst. He owned a motor bike and we often went round together to sporting venues and dances in the surrounding area, but after I met Barbara my local dancing activities dropped off rapidly. Whenever I was home Barbara and I danced most of the nights away.

As most of us were young, fit men we spent lots of our spare time playing football, tennis and cricket. A bunch of us who played and practised regularly together threw down a challenge to the rest of Beaumanor to produce a team to beat us. A match was arranged against a team calling themselves the 'Beaumanor Allstars' and they had some very talented players who played in local leagues, but on the day they were no match for us and we beat them 6-1. Our reputation was established.

In late September we were informed that the party for Cyprus had been selected and it included myself, the Dowsetts, Ep Jones and Frank Donnelly. Our departure date was to be early January 1950, subject to medicals, vetting procedures etc. I don't think Barbara was very happy at the thought of me going away for three years! I vowed I would get home to see her at every opportunity during the next few months and I did so, often swapping days off so that I could manage two or three days off together.

In October we received a £40 outfit allowance to enable us to buy clothes suitable for warm climes, and this was followed by another £20 trunk allowance. I remember buying what I thought was a classy brown suit made to measure at Alexander's the tailors in

Leicester. Money certainly went much further in those days, and after buying suitable shirts, shorts and underwear etc I still had money left.

One weekend I went home on a Saturday and went straight from the railway station to Blundell Park as Grimsby were playing Spurs. This was the great Tottenham Hotspurs team of 1949, which played a unique brand of football in a style of their own. Within the first few minutes the Grimsby centre forward Tommy Briggs had the much vaunted Spurs defence in tatters and had scored twice. The next time Briggs was going through the middle Alf Ramsey screamed "Stay with him" to the Spurs centre half and there was absolute panic in the Spurs defence every time Briggs had the ball. They did however eventually pull themselves together and made it two all. Alf Ramsey himself scored the winning goal in the last few minutes. He came out of defence and with everyone waiting for him to pass the ball he went through and scored a great winning goal. That was the nearest Spurs came to defeat in the league in the whole of that season, and they went on to even greater glories.

I was still travelling home to see Barbara at every opportunity and our romance was certainly blossoming. I managed to obtain four days' leave over the Christmas period, but needed to go back and work one night shift before I was entitled to another two days off. My friends the Dowsetts were in exactly the same position and needed to return from Wales to work one night shift. It was arranged that on Boxing Day I was to go over to North Cotes for a meal and to meet Barbara's parents, Norman and Ethel Phillipson. Norman had a greengrocery shop in Park Street, just inside the Cleethorpes boundary. Norman and Barbara came and picked me up in his car and en route to North Cotes we stopped to pick up Barbara's Uncle Bert and Aunt Cicely (about whom you'll hear more later). I realised I was being vetted, and was on my best behaviour. Barbara's little brother John and sister Pamela, aged five and six, were very hyped up, but it was Christmas and they were showing off. On this visit I also met another sister, Norma, who was thirteen. The oldest sister, Jean, was recently married to Bill Evison, a fisherman, and lived quite near to us in Tunnard Street, Grimsby.

I thought things had gone quite well at my first meeting with Barbara's parents, but I don't think they were particularly happy about her being involved with someone who was just about to go abroad for three years (I expect they thought it wouldn't last!). I didn't go back to work for that solitary night shift - I risked ringing in sick. When I returned for my last few days at work I was called in to see the Operations Officer, a pleasant man called Les Hadler (ex gallant 78). I fully expected a rocket, but instead he said words to the effect that the leave I had rung in for had been approved and then he winked. Slowly I got the message. Needless to say after that I always had a soft spot for him.

While I was being dealt with very leniently, my

colleagues Gerald and Leslie Dowsett, who had also been absent that night, were hauled up in front of the Commanding Officer. They were foolish enough to tell the truth and state that they had been drunk and incapable. The CO blew his top and said it was too late in the day to remove them from the draft, but he was sending a letter to Colonel Winterbottom informing him that these two men were unreliable and untrustworthy and must be watched at all times.

Our party of eighteen were booked to sail on His Majesty's Troopship the *Empire Windrush,* which was due to sail from Southampton on January 14th 1950. The *Empire Windrush* had been one of Hitler's "Strength Through Joy" ships built in the mid 1930s to enable ordinary Germans to enjoy subsidised holiday cruises. It had become a troopship as part of the war reparations agreement. Recently she has found fame in the TV series *Windrush* as the ship which brought the first West Indian immigrants to Britain after the war. Unfortunately some years later she met her demise when she sank in the Mediterranean after a fire. Luckily it was in calm waters and not too far from shore, so there was no loss of life.

I did manage to return home for a brief visit before we sailed. On the Thursday evening I said goodbye to a rather tearful Barbara outside her sister's house. We had earlier decided we wanted to become engaged and later sent the money for her to buy the ring. We embarked and set sail in the traditional manner of troopships, with regimental bands playing and streamers being thrown from and to the dockside. Thus began another phase of my life.

CHAPTER 5

SAILING INTO THE UNKNOWN

Our first morning at sea produced a fine crop of sore heads, as all the ship's bars had been working overtime the previous evening. Fortunately I had not been indulging, so I felt fine and decided to have a walk on deck before breakfast. There I came across one of our party, Peter Harris, hanging on to the rail and looking decidedly green.

Perhaps at this stage I ought to give you a brief rundown on the rest of our party and their service backgrounds:

Ken Blackley (ex Army)
Willie Backhouse (ex Army)
Ken Carling (ex RAF)
Casey Campbell (ex Army)
Maurice Cooper (ex RAF)
Bill Cooper (ex Army)
Frank Donnelly (ex Army)

Gerry Dowsett (ex Army
Les Dowsett (ex Army)
Peter Harris (ex Army)
Ep Jones (ex Army)
Jim Murray (ex Army)
John Mortby (ex RAF)
Danny O'Neil (ex Army)
Jim Purdie (ex Army/Gallant 78)
Duncan Small (ex Army)
Ken Spring (ex Navy)
Roy Ward (ex Army/Gallant 78)
Laurie Wilson (ex Radio College).

We were nearly all in the early twenties age bracket with one or two in the mid to late twenties. I shared a fairly comfortable four-berth cabin with Danny O'Neil, Jim Murray and Jim Purdie. Danny was an extrovert ex-service concert party entertainer with a good tenor voice and was always in demand at late night sessions aboard ship, so it was often between two and three in the morning when he staggered into his berth. Jim Murray was a pleasant, quiet and unassuming man brought up in the Middle East. His father was a Scot who had been an embassy official and his mother Lebanese. He spoke Greek, Arabic and French fluently and his talents were to become a great asset to our organisation for many years to come.

Jim Purdie was one of the Gallant 78 who had

started as a sixteen-year-old at Chatham just before the war. After the war he had to do National Service in Austria and then rejoined the War Office at Beaumanor.

Shipboard life was quite relaxing, with plenty of activities. The food was good and the drinks cheap. We sailed along the coast of Portugal and Spain in beautiful sunshine, with blue skies and scarcely a ripple on the sea - and this was mid January, quite a contrast from the weather we had left behind.

As we entered the Mediterranean and left the Rock of Gibraltar in our wake it seemed to be sunshine and relatively calm seas all the way. In the evenings people would usually congregate in the various bars and lounges, which were strictly segregated, Officers and Other Ranks. Rank is very important in the service mentality and even though we were civilians we were accorded the status of sergeants and used the appropriate amenities. Wives and families travelling to join their husbands adhered strictly to the use of amenities as per their husband's rank.

There was a daily sweepstake on the ship's run (the distance covered every day), which was usually over 300 miles. One morning on about our fourth day since we left Gibraltar we realised that the ship had turned round in the night and was now heading back towards Gibraltar. We were later informed that a wife travelling on her own to join her husband in the Canal Zone was missing, not having been seen since the previous evening. It was feared that she had gone overboard, either deliberately or accidentally. The ship retraced her course for twelve hours, but she was never seen again. Because of this delay our scheduled stop at Malta was very brief and no one was allowed to go ashore.

Our next port of call was to be Salonika, to pick up the last British troops in Greece. Our trip so far had been very smooth, but things took a turn for the worse as we headed into the Aegean. One mountainous wave hit us broadside on with a tremendous crash, and I thought we had struck a mine (a British destroyer had struck one in that area the previous year). The seas moderated the next day and a couple of days later we docked at Salonika.

There was much pomp and ceremony as the last British Forces came aboard to the music of Greek and British Army bands. Our next stop was Piraeus, the Port of Athens, and as we docked on another beautiful clear day the Acropolis and the Parthenon were clearly visible. At Piraeus we took on a few more servicemen en route to Cyprus or even Singapore.

As we began the last part of our voyage, shipboard life was becoming rather dull and one reason for this was that very few of us had any money, due to the very strict currency restrictions. Ten pounds was the maximum amount an individual could bring out of the UK. On the first night out from Piraeus, a few of us decided to try our luck at tombola, or bingo as it is now known. I had a winning line in very quick time and went on to complete a full house, to great applause from our table. I received five pounds for the line and thirty pounds for the full house, an appreciable amount in those days. I was touched for quite a few loans the next day, some of which are still outstanding!

As we sailed around the coast of Cyprus on another calm sunny day, Sunday January 29th 1950, it truly did look like a magical tropical island. We had expected to dock at Famagusta, but instead the *Empire Windrush* anchored about a mile out in Famagusta Bay. A series of tenders and small boats came out to transport us and our luggage ashore.

After we had negotiated the Cyprus Immigration and Customs officials we met our official welcoming party. This consisted of Colonel du Cros, temporarily Officer in Charge of Civilian Wing 2 Wireless Regiment, Royal Signals. He was accompanied by Eric 'Slap' Reedman, his second in command, who had brought out the first party of civilians six months previously. With them was Syd Naylor, a clerical officer who was our Admin Officer and he had also arrived with the first party.

We were given ten Cyprus pounds each and then we boarded the inevitable army three-tonner and followed Slap's little Ford saloon, to be deposited at the various guesthouses or 'pensions' which had been selected as our temporary or even permanent accommodation. I was dropped off at Christo's Pension along with the Dowsett twins, Maurice Cooper, Frank Donnelly, Jim Murray, Ken Blackley and Danny O'Neil. The Pension was a very large bungalow type building owned by

Christo, a Greek Cypriot who had been trained as a chef at the famous Savoy Hotel in London. He had returned to Cyprus to open his own little hotel and was assisted by his wife and his sister, a young village girl called Attoula. Every evening after he had prepared and overseen the serving of our evening meal he went to work as a chef at the Savoy Hotel in Famagusta. He certainly worked very hard and needless to say was a superb cook.

At our first evening meal we had soup, then a main course of chicken, which tasted marvellous, and then a huge bowl of Cyprus Jaffa oranges was placed on the table. We all took one and, following the lead of the Dowsett twins (seasoned Cyprus campaigners), we all washed our oranges in the little fingerbowls of water and dried them on our serviettes before peeling them to eat. Jim Murray winked at me and we all burst into fits of laughing when we realised how stupid we had been.

The next morning we were picked up by a three-tonner and transported out of Famagusta along the Larnaca/Nicosia road to Four Mile Point, so called because it was four miles out of Famagusta. This was the site of No. 2 Wireless Regiment, Royal Signals, and our establishment was the Civilian Wing of this with regiment. Our admin office was a Nissen hut divided into two, with Syd Naylor at one end and Slap and the Colonel sharing an office at the other. After a long session of filling in forms for transfer grants, collecting outstanding pay etc, we were allocated to our watches after a pep talk about discipline from Slap and the Colonel on the importance of getting on with our new army colleagues. We were then given the rest of the day off and transported back to Famagusta, this by the same method of standing up in the back hanging on to the framework whenever it became bumpy.

We spent the rest of the day walking around Famagusta and familiarising ourselves with the two main thoroughfares, Hermes Street and King Edward VIII Avenue, which housed lots of small shops and cafés, two hotels, the previously mentioned Savoy Hotel and also the Palace, which was off King Edward Avenue. At this time there was just one other hotel called the King George situated on Famagusta beach, a very pleasant place.

While we were meandering around town that day we passed the window of a local photographer and were amazed to see large photographs of Syd Naylor, Slap Reedman and several other colleagues already serving in Cyprus. We were not aware that only about six weeks before we arrived Famagusta had endured its worst flooding on record and members of the III 134 Civilian Wing had been instrumental in rescuing and helping lots of the local population. I usually wrote to Barbara every other day. I must confess I was missing her and was hoping she was missing me.

In our new environment there was always plenty to write about. The shift system was a four-day cycle which commenced with a one to six in the afternoon, the next morning was an eight until one returning the same evening for a midnight until eight in the morning. Then it was bed for some sleep before returning at six in the evening until midnight with the next day as a day off. I must admit I didn't like this system one little bit, but as it was the one the army worked it seemed we were stuck with it.

Frank Donnelly and I were the only ones from Christo's on "B" Watch, so we usually went to most places together during our off-duty time. Frank and I would often go down to the Famagusta beach to swim and do a little sunbathing and though it was considered winter by the locals the sea was not too cold for we hardy "Brits". Another place we frequented was the British Institute, to play table tennis or volleyball with some of the local young men. British Institutes were situated in many places throughout the Empire, allegedly to show other people just how good and effective the British way of life could be. British nationals abroad were encouraged by the institute managers to mix and be friendly with the locals and also to compete with and against them in various sports and games (this was I suppose a type of propaganda!).

The Civilian Wing now consisted of about fifty men, enough for me to begin to organise football matches against various teams within 2 Wireless Regiment. As we could field outstanding players like Duncan Small and Arthur Hicks, we soon had a formidable team. Most of our party had yet to travel much around the island, mainly because the local buses between towns and villages were erratic and always packed with locals carrying a wide variety of goods including fruit, vegetables and live chickens, some they had purchased at the market and others to sell there. Taxis were the best mode of transport and at the time they were mostly large American models, very comfortable but heavy on petrol, but at that time it was the equivalent of about twenty pence a gallon so it didn't seem to matter very much.

At work we were now in an entirely new signals environment which in many aspects was very different to the UK. There was plenty to learn, but it was very interesting and we soon became familiar with some of the different types of morse we were required to intercept. Because some of our colleagues had spent long periods in the Middle East they were quite happy to pass their expertise on and help us to adapt to some of the new styles of morse.

There were quite a few people in the Civilian Wing who were far too fond of drinking and bars and cabarets. Placing such people in an island like Cyprus where drink was cheap and they had a lot more money than in the UK was a recipe for self destruction, a fate which overtook quite a few of our number through the years. Our first casualty was Ken Blackley, who came out with our party and lived with us at Christo's. From the outset he was frequently absent from work, and one morning when he should have been on duty at eight he was still in bed at eleven when Slap and the Colonel called to see him. He gave them a lot of abuse, all in our earshot.. I thought the Colonel was going to have an apoplectic fit - he went purple with rage. Two days later Mr Blackley was back in England and out of a job.

The Civilian Set Room was manned by four watches A, B, C and D, with ten operators on each watch. The person in charge of our watch was called Eric Dobson, and he had arrived with the first party. He was also a member of the "Gallant 78" and his wife and six children had recently arrived on the island and were now living in Famagusta in a rented house. Eric was a pleasant, intelligent and affable character but a very poor disciplinarian, and most of the senior operators took advantage of him. His fall from grace, however, was brought about by his most junior operator, namely Ken Spring, one of our party. Ken was in the middle of the set room in front of Eric's desk indulging in a wrestling match with Brian Blacklock (note the name!) a young Intelligence Corps corporal who was assigned to our watch (every watch had an "I" Corps NCO. attached.) While this friendly fracas was going on in front of him, Eric was sitting at his desk doing a crossword. At this inopportune moment Major Bickerstaffe, the "I" Corps Commander, walked in and watched for a while with hardly anyone noticing.

The next day we were all called in and severely reprimanded, innocent and guilty alike. We were informed that we obviously needed discipline. This meant that Eric was banished to some menial task and

Frank Cameron was put in charge of our watch. Though we didn't think so at the time, the move was to our advantage. Frank was a Scot with a great sense of humour who could always manage to get the best out of people. Within a few weeks we realised that the change had been to our benefit.

As time progressed quite a few wives were coming out to join their husbands but downtown accommodation was in short supply. The Colonel came down to Christo's and asked us if we would mind if Danny O'Neil and Casey Campbell's wives could move in there until they could find more permanent accommodation. We could hardly say no, even though it was an all male-establishment. There were new married quarters almost completed at Four Mile Point, adjoining the 2 Wireless Regiment site. These were to be allocated to both military and civilian families. Roy Ward and Duncan Small's wives had recently arrived, so they had taken a short-term lease on a small two storey flat in Hippocrates Street, right on the beach. This was temporary until their quarters were ready. We often used to join them on the beach in front of their flat and thought what a great place it was to live.

Frank and I were both quite happy at Christo's, and though the food was excellent it was repetitive and we soon knew the daily menus off by heart. It cost about ten pounds per week to live at Christo's with laundry an extra, and as our weekly wage, enhanced by FSA (Foreign Service Allowance), was about £18 we managed quite well. I was however thinking in terms of saving as much as possible so that I could marry Barbara. Frank who was engaged to another Barbara (Shortland), a nursing sister at a hospital in Lancashire, had similar ideas.

There was another colleague on our watch called Henry Nuttall (ex RAF aircrew) who had arrived with the second party, he was also interested in finding fresh accommodation, so we agreed to look for somewhere suitable together. We contacted the landlord of the beach flats occupied by Roy Ward and Duncan Small and were informed that the ground floor flat was already spoken for, but he was willing to let us have the first floor flat as soon as it became vacant. Life continued quite pleasantly, with plenty of beach expeditions and sport. In those days Frank and I would often complete a night watch, play tennis for a couple of hours, then take a taxi back to Famagusta .Then it was a few hours' sleep and an early evening meal before going back on duty at six until midnight.

Because very few of us had our own transport, and there was no public transport, we saw very little of the rest of the island during our first few months, but shortly after this quite a few people became mobile. Henry Nuttall already had a motor cycle, but within a few weeks there seemed to be a series of motor-cycle owners including the Dowsetts, John Mortby ,Ken Carling, Ken Spring and Ep Jones. One of our second party indulged in a brand new Austin A40, so the rest of the island was beginning to open up to some of us.

The new married quarters were now ready and being allocated. This meant that the Wards and Smalls moved up to Four-Mile Point and our beach flat was available. The flat had only one bedroom containing three single beds, one wardrobe and one chest of drawers, a kitchen with a worktop, an oil cooker and an icebox. There was also a small Ascot-type heater for hot water. A small but adequate bathroom with a wood-fired boiler provided hot water. Most of the time we were there the water which was drawn from a tank on the roof and was already warm from the sun. Our monthly rent was £18, which was high by local standards, but this was mainly because it was in such a wonderful position. Shared between the three of us it worked out at about £1.50 per week each (the Cypriot pound was more or less equivalent to the English pound). It was agreed that I would be the treasurer and we all contributed £5 per week to cover food, electricity, ice (a block delivered every other day) and paraffin. I usually went to the market to buy our fruit, vegetables, meat and groceries carrying a large Cyprus wicker basket balanced precariously between us on the pillion of Henry's motor cycle. We always had plenty of fruit, grapes, apples, melons, apricots or plums - whatever was in season. We all loved bacon, eggs and tomatoes, but one of our favourite main meals was pork chop, mashed potatoes and tinned peas. Our butcher in the market used to carve us magnificent pork chops with little or no fat on them, three large ones for about 50 pence. I did most of the cooking and Henry and Frank did most of the washing up, but we each packed our own sandwiches for the night shift.

As we sat out on our verandah we gazed down on the Mediterranean lapping the beach about fifteen yards in front of us. There was a bathing raft anchored about 50 yards in front of us and more often than not we were its sole occupants. In those days very few Cypriots used the beach, except on Sundays when they tended to parade along the main thoroughfares and the beach, whole families dressed in their Sunday best. This was an idyllic existence, marred only by the fact that I was missing Barbara, so I concentrated on saving as much as I could to enable us to be married as soon as possible.

Friday was our payday, and I always gave Frank as much as I could to save for me in his local savings bank account (trusting soul that I was and still am!)

Most mornings Frank and I used to swim out to the Camel Rock and back. This rock was about three quarters of a mile away and though I was a relative beginner at swimming and Frank was a very strong swimmer, we always stayed together. The sea was usually like a millpond especially first thing in the morning, and alternating between breast and side stroke I improved every day. Swimming, tennis and a few games of football had been my only exercise during my first few months in Cyprus and I had done no running training at all, so I was a little dubious about entering the three-mile event in the Regimental sports. My swimming must have been very beneficial or the opposition was weak, as I won very easily and was consequently invited to run for the Regiment the following week at the Inter-Services sports at Nicosia. The meeting was held over two days. The first day was the team competition with two entrants from each unit collecting points according to their finishing positions. I can recall clearly that as the starter's pistol sounded for the three-mile event the Regimental band of the Oxford and Buckingham Light Infantry began to play. This made it very difficult to pace yourself as everyone was running to the beat of the music. On completion of the first of twelve laps I decided to make the pace and go to the front, followed by the two Ox and Bucks competitors, one of whom was a tall young Lieutenant who stayed with me right to the end and just edged in front of me in a very close finish.

I returned to Famagusta and did a night shift, as there was no leave available, but I had decided to return the next day as I fancied that I could win the individual event. My only sleep the next day was a fitful doze in the back of the three-tonner en route to Nicosia but I didn't really feel too bad - I was just keyed up. The race was much faster than the previous day's. I allowed the previous day's winner to lead until the last hundred yards and then went past him, but just when I thought the race was mine he came back at me and pipped me at the post once again.

I didn't realise that the Officer Commanding 2

Wireless Regiment, Colonel Winterbottom, was a spectator that afternoon, and afterwards he approached me and thanked me for representing the Regiment so well on both days. He also asked me how much training I had been doing. I told him none but went on to say that I thought I might have done better if I hadn't just completed a night shift. He said he was amazed to hear this and said that in future I should go through him and time off, not leave would be arranged. This taught me a valuable lesson which I often put to good use throughout my Civil Service career. If you have a request or a suggestion, or just an idea, try to ensure that it goes to the top.

Despite the fact that Frank was also saving for marriage, he weakened and acquired a motor cycle, but unfortunately it only lasted about two months. One evening we all went to the Hadji Hambis open air cinema, and I rode pillion with Henry as he was the more experienced rider. When we left the cinema only Henry's bike was there - Frank's had vanished. It wasn't very kind of us, but looking at Frank's face all Henry and I could do was to burst into uncontrollable laughter.

When we regained our composure we went along with Frank to the police station to report the loss. It was never seen again as a complete motor cycle, though parts of it did come to light in a cave near the village of Tricomo about nine months later. I believe Frank did receive some insurance money for his loss.

Most of the year Cyprus was an ideal climate for the

use of a motor cycle. Safety helmets were unheard of, but some people did wear goggles or sunglasses as a protection for their eyes from insects while travelling at speed. One day I rode pillion with Henry and we went first to Nicosia and then took the road to Kyrenia and visited the magnificent Abbey of Bellapais (Abbey of Peace) which is set up high on a cliff about three miles from Kyrenia. It is considered to be the outstanding Gothic monument in the Middle East. After this we went on to St Hilarion, which looked very much like a fairytale castle and is set on the very summit of a mountain peak over two thousand feet up. It was named after St Hilarion the Great, a sixth century Syrian hermit. The views from both Bellapais and St Hilarion were absolutely breathtaking.

Our next stop was Kyrenia just a few miles further on. It was a pleasant town with a horseshoe-shaped harbour and a well-preserved mediaeval castle. We then stopped at a roadside café for a beer and a meze before taking a pleasant ride back to Famagusta via the coast road. Frank, Henry and I used to have a weekly rendezvous with Arthur Hicks at a cafe in Famagusta called Fisherman's Cottage, which was near the beach and possessed an excellent tennis court. We had some excellent games there. I have mentioned Arthur previously; he had served at Sarafand in Palestine and at the end of the war was the goalkeeper for the 'Wanderers', a service team of mostly professional footballers serving in the Middle East which toured around entertaining the troops by playing matches against combined sides from the best local teams. The team included Tom Finney of Preston and England and other players who went on to become internationals.

Arthur was an outstanding goalkeeper, with a penchant for saving penalties. I have seen newspaper cuttings of many of his penalty saves including one from Tom Finney himself when their unit teams were in opposition. When he was demobilised he was offered professional terms by several English clubs, including Derby County, but he decided it was too precarious a way to earn a living and opted to join the War Office at Beaumanor instead. A couple of years later he was on his way to Cyprus with the first Civilian party. When we first arrived in Cyprus Arthur was not around, as he had a stay of several weeks at the British Military Hospital at Nicosia after being involved in a night club fracas in Famagusta. His jaw was broken in several places and he was wired up for quite a while. Shortly after this his wife Yvonne joined him in Cyprus and he was a reformed character in many ways, though still quick tempered. He still was very fond of Keo beer, and when we went for a meal at their place, as we frequently did, he used to amaze us with his ability to consume eight to ten pints in an evening with no apparent affect.

During the summer another party of civilians from Beaumanor arrived which included several members of Beaumanor's T A (traffic analysis) and CRR (compilation of reports and records) sections. These people were CROs (Civilian Radio Officers) employed mainly on day shifts at Beaumanor, but they had built up quite a lot of expertise in their own special fields. They immediately went on to days and integrated with the "I" Corps contingent already in situ at 2 Wireless Regiment. Included in this group were Dick Reedman (Slap's brother), Ron Denny and Wally Cairncross, who became good friends of mine.

Another member of that party was Tom McMinn, who also became a good friend. He took up residence at Christo's and a couple of years later he married Attoullah, Christo's sister (he was given a couple of donums of land in her village as a dowry).

By the end of that first summer I was very tanned without ever getting burnt, probably because I had started gradually almost as soon as we arrived. In those days sun cream was used by very few people - fortunately we know better these days.

Life continued in a most pleasant fashion. The three of us were very compatible, considering we were three bachelors living in very close proximity to each other. I was still managing to save a reasonable amount every week. A night out in the Turkish quarter of the old city of Famagusta cost the equivalent of 25 pence in today's UK currency. For this amount you could obtain an excellent meze consisting of all kinds of fruits, chips, spicy flavoured dips, octopus and Cypriot bread washed down by a couple of pints of local Keo beer. The cinema only cost about 15-20 pence depending where you sat.

Up to this time I had given very little time or thought to the political situation in Cyprus but I was aware that the church had organised a plebiscite in 1949 which had resulted in an overwhelming vote in favour of "enosis" or Union with Greece, and this result had been forwarded to the United Nations. Since we had arrived we were always seeing such slogans painted and posted all over the place, and as fast as they were cleaned up they appeared somewhere else.

In October 1950 the Bishop of Kition was elected Makarios III at the age of only 37. He immediately made clear his position as Ethnarch with a pledge to work relentlessly for union with Greece. Perhaps it might be as well to give you a little bit of background regarding the Archbishop. He was born Michael Mouskos into a peasant family living near Paphos. He was educated at the Pancyprian Gymnasium and then at Kykko monastery. In 1938 he was made a deacon of Phanoremeni Church. Strangely enough he spent the whole of the second World War in Greece. The World Council of Churches then selected him for a two-year scholarship at Boston Theological College and it was while he was still in the USA with his studies unfinished that he was elected Bishop of Kition. On his journey back to Cyprus he called in for another two months in Athens. Before leaving he stated that Cypriots were determined to achieve enosis.

Several years later it came to light that during his latest visit to Athens he had had several meetings with

Colonel Grivas. I first saw the Archbishop in person when he came to conduct a service at the Greek Orthodox Church of Ayios Triada, which was quite near to where we lived in Famagusta. Little did I know just how much the Archbishop's machinations would affect my next tour of duty in Cyprus.

During the rest of my first tour things were fairly quiet politically, I think because the majority of Cypriots entertained high hopes of United Nations intervention to aid their aspirations of union with Greece. The outbreak of the Korean War in the early summer of 1950 had little impact on us in Cyprus except to place us on a higher state of alert. A few weeks later I received a letter from my brother Tom informing me that was shortly embarking for Korea as a sniper with the "Tigers", the Royal Leicestershire Regiment. My last news of Tom had been that he had joined the Regular Army and was a Physical Training Instructor, yet here he was on his way to Korea. Of course I followed the fortunes of the United Nations forces in Korea with much more interest and concern knowing my brother was serving there. Yes, I renewed a dialogue with the Lord on his behalf (how predictable I was, and I must confess still am).

I now began to take an interest in hockey, a game I had never played before. This came about because Civilian Wing had some superb hockey players, who had developed their skills serving in places like Sarafand and India. These included Slap and Dick Reedman, Casey

Campbell, Ron (RPL) Smith, Slim Braithwaite and George Davison. Because there weren't enough of them to make a team, footballers such as Len Tovey, Steve Lavelle and myself were pressed into service, with the core of expertise and brilliance aided by the enthusiasm of the beginners. Civilian Wing soon became a very good team. In early October, after torrential rains in late September, the Island Cross Country Championships were held at Karalaos, which is situated between Salamis and Famagusta. My nemesis, Lieutenant Payne of the Ox and Bucks was also in contention. Halfway through a quagmire of a course, sitting comfortably on his heels (so I thought), one of my running shoes came off as I ploughed through ankle-deep mud. Foolishly I spent what seemed an eternity searching for it, to no avail. As it was a team race it was essential to finish the race to collect points for your team. Like an idiot I ran on in one shoe to finish about halfway down the field of about one hundred runners. First to the winning tape was of course Lt Payne, and his regiment also won the team event.

My foot, which hadn't bothered me very much on the way to the finish, was now in a terrible state with lacerations and huge blisters. I received some first aid from the medics in attendance, but couldn't put my foot down for several days. I had to take a few days' sick leave, which didn't go down very well with the Civilian Wing hierarchy, but because I was representing the Regiment they couldn't say very much.

By a strange coincidence, during my sick leave I began to read Leon Uris's *Exodus*. There I was reading about Bruce Sutherland only a few doors away from where his desk had been in his house in Hippocrates Street. I went on to read about the detention camps in the shape of huts and barbed wire enclosures at Karalaos, the very ground I had been running over a few hours previously. This made the book live for me, and I enjoyed it from cover to cover. Uris had researched his Cyprus details meticulously and I considered how easy it would have been for me to become a Zionist the way I felt at that time (did I hear you say young and impressionable?). More of Exodus later.

At the beginning of November Eric Dobson was looking for people to cast in a pantomime production of "Sinbad the Sailor". He had apparently produced and directed a wonderful pantomime the previous year with a cast which included Derek Nimmo, who was at that time serving in the "I" Corps. Reluctantly I agreed to participate and Ken Spring and I were cast as a pair of card players at the front right of the stage sitting either side of an upturned barrel on a couple of small stools. We remained there throughout the whole performance, making jokes and caustic comments at appropriate times. Also included in the cast were Wenda and Cynthia du Cros (the Colonel's daughters), Pam Ward and Sylvia Lavelle. Male cast members included Joe Bainbridge and Graham Offen ("I" Corps) and Jim Purdie, whose wife Edith was the makeup lady. We were scheduled for three performances and played to full houses (captive audiences), and we were all looking forward to a final Saturday evening performance to be followed by the traditional celebration.

Great drama then ensued. With half an hour to go before curtain up there was no sign of Jim Purdie, who was playing one of the romantic leads, neither was Edith in attendance. The story was that Jim had last been seen heading for the old city earlier that afternoon on his motor bike, allegedly to bring back some bread. With only ten minutes to go, Eric in desperation said to me, "You know all Jim's lines and you also know the words to his song, so please don't let me down!" So in the best show business tradition, I stepped in. I wasn't nervous and everything went well, even my rendition of *I Wonder Who's Kissing Her Now*.

The Purdie mystery had an unfortunate ending. Their non-appearance on the final night culminated in an unholy row which resulted in practically every bit of crockery in their married quarters being smashed. Friends and the hierarchy tried peacemaking and intervention with no result, and within a very short time Edith was on her way back to England and their marriage was virtually over. In retrospect it seems a bit unfair when Jim was probably equally to blame. I think official thinking was that the department had invested in a three-year tour from Jim and he still had a couple of years to go.

Henry, Frank and I were invited to the Cooks' for

Christmas dinner. Ralph Cook was on our watch, a vicar's son, ex-aircrew and Radio College. A likeable rogue, he was married to Wink (Elsie) and had a baby daughter called Jacqui who was aged about five months. We had an enjoyable day and an excellent meal and it was much appreciated.

The lease on our flat was due to expire in January, and though we had enjoyed living there we now considered it might be time to make a move. We knew there was a large bungalow available just off the main Larnaca and Nicosia road which was en route to Four Mile Point. Our idea was that Ken Carling and Maurice Cooper would share this new abode with Henry, Frank and myself and that we would employ a housekeeper to look after us. The plan came to fruition in late January and we acquired ourselves a pleasant middle aged Greek Cypriot housekeeper called Maria. she spoke very little English but she understood that she would clean, cook and do our laundry, while we would see to our own breakfasts. Maria did our shopping or ordered it and had it delivered. I relinquished the financial reins and I believe it was Henry who then took charge of the purse strings. I don't remember just how much we paid Maria, but I know it was above the going rate yet still ridiculously cheap.

Maria's son, who was a waiter at the King George Hotel, negotiated her wages and hours with us. She arrived about nine in the morning and finished at seven in the evening, with Sunday off. By the end of the first month we discovered that we were much better off all ways, including financially. This was the time when I asked Frank how much I had managed to save in his account and was pleasantly surprised when he told me it was more than £250. I then decided to open my own account at the Ottoman Bank in Famagusta and made the momentous decision to write to Barbara's parents and ask if she could travel out to Cyprus and marry me. I wrote to Barbara and told her that we now had enough money to get married and that I was busy composing a letter to her parents. I was well aware that this could be the most important letter I would ever write.

Barbara's air fare from London to Nicosia was £119 and if I made it up to £125 it would cover her rail fare from Cleethorpes to London. This would leave me with £125 plus whatever I could save before she arrived. As soon as we were married I would go on to the Married Unaccommodated rate of Foreign Service Allowance (FSA), which would give us about £30 a week to live, providing a very comfortable standard of living, or so I thought.

A week later I had completed my masterpiece and posted it. At the same time I wrote to my parents telling them what I had done and what we were hoping for. To their credit they arranged to see the Phillipsons and plead my case. All I could think of was that if Dad had a few drinks beforehand the meeting could be counterproductive.

About five weeks later I received a reply which had

been written by Mrs Phillipson. It was quite a long letter, which stated that they were not really happy about Barbara coming out to marry me, especially because we had known each other such a short time in England. However after much thought and deliberation they had decided to let Barbara come because they knew that she had never really been happy since we had been apart. They agreed that I could go ahead and make the necessary arrangements.

It is not possible to put into words just how happy I was at this news. Everyone must have been fed up of me telling everyone, often more than once.

One evening shortly after this, the rest of the lads said they had something they wanted to discuss with me. Henry acted as spokesman and said that as I had been signatory to the contract, which had another ten months to run, I would have to pay my share of the rent for another ten months. My face fell, but then Frank snorted and I thankfully realised that they were joking. I sent Barbara her fare and waited with bated breath to see just how soon it could be arranged for her to travel to Cyprus. The Cooks had offered to host our wedding at their married quarters and also to have Barbara stay with them to complete the necessary fourteen days residence in Cyprus before we could be married. Soon after this I heard from Barbara that she would be arriving on May 3rd, which meant I had just over a month to arrange everything.

My first task was to find a church. The new church

at Four Mile Point was still unfinished, but I knew there was an English church in Famagusta near the Savoy Hotel, though in my fifteen months in Cyprus I had never attended it. I knew that a colleague of mine, Ted Kingston, and his wife Pat attended on a regular basis, and it was thanks to them that our wedding service was arranged, for eleven o'clock on Saturday 19th May 1951 at St Mark's Church. I had to ask permission from Colonel Winterbottom to marry and also to our office for three days' marriage leave, because I was an unestablished civil servant. Had I been established I would have been given six days.

I couldn't decide which of the Dowsett twins to have as my best man, so they tossed a coin for it and Gerald won. They had recently traded in their Triumph motor cycles for a brand new Triumph Mayflower saloon which they took turns at driving. A never-to-be-forgotten incident which occurred about this time concerned George Dalgarno, who had arrived in Cyprus as a member of the first party of civilians, a married man with two young children. He lived in quarters at Four Mile Point and rode a powerful Norton Dominator motor cycle. On this particular day he called in at our bungalow and was having a chat with Frank and me. He knew that I was going to be married soon and he intimated that though his own marriage wasn't particularly successful he still considered it to be a worthy institution. Frank and I commented afterwards that it was refreshing to hear him conversing intelligently, as he normally poked fun at or was sarcastic about everything.

Just before George left he told us that it was his 30th birthday and he was now on his way to Famagusta for a couple of celebratory drinks before going on duty at one.

About three quarters of an hour later we heard a motor cycle going full throttle along the Larnaca Road and about half an hour after that Frank and I walked into Famagusta. As we passed the police station a policeman we knew came over to speak to us and said he needed our help to identify someone he thought we might know. We walked across the road to the local hospital and we were ushered into a room with doctors and nurses surrounding a body which was threshing around and intermittently singing and then shouting the foulest oaths imaginable. Yes, it was George Dalgarno. They had shaved the top of his head and his brain was clearly visible. He had tried to negotiate the bend opposite the soft drinks factory at an excessive speed, and had been thrown off and landed head first on one of the few stones strewn around a sandy piece of ground. In those days only professional riders wore crash helmets.

George was transferred to the British Military Hospital Nicosia, where he died two days later without regaining consciousness. It was quite a shock to everyone, but particularly to Frank and me. George was buried the very next day in accordance with Cypriot regulations, and a week later Mrs Dalgarno and her two children were on their way back to England.

One evening Frank, Ken Carling, the twins and I went to the cinema to see a film about the life of Rogers and Hart, the composer and lyricist. We were seated in the open air near the back of the balcony which consisted of about ten tiers of wooden backed cane chairs. There were very few people up in the balcony, probably because they were the most expensive seats. Les Dowsett was sitting with his feet over the back of the empty seat in front of him. During one of the many breaks to change reels and sell ice cream and cold drinks he leaned forward to beckon to the boy who was selling the refreshments. As he did so his chair pitched forward and he went over the top on to the chair in front and continued riding the crest of the toppling chairs in a domino effect for about eight rows until he reached the balcony rail, which fortunately was reasonably high. Everyone on the balcony was watching aghast, and the people below were looking up to see what the commotion was all about.

At this point, Les with magnificent aplomb, stood up, dusted himself down, walked back up the balcony steps and regained his seat, which we had righted for him. Just as he was sitting down his brother Gerald gave him a savage punch in the ribs and remarked, "That's for showing me up!" The rest of us couldn't stop laughing for ages afterwards, but the twins were not amused.

It was during this period that two more members of our third party resigned. The first to do so was Danny O'Neil, who had saved a few hundred from his wages and opened up a bar in Famagusta which he called the Ship Inn. Danny and Dizzy, his wife, were both extroverts and initially seemed to be doing good business, thanks to Danny's flair for entertaining. The second one was Casey Campbell, who resigned after being disciplined for excessive sick leave and poor timekeeping. He was a fine operator but rather a flamboyant character and easily led astray. His wife was a well-educated girl whose parents had died recently, leaving her a considerable sum of money. They had three young children and I'm sure Casey was hoping she would set him up in a similar establishment to Danny's. I think he was given a small amount, but not enough to open a bar. His wife and children returned to the UK and I think she later divorced him and married again.

Casey worked for Danny for a while and then gradually drifted around doing casual bar work. He actually lasted about ten years in Cyprus before he died. I saw him in Cyprus in 1962, when he looked like a beach bum. Danny only lasted about five years before he died of cirrhosis of the liver as a result of years of drinking to excess.

The time was fast approaching when Barbara was due to arrive, and Ralph offered to run me to Nicosia airport to meet her - fortunately we were on day off. The journey to Nicosia in that little Ford saloon seemed to take forever, but Barbara's flight actually landed bang on time.

My greeting to Barbara as she stepped off the plane was "Why on earth have you cut your hair?" It's a wonder she didn't go straight back, as she was feeling rather queasy after an overnight stay at a hotel outside Athens, having been transported there in a rickety old bus, and for days after this the smell of orange blossoms and fried food made her feel nauseous. The flight had also made a short stop on the island of Rhodes, where zealous customs officials had searched her suitcase so vigorously that they had disintegrated a box of sanitary pads.

I apologised for my remarks about her hair and we began to enjoy being together again as Ralph drove us back to Famagusta. There seemed to be a thousand things to do and arrange before the 19th of May. Probably the most important was to arrange to appear before the Colonial Secretary to repeat after him and then sign a document which in essence stated that we were both free to marry each other. To our shame we both got the giggles, and had great difficulty in completing our utterances. Heaven knows what he must have thought. Incidentally the Colonial Secretary was Fletcher-Cooke, who went on to become a leading United Nations official.

Wedding invitations turned out to be a very tricky subject and had to be strictly limited to sixty guests, mainly because the Cooks' married quarters were not very large. Barbara didn't really know anyone, so selection was mainly due to me, aided and abetted by

Ralph and Wink. Little did I know that one person who wasn't invited would harbour a grudge for the next fifteen years!

We then began looking for a place to live in as soon as we were married. We soon found what we thought would be an ideal place for us. It was a small semi-detached bungalow, fully furnished in Cypriot style, not far from the beach, and it would be ours for the ridiculous sum of £8 per month if we agreed to stay for at least a year. As we were about to sign the lease we were informed that a married quarter would shortly become vacant and that we would be expected to move in. We were very disappointed!

We had arranged to spend our honeymoon at the Dome Hotel in Kyrenia and friends Walter and Betty Topham, a wonderful but very naive couple not much older than us had volunteered to transport us there after our reception. Gerald and Les offered to come to Kyrenia to pick us up afterwards (as you'll discover, things didn't quite work out that way). Henry had agreed to give the bride away and Bernard and Edith Braithwaite were delighted to provide Barbara's only bridesmaid in the person of Janet, their four-year-old daughter.

The day dawned bright and clear, as you might expect in Cyprus in mid May. As I was on my way to the church with Les driving and best man Gerald sitting in the back with me I must confess I did say jocularly, "What am I doing here? Drive me to the hills". I did feel a little nervous. While we were waiting in the church the Rev. W T F Castle had a little chat with me and was very reassuring. The church was quite full, including lots of friends who we hadn't managed to invite to the reception. I saw Henry and Barbara's faces appear momentarily in the church entrance and then vanish, to reappear a few seconds later. Apparently Janet had caught Barbara's bridal train on something, but Henry thought Barbara was hesitating because she was nervous and was trying to propel her forward.

The obstacle was cleared and Barbara and Henry came down the aisle. Barbara looked marvellous. The ceremony was more meaningful to us because we knew our families and friends in England were having a church service to coincide with the time of our wedding, followed by their own celebration.

There were lots of interested Cypriot onlookers as we left the church and had our photographs taken. Brian Hague was our official photographer, taking pictures in colour with a new camera. It seems strange looking back, but one of my most vivid memories of our reception was of the bath in Cook's house which was filled to the brim with cans and bottles of various types with two huge blocks of ice sitting on top of them. We had a beautifully-decorated three-tier wedding cake which had been baked for us by Yola Murray, Jim's wife, and given to us as a wedding present.

When the time came for us to leave we set off in the Tophams' car festooned with the usual traditional tin cans, old shoes and graffiti. As soon as we pulled out of the married quarters we stopped and disconnected our appendages before setting off towards the coast road to Kyrenia via Lefkonico. When we checked in at the Dome Hotel, Betty and Walter insisted on carrying our bags up to our room. When we opened the door Betty proclaimed in a loud voice, "Walter, they've got single beds! They must have a double bed". Walter was promptly dispatched to see the manager and insist that we were moved, but about ten minutes later he returned to inform us that there wasn't a double bed in the whole of the hotel. Betty lamented once more upon our misfortune and then reluctantly left.

We had our evening meal in a beautiful large dining room overlooking Kyrenia harbour. The room was crowded, mostly with Americans, some of them tourists and some who worked locally. After dinner we had a walk around the town. There was a pleasant sea breeze and it seemed a thoroughly pleasant little town. We were not really impressed with the Dome, so during our walk we looked in at the Bristol, which was the only other hotel, but there were no vacancies.

It had been a long and hard but exciting day so we decided to go to bed early. After we had showered and pushed our beds together we pretended to read for a little while, then tried unsuccessfully to make love. Barbara then asked me what the button was at the side of her bed, and I said that if she pressed it she would find out. A minute later there was a knock at the door and a waiter was asking what we required. All I could think of was,

"What time is breakfast in the morning?" We collapsed into hysterical laughter and eventually fell asleep.

Next morning after breakfast we paid our bill and hired a taxi to take us to the Forest Park Hotel, which was about 70 miles away in the Troodos mountains. It was a wise move. The Forest Park was a magnificent hotel, less than half full, and the service was wonderful, the food out of this world. Our lovemaking came right and we had four wonderful days. Our bill came to £18, and that included a tip!

We had managed to get word to the Dowsetts that we would meet them in Nicosia and not Kyrenia, and they duly met us in the restaurant of the Imperial Hotel. while we were eating our lunch something one of us said started us all laughing. Unfortunately our waiter, who had a bad squint in one eye, thought we were laughing at him, and this made us even worse. In the end we had to leave a lot sooner than we intended. It was all innocent but very embarrassing.

On our return we were booked in at the Savoy Hotel in Famagusta to await our quarters becoming available. It was another excellent hotel, but after we had paid the bill for the first week we decided we couldn't afford to stay there any longer as it might be another two or three weeks before we could move up to Four Mile Point.

Our next move was to the Middle East Hotel, a small pension in a street off Bermes street. It was run by a Mrs B, an Armenian Jewess who along with her husband had been interned in Karalaos until the state of Israel was declared and her husband was now running several orange groves in Cyprus. The hotel was clean and efficiently run - it had been used and recommended as a halfway house by several members of Civilian Wing. Mrs B's food was renowned and various people used to come in for their evening meal. One regular was Bill Page, a member of the first party.

After we had been in residence about a week, Barbara was reading aloud to me a letter which had just arrived from her mother in which she said that she hoped to get our wedding presents off soon. Jokingly I lunged at Barbara on her bed (she had told me they were already on their way), and as I did so the bed collapsed beneath us. Fortunately neither of us were hurt, but we laughed and giggled into the early hours anticipating what Mrs B would say, and how right we were!

The next evening we were sitting outside on the verandah with Bill Page at our table enjoying the usual high class fare. A few minutes later Mrs B appeared with the main course. She said to Bill, "Have they told you they have broken my bed? It was new and British made". Bill laughed for ages (he had a hearty laugh) and of course the story went the rounds, no wonder with Mrs B telling every guest.

When we left we offered to pay for a new bed, but Mrs B wouldn't hear of it. We parted on the best of terms, promising to return for an evening meal in the near future, though we never managed it.

We were scheduled to be "marched in" to our

quarters at 1000 hours on the Monday morning. This meant you would take over your quarters, check the condition of furniture, cutlery and crockery etc. The standard routine was for the outgoing occupant to be "marched out" at the same time and items checked and agreed on at the same time. However as the ingoing occupant was a civilian with a sergeant's status and the outgoing occupant was an officer, such a handover just wasn't on. This was probably just as well, because so many items left a lot to be desired. The child's bedroom stank of urine and the mattress and bedding were badly stained. Quite a few items were withdrawn because officer's quarters were at a higher standard. It was however a very well situated two-bedroomed house looking out over the wadi (valley).

We soon settled in, and as you might expect life seemed very good. The only drawback was that Barbara had never been away from home before and as she was often left alone she sometimes felt homesick. To help to alleviate this we acquired a young male cat called Dabsy from Sheila and Jim Southwell and a dog called Socksy from Arthur and Yvonne Hicks. We attended lots of dances at Four Mile Point and at various local units. We also went to the beach at Famagusta whenever the opportunity arose. The church at Four Mile Point was now completed and Barbara soon had me attending whenever I was off duty on a Sunday morning.

One of the first things we did when we had settled in was to send thank you letters to people who had sent us wedding presents. At the same time we sent home to England a number of small packages containing wedding cake. A few weeks after this Barbara opened the tin which contained what remained of the wedding cake and a crowd of small moths flew out. Our worry then was that friends and family at home might be opening similar packages of moths, or even worse eating cake and then discovering them. Sure enough letters from home confirmed that this had indeed happened. Apparently it is not an uncommon occurrence in the Middle East. (We didn't tell Yola!)

By August we knew that Barbara was pregnant, which made us both very happy. By coincidence our next door neighbours, Denis and Connie Corless, were also expecting their first child at about the same time. Denis had arrived with the 4th party and we became very good friends. Barbara soon had to cope with bad bouts of morning sickness which sometimes went on all day. Amazingly enough, when a bout subsided she usually fancied a fried egg placed on a piece of bread. The frying fat was then poured over it and the plate edged with slices of cucumber. I usually prepared it for her, but it never looked very appetizing to me.

In October 1951 a crisis occurred when Egypt abrogated her 1936 Treaty with Britain and our troops in the Canal Zone had their local supplies of fresh food stopped. This meant a high state of alert for us operationally, and along with quite a few of my colleagues I had to adopt a new temporary shift system which omitted night shifts. Barbara welcomed not being left alone at nights, as the braying of the donkeys in the wadi and the screeching of the owls which often landed on our bedroom windowsill made her nervous. The downside was that I had to spend more time away from her during the day.

During this period Jim Purdie was keeping company with a girl called May. She was married, but her husband was a sergeant who had been posted to the Canal Zone. One day we had arranged to meet them at a bar cum restaurant called the Trianon. When we arrived May was already there, but there was no sign of Jim. We sat there for almost two hours and then decided we had better depart, because I was on duty at six. As we passed the police station we asked our taxi to stop while I made a few enquiries about any recent accidents, knowing Jim was on his motor bike and with the fate of George Dalgarno fresh in my mind. The desk officer asked, "Is your friend's name James Thomas Campbell Purdie?" When I said it was he went on to say that Jim had been involved in a collision with a car and he had been taken to BMH. One of his legs was badly lacerated, but he wasn't thought to be seriously injured. His bike, however, was a write off. We both breathed a sigh of relief and wondered just how we could let May know what had happened.

The liaison didn't last much longer because her husband returned from Egypt.

Another significant happening was that Frank and

Barbara's romance, which had been extinguished, suddenly flickered and then burst into flame, so much so that Frank came over to see us and informed us that his Barbara was arriving in a couple of weeks' time and he was hoping she could stay with us until they were married. The original breakdown had been because Frank, as a Roman Catholic, had insisted that any children must be brought up as Catholics. Barbara would have none of this a few months previously, and we were amazed that she had now capitulated.

We agreed that she could stay with us and also that we would host a small wedding reception. Les Dowsett was to be best man. Yola and Jim were also very involved as they were also Catholics. Frank and I had been close friends, but after the three weeks leading up to the wedding things were never the same. It wasn't just Barbara who moved in - Frank also practically lived at our house for the next three weeks, going to work from their and usually sleeping on our lounge carpet. We would whenever possible go to bed early, leaving them alone, but we would get up next morning to lounge littered with empty glasses, full ash trays and empty plates with crumbs on them streaming with ants. Frank smoked a pipe and Barbara cigarettes, and there was always ash all over the place, plus cigarette ends floating in the toilet. It was an absolute nightmare, especially with my Barbara feeling the way she did. All the hints we dropped fell on deaf ears, and it was obvious that after this our relationship could never be the same.

To help us celebrate our first Christmas together we felt we needed a Christmas tree, a tradition which was unfamiliar to the Cypriots. A few days before Christmas Ralph said to me "Come with me and we'll both get one". We drove to a small wooded area not far from Salamis and there we cut down a couple of small spruce trees. Barbara was most unhappy about our method of obtaining them, but she did decorate ours beautifully. We invited Ken Carling to spend Christmas day with us, and Barbara cooked a goose with all the appropriate trimmings. Our dog Socksy had the remains of our Christmas pudding with lots of fortified sauce and after a few minutes he was staggering all over the place.

Most of the people who lived at Four Mile Point took a pride in their gardens, though they were relatively small. The soil was sandy, stony and lacking in nutrients, but despite this flowers such as zinnias, geraniums and burning bushes seemed to thrive. Tomatoes also did very well and we had a crop of them in our garden from the remains of a tin of cooked tomatoes workmen had thrown down while building walls round our gardens.

By the end of May the wadi was usually dry arid sandy scrubland as far as the eye could see. Towards the end of the year, within six weeks of the first heavy rains, it slowly turned green and produced a profusion of different types of wild flowers which were wonderful to see. We used to go for long walks across the wadi with Socksy and we often came across shepherds with large flocks of the Cypriot fat- tailed sheep, usually with a scruffy-looking mongrel in attendance which ran for its life at the sight of Socksy (who was a coward himself.)

Dabsy was by this time a very fine large cat with quite a few unusual habits. He could stand up and open any door in the house. He loved raw tomatoes and was in the habit of knocking one off the kitchen worktop to let it burst on the tiled floor, when he would eat every morsel. In the evenings he loved to sit on Barbara's lap and nestle up against her bump. If she hadn't spoken to him or caressed him for a few minutes he used to put one of his forepaws to her lips and pat her mouth until she did so.

On Barbara's 21st we had a little celebration at home. The twins and Wally Cairncross came up for the evening and Barbara cooked us a lovely meal. I remember buying her an Oris watch from the garden shop in Famagusta for her birthday.

In the previous few months the Egyptian situation had escalated, and it was brought to a head when British troops in pursuit of terrorist suspects surrounded the police station in Ismailia. When the police refused to surrender the suspects our troops opened fire, and in the ensuing battle 50 Egyptian policemen were killed. The next day serious rioting erupted in Cairo directed against British targets or places associated with Western influence, which included the famous Shepheard's Hotel, which was burnt to the ground. King Farouk appeared weak and helpless, and it was no surprise when he was deposed by a coup of his army officers which included Nasser and Neguib.

In March the first party packed their bags and departed a couple of months before their tour expiry date. A fresh contingent had just arrived from Beaumanor. The Braithwaites stayed with us for the last couple of nights before they left, which was a bit of a squeeze because besides Janet they now had another daughter, Katherine, who was now about eight months old. This began a close friendship which lasted for 45 years. They also brought with them a dog which we agreed to look after until someone in the Regiment could be found to take him over. Major was a small white Spitz who had been with a German unit captured by the Allies in Italy in 1944. 2 Wireless Regiment took him over as a mascot and after the war he transferred with the Regiment to Sarafand in Palestine, eventual finishing up in Cyprus. Bernard, who had been a sergeant with the Regiment during the war, remembered Major well and took him over when they moved into their quarters at Four Mile Point in 1950. He was an incredible dog - so obedient, he seemed to know what you were thinking. He soon settled in with Socksy and Dabsy.

One day down on the beach a large dog was digging near Stephen's carrycot, sending showers of sand on to him, I shouted to frighten it away and in a flash Major had it down on the sand with a death grip on its throat. He would surely have killed it if we hadn't intervened. Major then just went and laid down beside Stephen, as if to say "I've done my job".

In the set room we were still very busy and overtime was on offer, something that was new to me at that stage of my career. However the thought of working on one of my precious days off was anathema to me, and to Barbara too. About a week before the baby was due I was still on my special shifts. It was Saturday evening and I was supposed to finish at midnight. My supervisor, Jim Collins, told me to go home half an hour early as everything was quiet. It took me about six or seven minutes to walk home and when I got there I found Barbara lying in bed looking white as a sheet, though she seemed quite calm. She told me that she had felt strange all evening cleaning through the house and doing various jobs. She'd had a show on the Thursday but the consultant had said there was nothing happening.

I had only been home a few minutes when Barbara got out of bed to go to the toilet and as she did so she deposited what looked like a large dark brown cowpat of clotted blood on the tiled bedroom floor. When she sat on the toilet she thought it was the baby coming and tried desperately to hang on but couldn't. It was another huge clot. I had to dash down to the guardroom to ring for the duty Medical Officer (no one had a phone in those days). About an hour later the MO arrived in the duty three-tonner and apologised because there was no transport available. When he examined Barbara he said he didn't think the baby was imminent, but to be on the safe side we ought to get a taxi and go to BMH. He also thought we were exaggerating about the amount of blood she had lost, because her temperature was practically normal. So it was back to the guardroom to call a taxi, and off we went to Nicosia.

We arrived at BMH about three in the morning. I was assured that everything was all right and that I should go home and telephone about midday. I returned home and slept until twelve, then rang the hospital to be told that everything was fine and that nothing was happening.

A few minutes later the twins rolled up, as they had heard that Barbara had gone into hospital. When I told them there was no news they suggested I might as well go with them to watch a car rally in Famagusta. At about three I was watching Adam Prastitis, a local car dealer, carrying out some intricate manoeuvres in his Jowett Javelin saloon when I saw the MO striding towards me. He had been trying to locate me all afternoon. He was very apologetic, but said he needed permission from me for Barbara to have a Caesarian section, which was scheduled for four o'clock. He told me that the placenta was partially blocking the birth canal and this was preventing the baby from being born it was also the cause of all the bleeding. This had been suspected since the consultant had examined her on the previous Thursday, but our local MO had never been apprised of the situation, or he would have insisted on an ambulance and a doctor to accompany her to hospital.

To cut a long story short, our son Stephen was born normally a few minutes before four with the theatre staff standing by just in case. Only a couple of hours previously our next door neighbour Connie, who had just had her son Barry on the previous Tuesday, was telling Barbara how lucky she was to be having a Caesarian. She likened her own birth experience to having a knife drawn repeatedly through her vital parts.

When I rang at five I was given all the good news. I sent my love and said I'd be along to see them the next afternoon. The twins were going on duty at six, otherwise they would have taken me. when I told Dick Reedman (Slap's brother) my news he didn't hesitate - both he and his wife said that I must go and see Barbara and the baby now, that Barbara would be dying to see me and for me to see the baby. Dick said he was ready to take me there and then so, I accepted with alacrity. It was a kind offer which I have never forgotten.

Of course Barbara was very pleased to see me and I was allowed to see Stephen. At BMH baby viewing was strictly by appointment, and if during visiting time a mother had to feed her baby the ward was cleared. Stephen looked perfect, with no marks or wrinkles and he had a thick mop of black hair, which eventually all rubbed off and became blond.

In those days having a baby meant ten days in hospital. For the first few days I was able to have a lift with Denis, who was visiting Connie. I managed every other day until I went up on the Thursday and brought them home in a taxi. On the Saturday night we arranged a baby sitter in the shape of Julie, our Cypriot cleaner.

Barbara fed Stephen and we went off to a big regimental dance at Four Mile Point. Looking back now it seems highly irresponsible, but we both loved dancing and felt that we needed a break. We were back home before eleven, having thoroughly enjoyed ourselves. During the evening the MO looked at us amazed as we flung ourselves around. He came over to our table for a friendly word and apologised once again for the mistakes the night before Stephen was born.

Shortly after this I returned to normal watch keeping and we began to settle into a more routine pattern of life. To obtain a birth certificate for Stephen it was necessary to go to the village of Pallouriotissa, close to BMH, find the Mukthar or headman of the village, and ask him to issue one. I had a cup of Turkish coffee with him, gave him the details and he completed the appropriate Cyprus birth certificate. I believe he kept the small fee involved as one of the perks of his job.

Until a special act of Parliament which was passed some years later, Stephen and several hundreds like him had to be registered at Somerset House. Technically Stephen had dual nationality and if he had been living in Cyprus at the time of the Cyprus-Turkish conflict he could have been called up for National Service in the Cypriot Guard.

Stephen was an amazing baby. Of course all parents say that, but he really was. By the time he was three months he could reach any place he wanted to by rolling over and over, usually clad only in his nappy. At four months he was crawling all over the place and beginning to stand up. He was wearing his little knees out, so Barbara made him a tiny pair of dungarees to help protect them. Connie next door sometimes used to ask if she could borrow him for a while to show visitors how forward he was. It's a good job Barry wasn't old enough to understand, as it could have given him a complex.

We had another celebration when Stephen was christened at St Andrew's church at Four Mile Point by the Chaplain, Howard Cole, whom we met again 23 years later when as Senior Chaplain to the Forces he came to preach at Stanley Fort Garrison Church, Hong Kong.

Our tour was rapidly drawing to a close and we were trying, not very successfully, to save a little to help us make a start in England. Saving in that last year had been made particularly difficult because in January 1952 as non-industrial civil servants we had been compelled to have our salaries paid to us on a monthly basis. It seemed very difficult after a weekly wage. Advances of pay were available initially for anyone who had no savings and couldn't manage, and it was surprising how many couldn't, especially among the alcoholic fraternity.

Our repatriation date was mid-November, much earlier than we expected, supposedly because of aircraft availability. Connie and Denis put us up for our last two nights and they truly were nights to remember. We were constantly under attack from mosquitoes. Stephen's cot was covered by a net, but we had no protection and we really suffered.

The story of our return flight beggars belief. Because of problems at Nicosia Airport our chartered aircraft had landed at a small emergency airfield near Tymbou, a small village on the Famagusta side of Nicosia. As it was a charter flight and hadn't landed at Nicosia, it had been unable to take on fresh provisions and the only refreshment available to passengers was tea or coffee. There was only one small building on the airfield and we had to congregate there until it was time to board for a four o'clock take off. It was almost take-off time when John Mortby, Ken Carling, Ken Spring, Maurice Cooper and Pete Harris rolled up in a taxi after a last-minute bar crawl in Nicosia. I'm convinced it was a DIY take off with no ground control restrictions. There were about eighty passengers, mainly third party civilians, supplemented by a small army contingent which included a Major and his wife who sat opposite us. Laurie and Celia Wilson had their baby daughter with them. She was roughly the same age as Stephen, but they had brought no food with them, expecting naively that baby food would be provided. Barbara had brought plenty with us so we were able to give her some.

Because of bad weather we were informed that it was necessary to fly at 12,000 feet. That seems nothing nowadays with pressurised airliners flying at heights in excess of 30,000 feet, but our problem was that the heating in our aircraft was totally inadequate and most people were cold, especially if they were anywhere near the aircraft door, as we were. The stewardess told us there were no blankets available, so Les and Gerald gave Barbara their overcoats to put round her legs.

After about six hours we made our approach to Luqa airport Malta. Our plane seemed to bank very steeply as we came in to land between what looked like two narrow parallel lines of landing lights, and we all breathed a sigh of relief when we touched down. We were ushered into a very unsalubrious restaurant where a meal was served which consisted of egg, chips, beans, bread and butter with tea or coffee. Most of us were so hungry we cleared the lot. We agreed however that the airport should have been called "filthy Luqa".

Our next wait was for transport to take us to an overnight service transit camp. After quite a wait an old bus arrived and we duly climbed aboard. This time the Major and his wife sat in the seat behind us and Stephen succeeded in making them both smile and talk to him, something he hadn't managed on the flight from Cyprus to Malta, but not for want of trying. After about half an hour's journey we stopped and thought we had arrived – no, this was the officer's transit accommodation and we had another half hour in another before we reached our destination.

The camp was basic but clean. Our sheets felt damp, but we soon fell fast asleep. We had an early call and after a reasonable breakfast we were told that our pilot was not happy with his engine and it would need to be checked out. There would be no chance of taking off before late afternoon, so we were free to go and have a look around Valetta. We shared taxis and had a pleasant sight-seeing stroll around the town. We finally boarded our plane about four, and it was nearly five before we took off.

About five hours later, after circling around for what seemed ages, we landed at Stansted Airport. The customs officers here were unbelievably thorough (possibly because they knew we had taken off without customs control at Tymbou). The Dowsetts stated they had nothing to declare but they were not believed, and their belongings were meticulously searched. Ken Carling declared that he had nothing, but when they found an empty Rolex case in his luggage they took him away and strip-searched him. We had to wait for him before our bus could set off for London, having had a decent airport meal.

It seemed a long journey into London. Because it had been such a long and tiring trip a few tempers were frayed and voices were raised. I remember hearing Pam and Roy Ward arguing about meeting Pam's sister. Eventually our bus trundled into Goodge Street, London Services Transit Centre, which adjoined the underground station. We were then rerouted to various hotels which had appropriate vacancies. Ours was a good hotel near King's Cross, handy for our train journey north.

It was now nearly two in the morning, but we opted for a seven o'clock call so we could catch a through train for Cleethorpes which left King's Cross at 8.05. Bill and

Anne Cooper, along with Laurie and Celia Wilson, had decided to take their time and have breakfast in the hotel first. How we wished we had. Thanks to a "pea souper" fog and London traffic, we missed our train by about three minutes. There was nearly two hours to wait for the next, so we went into the station restaurant and had an excellent breakfast. Stephen had been on mixed feeding for quite some time and he enjoyed the egg, cereal and hot milk they provided.

The fog lifted a little and our train left on time. We tried to settle down and relax, but Stephen had other ideas and was very active throughout the journey. He was just seven months old the day we arrived in London.

So began another phase of our lives.

CHAPTER 6

ENGLAND MY ENGLAND

As we sat on the train from King's Cross to Cleethorpes on a cold foggy November day, I couldn't help wondering how we were going to fare in austerity Britain after three years in an island paradise with an abundance of sunshine and no food shortages. Barbara's parents had just moved from North Cotes into a large old house in Cleethorpes which had formerly been the residence of the local RC priest. There had been plenty of work to make it shipshape and they had only moved in the week before we arrived.

It was strange at first living in the same house as my in-laws. Though I was soon on good terms with Barbara's father Norman, there was initially a veiled hostility between her mother Ethel and myself. Our first skirmish took place when I used all the hot water having a bath after playing football (in the same team as my old pals Bob Potterton and Bill Todd). Another source of irritation to her was my ridiculous habit of having three teaspoons of sugar in my tea or coffee. Usually I didn't bother to stir it, as was shown by the amount in the bottom of my cup. However I suspect the main reason for the friction was that we had told her we had a flat to go to in Loughborough and could only stay for about ten days. Barbara was convinced that her mother thought mother and baby would be remaining at home with Granny while I went back to work and to look for accommodation.

Ethel had arranged for a reporter and photographer from the *Grimsby Evening Telegraph* to interview us about life in Cyprus. This set alarm bells ringing, because I remembered the cutting sent us from the *Telegraph* concerning Stephen's christening, saying the Dowsett twins were his godfathers. I had expected repercussions from the War Office about this, but nothing was said. This was the result of showing Barbara's sister Jean my notice about being posted to Cyprus. She had noticed that it originated in a certain Military Intelligence department in London and she had never forgotten it. The reporter asked me lots of probing questions about the political situation in Cyprus and asked me whether I thought the Cypriots would ever achieve "enosis", but there was very little I could tell him at that time. A few nights later an edited and very distorted account of our interview appeared, accompanied by a photo of Barbara, Stephen and myself.

Those ten days back home were quite hectic as we tried to go and see my Mum and Dad as often as possible, plus trying to fit in seeing as many old friends and relations as we could on both sides. Unfortunately I did have one major altercation with Ethel because I took Stephen over to Jean's house to meet her husband Bill, who had arrived home from sea the previous evening. He was just about to go down to the fish docks to see how much their catch of fish had made and pick up his wages and his share of any profits. Jean insisted that I accompany Bill and said she could easily manage Stephen, who was playing happily with her daughter Janet. It turned out that Bill had made a good catch and so we called and had a couple of pints. Of course we didn't stop at a couple and we were both well away by the time we called a taxi to take us back home. Jean was fine about it but Barbara's mother went ballistic and tore into me. The main thrust of her tirade was that I had dumped Stephen on Jean and gone off drinking with Bill. I then unleashed a few home truths of my own. It must have been awful for Barbara listening to us arguing.

The last few days were not very comfortable and we were pleased to board the train for Loughborough. Our flat was a ground floor one in Gladstone Street and consisted of a front bedroom, a living room and kitchen with an outside toilet and a small garden. The upstairs was occupied by an Asian couple, who were quite pleasant except for grumbles that the water was never hot enough for them. The arrangement was that whenever they needed a bath they gave us an extra bucket of coal to put on our living room fire, which heated the back boiler. The owners of our flats were a Mr and Mrs Hasenfuss, who owned a pork butcher's shop in Ward End, Loughborough. This was very much austerity Britain, with many things still rationed, so when we used to go into the shop to pay our rent and were offered extra off ration bacon, ham and eggs, we couldn't refuse. Coal was also rationed, but as we had just returned from warmer climes we were given an extra allocation for three months.

Outside in the coal shed there was an old cycle. I repaired a couple of punctures, bought a front and rear light and a couple of mornings later at 6.15 I was en route to Beaumanor. It was cold, dark and frosty and my ears sang. I had forgotten that England could be so cold, and here I was back on Beaumanor's dastardly seven-week cycle a couple of weeks before Christmas.

We had our Christmas dinner with the Braithwaites, who had managed to acquire a new council house in Woodhouse Eaves. Straight after dinner I had to go and work a 1400-2230 shift. We had quite a few visitors while we were in our flat.

My brother Tom was now a PTI stationed at Warwick and had become very friendly with the Turpins, Jackie, Dick and Randolph. I think it may have been their influence which made him consider boxing as a career when he left the army. My brother Terry was also now in the army and he came to visit us while he was on embarkation leave before leaving for Korea, so we were pleased the conflict was over. A short time after this my mum visited us with my sister Thora, who was now in the QARANC (Queen Alexandra's Royal Auxiliary Nursing Corps) and shortly due to sail for Hong Kong, where she served at the British Military Hospital in Bowen Road.

By the time we had spent a few weeks in our flat we had decided that we were living just a little bit beyond our means, as we were paying two pounds ten shillings a week rent, had no furniture of our own and considered it was time we acquired some. So we decided to look for some cheaper accommodation. We answered an ad in the local paper which stated "Good accommodation available for only one pound and ten shillings per week plus some cooking and cleaning". The house was in Storer Road, not far from the College, and was owned by a Mr Austin Couldery, a teacher at Loughborough College Grammar School. He already had a lodger called Eric Campbell who was a lecturer at Loughborough College. The accommodation was quite good, with a good-sized bedroom for us upstairs, a sitting room downstairs and a shared kitchen. Barbara was expected to keep the house clean and provide meals most week nights, with the costs to be shared. It was an arrangement doomed from the start and it lasted only six weeks before it became too much of a burden for Barbara, so she took Stephen with her to Cleethorpes while I resumed temporary residence in the house at Beaumanor.

It transpired that there was an advantage to being homeless, as it gave us extra priority points on the Beaumanor housing list. Within six weeks we were allocated a wooden hut at Woodhouse Eaves. This was one of about forty which had been provided to house the ATS girls who worked at Beaumanor during the war. They stood on a little plateau at the top of Brand Hill, surrounded by copses. When the war ended and the girls were demobilised the camp was left deserted for quite a while.

This was a time when there was a great housing shortage, and it was not unknown for squatters to move in and take over unoccupied accommodation of any description. The hierarchy at Beaumanor received information that a group of squatters were on their way from Leicester to occupy the Brand Hill site. This was in the middle of the afternoon. They phoned down to the set rooms and said that anyone interested could be released from duty to hotfoot it to Brand Hill (about a mile and a half distant) and occupy the hut of their choice. When the squatters from Leicester arrived the huts were no longer vacant and the police were in attendance to prevent any trouble.

Eventually Barrow-on-Soar Rural District Council took over the site, providing street lighting and the usual amenities, and began charging a nominal rent. When I met Barbara and Stephen at the railway station, Stephen was only eleven months old but he ran towards me at breakneck speed. He certainly hadn't forgotten me.

While in Storer Road we had bought a new three-piece suite on hire purchase and Mr Couldery had let us keep it there until we found somewhere to live. We then returned to the same store and bought a sideboard, dining table and chairs, a double bed and some lino, all also on HP. We also arranged for the furniture van to pick up our suite at Storer Road and deliver it at the same time. Our new home consisted of a bungalow type wooden hut with a large L-shaped living room dominated by a large coke-burning pot-bellied stove. There was a small kitchen with an electric cooker at one end of the living room and two small bedrooms at the other end. there was an annexe between us and the next hut which contained two toilets and one shared bathroom with hot water being provided by another stove in the annex, lit by whoever wanted a bath.

When we had been there a few days I attended an auction in Loughborough and picked up a washing machine which boasted a wringer and a hand-operated agitator, this for a bid of four pounds and ten shillings. I also secured a length of good haircord carpet for another one pound and ten shillings, I must also mention that I had to pay a further half a crown for delivery. The carpet went well over our lino and Barbara was overjoyed with her washing machine.

We soon settled in what was truly a most beautiful spot; there was even an allotment for me within fifty yards of our hut. Despite the dreaded shift pattern and the fact that money was tight we were very happy. My salary was £32 per month and our HP payments were £8 a month. Fortunately our rent was only ten shillings and threepence a week including rates, but we had a quarterly electric bill and we had to buy coke for the stove, so we had to budget carefully.

Our immediate neighbours were Gladys and George Davison, who had a five year old son called Alan; they had been in Cyprus with the first party. 1953 was a glorious summer and we often went for picnics in the woods at Swithland. We had lots of visitors from both our families and Norman and Ethel often came to see us in what we considered was their opulent Humber Hawk. Sometimes Pam and John came with them and they loved it too. My parents were supposed to be coming to spend a few days with us on their own, but when we met them at the station they had my sister Valerie with them and also my brother Tom and his girlfriend Irene, who had run away from her parents in Birmingham and had turned up on Mum's doorstep.

They stayed with us for about five days, greatly stretching Barbara's ingenuity and resourcefulness in feeding and accommodating them. Tom had left the army and had just embarked on a professional boxing career. He easily won his first two fights, so while he stayed with us he was out road running with me and dad accompanied us on my bike. In his next fight he was beaten by a boxer named Ernie Maitland who was a National Coal Board champion and a seasoned professional. Tom's nose was badly damaged and wisely he decided to call it a day and turned his attention to bodybuilding and weight lifting.

This was the summer of the conquest of Everest and the Coronation, and I remember one of our neighbours, Winnie Denton, organised a big outdoor party. I also remember that George Davison and I travelled to Trent Bridge and saw a glorious day's cricket in the Test against Australia in which Alec Bedser bowled magnificently. When the third party returned to the UK the majority of them immediately volunteered for another tour to Cyprus. Quite a few of the second party did likewise, but very few of the first party volunteered, possibly because most of them had been allocated good quality council houses in the beautiful setting of Woodhouse Eaves.

Money was often tight for us and there was rarely anything left at the end of the month, especially if we had entertained visitors. When Norman and Ethel came it was usually a bonus, because being a grocer he invariably brought a large box of groceries. On one occasion I took a day's leave after a rostered rest day and spent two days carrying chaff during threshing at a nearby farm. It was dirty, back-breaking work, but the five pounds I earned was more than welcome.

One October evening I was on a 2-10 afternoon shift. George Davison and I had travelled to work on our bikes in torrential rain and it carried on incessantly. At about seven in the evening we were all sitting at our set positions in "M" Hut when a torrent of water swept through the set room. George, who was sitting across the room opposite me, intimated that if the power shorted we could all be electrocuted. Almost immediately the power went off and we were in the dark. There were about forty of us in that room, but I was first out of the door, almost bumping into Slap Reedman and Ollie Pearce, who were yelling to us that we should assemble in the main hall as quickly as possible. We had to wade through to the bike sheds and push our bikes round to the front of the house.

A few minutes later Ollie (who was second in command at Beaumanor) came across and told us all to go home and dry out. This happened to be the night that Wolves were playing Honved, and as George had a TV we were able to watch most of a thrilling match which resulted in a victory for Wolves.

One winter morning I arrived home after a night shift at about 7.15. Barbara said she'd had a terrible night as a rat had been trying to get into our bedroom. It had been snowing intermittently and the wind was howling, and every time the wind howled the rat scratched and gnawed and tried to get in to our bedroom. Barbara was ashamed to tell me that she had moved into Stephen's room and had placed our newly-acquired kitten in our bedroom.

I was very tired and a little sceptical and jumped into bed. I was just dropping off to sleep when I heard scratching and there, clearly visible coming through the corner of the room, was the nose and whiskers of a rat.

I grabbed my shoe and gave its nose an almighty whack, and it gave a loud squeal and vanished. The council ratcatcher came and laid poison bait. I filled in the hole and we had no more problems.

We did however have a problem with our electricity bills, which were always much more than those of anyone around us, all of whom enjoyed more or less identical facilities. After a year of excessive bills we insisted that our meter was checked. When it was eventually checked it was discovered that four of the adjacent street lights were running off our meter! We came to an amicable agreement and received a good rebate and a much-reduced quarterly bill.

I then began to have trouble with a minor cut on my hand which refused to heal, so I went to see Dr Wykes, who was also the official War Office doctor. He advocated leaving it uncovered to let the air get to it. A few days later I woke up with the cut hand covered in lesions and itching like mad. By the next day it had spread to my other hand, and when I went to see Dr Wykes he said "What a bloody mess, I'll get you a specialist appointment as soon as I can".

I had expected he would sign me off work, but he said it wasn't necessary as it wasn't contagious. I went to work with bandaged hands and of course I found it difficult to write, especially at speed. My hand often bled and there were loads of little flakes of skin all around my set position, so no one wanted to sit anywhere near me. The duty officer rang Dr Wykes and received another assurance that my problem was definitely not contagious, but sent word that I should attend his surgery next morning.

The next day when he saw me he actually signed me off sick for a few days and prescribed an ointment in a tube which he hoped might help to alleviate the almost unbearable itching. The prescription was a forerunner of the modern Betnovate, and when I spread it on my hands and lightly bandaged them before I went to bed the itching began to ease. The next morning my hands had undergone a remarkable transformation. The lesions had healed and the blisters had hardened, but it took several weeks before my hands regained their sensitivity.

The time was fast approaching when I had to take a morse test, as part of my upgrading from CR02 to CR01 (Civilian Radio Officer). This was necessary to make me eligible for the last three yearly increments of my pay scale, the other two parts of the exam to be taken at Bletchley at a later date. Though I had been practising quite a lot at speed for several weeks on the actual test day I was quite keyed up, knowing how important it was financially. There were about a dozen of us taking the test. The code and the cipher (figures) had presented no problems and the last part was plain language. It could be any language, French, German, or even English, the trick was to always read three or four letters behind and never try to anticipate, especially in English.

Seated next to me was a Scot called Wally Johnstone

and halfway through the test his pencil snapped. He snatched the pencil from the chap on his right and carried on writing. The room was in uproar and it was several minutes before the laughter died down and a new plain language test could be begun. I did pass that test, but it was almost four years before I attended my upgrading course at Bletchley.

Barbara was by this time expecting again and the baby was due towards the end of January 1954. Barbara Anne was born at Brand Hill on the evening of Sunday January 31st during a period of gales, storms and torrential rains over the whole of Northern Europe. That same night Uncle George lost his life on the Grimsby trawler *Laforey*, which turned turtle in a Norwegian fiord as she ran for shelter from the storm. All hands were lost and no bodies were ever found. Aunt Ethel was never quite the same after this, because she was convinced that he was such a good swimmer he couldn't drown.

The following summer our finances received a healthy boost when we received almost £200 for a backdated increase in FSA for the last two years we had been in Cyprus. Barbara's parents came quite frequently. Norman was very fond of a day at the races and usually turned up when there was a meeting at Nottingham or Leicester. If I was off duty I went with him, but my betting was restricted to a couple of small each-way wagers. Norman had a way of making friends with everyone, especially in the local hostelries when he was playing darts or dominoes. During the next twenty years he became very well known and liked by quite a few of my colleagues and the pub locals wherever we happened to be.

We received our preliminary orders for Cyprus in October and were scheduled to fly out sometime in February 1955. A few weeks before we were due to go we placed our relatively small amount of furniture in store and Barbara and the children went to Cleethorpes while I moved into the house at Beaumanor, commuting whenever my shifts would allow. I shared a room in the manor with Bill Cooper and Duncan Small, also due to go to Cyprus, and they had made similar arrangements. The Dowsett twins had not volunteered and seemed quite happy with life in England at their "digs" with Mrs Bowler in Woodhouse Eaves.

There were hints of possible trouble to come in Cyprus with news of the British Navy intercepting the *Ayios Georgios* off Cyprus, which was carrying a cargo of arms and ammunition from Greece. Our return journey to Cyprus was at a much improved standard with a non-stop eight hour flight on a Britannia turbo prop aircraft. We were met at Nicosia by members of the various watches we had been assigned to. Quite a few of the Civilian Wing now had their own cars, and they had generously offered to come and meet us. I remember that Bill Scarth came and picked us up and transported us to the King George Hotel, which was on the beach at Famagusta. Also staying with us were

Ralph and Mary Burrows, Len and Jean Tovey, Denis and Connie Corless and Ron and Marjorie Hedges. Almost straight away we had the offer of a bungalow which was just about to become vacant, as Denzil Lewis and his wife Barbara were just about to move into a quarter at Four Mile. The bungalow was semi-detached in Apostolous Marcou Street (St Mark) in the Stavros area and the bungalow adjoining ours was the local police station. It was quite spacious, and when we moved in during the last week in February it was a great contrast to cold midwinter England - all we needed was a single sheet as a bedcover.

We soon settled in and the policemen made great friends with Stephen and Anne and were always feeding them with local bread, cheese and fruit. Fortunately they still ate their normal meals, so there was no need to intervene. Transport to and from work was still by army three-tonner, which picked up and dropped off in Famagusta centre. I always walked, meeting Len Tovey and Ralph Burrows en route.

After a few weeks we discovered that an enterprising Turkish Cypriot had imported a couple of old single-decker Leyland buses from England and was starting a service between town and Four Mile Point. It proved very successful, especially with people who had previously used taxis. We soon became very friendly with the Turkish driver and often when we had completed our six to midnight shift he would drop us off at our doorsteps, or as near as was possible. More and more EOKA slogans were appearing all over the island and as fast as they were removed they reappeared. At the opening of the Ayios Georgeos case at Paphos, hundreds of schoolboys mobbed the courthouse shouting "Enosis!" and "Englishmen go home!" The police had to make several baton charges. This meant that Grivas's efforts to stir up the Cypriot youth had at last produced results. In the court at Paphos six Greek Nationals and seven Cypriots were charged with trying to overthrow the Colony's constitution by revolution or sabotage. The prisoners were refused bail and the case referred to the Assizes. It was later revealed that on the 29th March Colonel Grivas met the Archbishop and agreed that the campaign would definitely start on the last night of the month, 31st March 1955.

In the early hours of the 1st April there were a series of explosions throughout the island. Many police stations were targeted and at the Cyprus Broadcasting Station bombs seriously damaged the transmitters. The bombs thrown at the main police station in Famagusta failed to go off. I was on the morning shift and had heard the news of the bomb incidents on the early morning Forces Broadcasting Service. When I returned home at about one thirty there were already workmen erecting a barbed wire perimeter fence around our bungalow and the police bungalow. A few hours later floodlights were installed, to enable the adjoining undeveloped land to be illuminated during the hours of darkness.

The police station was manned by two sergeants, one Greek and one Turkish, along with six constables, two of whom were Turkish. One of the sergeants came over to see us and suggested that in view of the threat to police stations and British Service units we should be extremely vigilant. He required a list of my shift rotas in advance and said he would need to know if we were expecting any visitors, especially during the hours of darkness.

The first few weeks of April were a period of uneasy calm with the expectation that things might happen at any time. EOKA leaflets signed by "Dighenis" (Grivas) threatened all sorts of dire consequences for any locals helping the British. A one day general strike was called, commencing at midnight. When Ralph and I came off duty just before midnight we thought we might have to ask for army transport to travel home, but we were pleased to see our friendly bus driver waiting for us. We were the only two passengers on the bus.

As we came into Famagusta and approached the Land Gate at the entrance to the Old City (Turkish) we would normally have turned right and followed the road in past the main police station, but there was a barrier across the road. I thought our driver was going to drive straight through, but at the last moment he decided to stop. Immediately several belligerent-looking Cypriots jumped aboard and manhandled our driver off the bus, then gestured that Ralph and myself that should also alight. We did so, with Ralph grasping his bag tightly as it contained “Clicky Ba”, an old baseball bat for use in emergencies. We walked about two miles home and the town was thronged with people, mostly male, and of course not a policeman or serviceman in sight. It was a little unnerving.

During June and July things began to look more ominous. Bombs were being thrown into bars frequented by servicemen and expatriates. Jock Chrystal, a friend of ours, was sitting out on his verandah one evening having a drink with his wife when a bomb was thrown on to the verandah. He was attempting to kick it away from his wife when it exploded, severely injuring his leg and foot. He spent a few weeks in BMH at Nicosia and then was shipped home.

While we lived at Stavros the most disconcerting shift for me was the night shift, because it entailed leaving a brightly-lit barbed-wire enclosure to walk about a mile to town, Ralph had already moved to Four Mile, but I always met Len near Stavros church and we walked the rest of the way to town together. .

One particular evening quite a few bombs had been thrown and there had been sporadic gunfire. As I approached Stavros Church I was carrying my
bag, which contained my headphones, sandwiches and a flask of coffee, when a blinding light was shone in my face and I was challenged with “Halt! “Stammata!” “Durr!” This was the mandatory call to stop in English, Greek and Turkish. I froze. I was approached by a corporal and two privates of the Green Jacket Regiment

who were on foot patrol in the area. Despite the fact that I was obviously British they searched me and my bag. When they were satisfied about my identity they told me to be on the alert, as they had already been bombed and shot at twice that evening. They told me to keep alert and sent me on my way.

There was no sign of Len at our usual meeting place so I walked on in the semi-darkness. As I walked across an alleyway between two buildings someone threw themselves at me yelling "EOKA"! It was Len, carrying out what he thought was a practical joke. There is no doubt in my mind that if I had been carrying a Sten gun or a revolver Len would have either been killed or wounded. By coincidence, only a couple of weeks previously most of us had turned down the option of carrying arms because of the worsening situation. Len was abject in his apologies and said he realised straight away what a foolish and stupid thing he had done.

One member of the Civilian Wing who did take up the option of being armed later went to jail in Cyprus for six months because someone stole his revolver. I appreciate how stupid and careless he was but I thought the sentence was very harsh, especially when officers who had committed the same offence weren't even court martialled. I'm sure the judge decided to make an example of him to deter other people with firearms. He served his sentence in full, was sent home and I believe he left the job.

One day the Greek lady who lived opposite us came

The original evacuees at Middleton Hall.
Back row: JR, Tom, Charlie Aldred, Alan Batty, Maurice Batty.
Front row: Frank Mould, Geoffrey Carter, A D M Dakin, 'Squeak' Mould, Norman Deering, Geoffrey Laurence.

The Ryan family just before leaving Loughborough for Hong Kong, 1967

Beverly, Richard, Anne, Stephen and Louise at our ruby wedding, 1991

Terry, Valerie, JR, Thora and Tom

James and Barbara, 1992

With eleven of our grandchildren at our golden wedding celebrations, 2001

across to see us, accompanied by her daughter, who spoke excellent English. Through her daughter she begged us not to sleep in the bedroom which adjoined the police station, because she was concerned for our safety. The lady was Mrs Lordos, the mother of the Lordos brothers, business entrepreneurs who now rate among the wealthiest men on the island.

During this period of tension I sometimes walked home alone if Len was on leave, and this particular night it was well after midnight as I approached our bungalow. I waved to the policeman on guard and let myself in very quietly. I didn't put the light on and crept down the corridor to our bedroom in complete darkness, thinking that Barbara must be asleep. Halfway along I bumped into her. She let out an almighty shriek and lashed out at me. When she realised it was me, I was castigated for creeping in with no lights on. Barbara said it had been a terrible evening with bombs and gunfire since eight o'clock.

It shows how nerves and tension can build up, because there had been no terrorist activity at all that evening. The noise Barbara had heard was coming from a "Wall of Death" show which was on a site near the market in Famagusta.

Soon after we arrived we saw some Alsatian pups advertised and duly selected a bitch whom we christened Janey. The children loved her and she was rapidly developing into a beautiful dog. Unfortunately the area around was scrubland, and several of our

Cypriot neighbours kept free-range chickens. Janey escaped a couple of times and one day she caught and killed a chicken. I tried to chastise her with the dead bird in front of her, but didn't make much impression.

The next day I was coming home from an afternoon shift and as I walked the last few hundred yards I met the owner of the dead chicken, a young Cypriot businessman also walking from work. I apologised profusely for her behaviour and said I would pay for the chicken. He said it wasn't necessary and that it was only natural that a young dog should chase chickens. While I was apologising I could see Barbara in the distance waving frantically. When I reached her she told me that the children had just let Janey out and she had immediately killed another chicken. Five minutes later the young Cypriot was knocking at our door saying that she was a killer and must be destroyed.

Very reluctantly, because we could find no one to take her over, we took her to the vet in the Old City. He took one look at her and said that she was too beautiful to be put to sleep and if he couldn't find a good home for her he would keep her himself. This of course was an ideal solution, and about a year later we saw her outside the vets and she really looked a magnificent animal.

As the summer progressed law and order began to deteriorate even more, and there was a steady trickle of families opting to transfer from the private hirings in Famagusta to the relative security of the quarters at Four Mile Point. I said relative, because the RAF signals unit just a few hundred yards away from our site at Four Mile was bombed. The police station at Paralimni about three miles from Stavros was attacked; here they tied up five policemen and escaped with all their arms and ammunition. In retrospect paralimni was noted as a hotbed of EOKA activists and one can't help wondering about collusion. It was common knowledge that EOKA had penetrated the police force and other Government departments, including Special Branch, three of whom were murdered. Many other Greek Cypriots in positions to expose EOKA were silenced by intimidation.

We were advised that as we lived in a very vulnerable spot we should relocate to Four Mile as soon as a suitable quarter became available. We moved at the end of September on a day when a general strike was in progress. Our transport was yet again an army three-ton lorry. Barbara and the children sat in the front with the driver and I stood up with our belongings in the back. As we drove through Famagusta we were greeted with boos and catcalls followed by a shower of stones, which was a little unnerving, so we were pleased to draw up in front of 1, Sutherland Road, Four Mile Point, which was to be our home for the next two and a half years.

Also in late September, a mob of Cypriot youths overturned a Jeep with three British soldiers in it as they entered Metaxas Square. They then proceeded to burn down the British Institute with only token intervention by the police and none from British troops. It was then announced that Sir John Harding CIGS would b e

Governor of Cyprus and Sir Robert Armitage would be released from his thankless task. Sir John arrived on the 3rd October 1955 and shortly afterwards EOKA pulled off a major coup by seizing a large consignment of arms and ammunition at Famagusta docks.

On the 28th October there was widespread rioting in all the large towns and mobs of stone-throwing schoolboys had to be dispersed by troops using truncheons and tear gas. In November a special Assize Court was set up and extra judges brought in, mainly from England and Ireland. This was to deal with the huge backlog of offences against public order and security. Makarios stated that Cypriots would never abandon their struggle, even if the whole island was converted into a giant prison. Shortly after this, sixteen leading EOKA men escaped from Kyrenia Castle. They had the audacity to complain about the absence of sheets on their beds, and when they were provided they promptly tied them together and lowered themselves to freedom.

On the 26th November the Governor proclaimed a State of Emergency because of the widespread disorder, and terrorist outrages. Several policemen had been shot in the back at various times in Ledra Street, Nicosia. The death penalty, previously used only for murder, was now extended to other offences including discharging firearms at persons, throwing or depositing bombs. The unlawful possession of firearms or explosives could mean life imprisonment. Offenders under the age of eighteen could be sentenced to whipping.

All troops were now on active service and liable to court martial for any serious offences. Also included in the emergency regulations were the powers to impose curfews and to levy collective fines on towns whose inhabitants resorted to riotous or unlawful behaviour. Within the next few months it became necessary to invoke the majority of these regulations.

This then was the unstable backdrop as we tried to settle down and enjoy the rest of our tour. We were advised not to go off swimming or picnicking to remote places. We hadn't a car, so we were not likely to do this, so it wasn't really a restriction for us. Our house was only a few yards from the entrance to the quarters on the main Famagusta to Nicosia road. Ralph and Mary Burrows lived in a quarter exactly opposite to us. Sport and work had now become the dominant factor in most of the men's lives. Looking back, it couldn't have been very pleasant for our wives, because most of us were obsessed. The Civilian Wing now had an excellent hockey team which competed in the Major Units League and had beaten practically every team on the island, despite the fact that our team was drawn from mainly just one watch "B", with a strength of about fifty people. We also competed in the Regimental hockey, football and cricket leagues, and quite a few of us played tennis and participated in Regimental athletics too.

One morning I went to Famagusta on the bus, taking Stephen with me. As we walked along Hermes Street we heard a lot of noise and shouting and as we approached one of the intersecting streets we saw a lot of young Cypriots running across. About a minute later, just before we reached the intersection, we heard, then saw, two soldiers running fast with their boots resounding on the road surface. As they came directly in front of us they raised their guns and fired several shots. We heard screams of pain and the two soldiers turned and ran back in the direction they had come from.

Almost immediately Stephen and I were surrounded by dozens of Cypriots who demanded that I witness what our soldiers had just done. I then saw the young man who had been wounded. He was groaning and bleeding profusely and a chemist from a nearby pharmacy was administering first aid. This young man was a cobbler who plied his trade in an open-fronted shop in that side street and obviously had nothing to do with the soldiers being stoned. I was concerned that Stephen, who was holding my hand had, witnessed the whole incident, and I wanted to get him home as soon as possible. A couple of Cypriots whom I knew came up to us and begged me to testify to what I had just seen. I said that I would if called upon to do so - fortunately I was never asked.

This incident took place at about 11 am and when we returned home I told Barbara what we had seen and we listened to the BBC World News at One to see if there was any mention of the incident. The main headline was that British troops in Famagusta had been forced to open fire as they had been surrounded by a mob and were under a heavy stone and missile attack. Seeing is believing.

During the next few months there was intermittent trouble in most of the large towns, which resulted in curfews and collective fines. It was also revealed that the person responsible for the murders of several policemen and servicemen (usually shot in the back) in Ledra Street Nicosia was Nicos Sampson, who was in hiding. Nicos was a young Cypriot whom quite a few of us knew from our first tour. He drove around in an open sports car and frequented the bars and nightclubs of Famagusta. He was supposed to be a newspaper reporter and he seemed a pleasant young man. He was eventually captured after an anonymous tip-off in a house in a village near Nicosia.

Unfortunately when he was arrested he was badly beaten and then thrown into the back of a security vehicle, unconscious, on a cold wet night. When he was formally charged in Nicosia the next day his injuries were apparent for all to see, including lots of international press reporters. Ironically this saved his life. When the trial judge passed sentence he said that even though he had been found guilty by the jury on several counts of murder he had no option other than. to commute the death penalty to life imprisonment because of the pre-trial brutalisation. This taught the security forces a lesson, and they instigated strict guidelines of procedure when arresting suspects. Nicos Sampson briefly became President of Cyprus after the coup which precipitated the Turkish invasion of the island in 1974.

During the early days of the Emergency, most men still used to go shopping in Famagusta during the day, though we were always on the alert. I remember walking along a fairly crowded Hermes Street when there was a sudden burst from a pneumatic drill on a nearby building site. Many of us hit the deck at great speed and then sheepishly picked ourselves up and dusted ourselves down. Soon afterwards we were advised that male personnel should remain in camp or quarters and that only women should go into town during daylight hours for shopping purposes. The best part of the beach was wired off especially for our use, with armed guards patrolling the perimeter.

On the 6th March 1956 Barbara and Mary Burrows had travelled on the bus to Famagusta on a shopping trip, Ralph and myself remaining at home to look after the children. Before they had completed their shopping, the Military Police approached and advised them to return to camp straight away. As they made their way to the bus pickup point they were surrounded by a crowd of hostile, jostling teenage Cypriot girls refusing to let them through. Mary was a large formidable lady (ex Roedean) with a heart of gold. She immediately cut a swathe through the middle of the girls wielding her umbrella, and with Barbara in close attendance they thankfully reach their bus. The reason for the widespread disturbances turned out to be the arrest and deportation to exile in the Seychelles of Archbishop Makarios.

To help alleviate the boredom of being confined to camp, a number of entertainers came out from the UK with supporting concert parties, and we were introduced to people such as Chic Murray and Maidie, Stanley Baxter (before he was famous), Jimmy Wheeler, Lita Rosa, Gary Miller and lots of others. I don't know if it was because we were starved of entertainment, but we thought every show was marvellous.

There was one tragic incident near Famagusta when a bomb was thrown into the back of a lorry full of soldiers on their way to see a Jimmy Edwards show at the Golden Sands Camp. Several of them were killed or badly injured.

Jehovah's Witnesses were quite active in Cyprus at this time and Barbara and I started a course of study with them. We had been impressed with their demeanour and outlook and the way they always seemed to be enjoying life. After about a year we decided that our views were not compatible and said farewell to Brenda and Joan, a couple of really lovely people. Mr and Mrs Matthews were a Jehovah's Witness couple who used to visit Ralph and Mary. They weren't on a regular study basis but used to drop in on the Burrows, often out of the blue and at inconvenient times. One day the Burrows had just returned from a day at the beach when they saw the Matthews parking their motor cycle outside their quarters. The children were told to hurry up and hide upstairs while Ralph and Mary kept quiet in the hall. The Matthews knocked several times, then went round the house peering through the shutters. Fortunately they didn't hear the suppressed giggles. About a couple of weeks later the Matthews called again, and the door was opened to them by young James Burrows. He proceeded to tell them "It was so funny last time you came, we all hid and we couldn't stop laughing". Ralph and Mary wanted the ground to open up and swallow them.

Summers in Cyprus are usually long and hot, but 1956 was exceptionally so, and on two successive days in August temperatures of 118 degrees Fahrenheit were recorded at Ayios Nikolaos, the official name for the Four Mile Point area. Normally the highest temperatures are in the Nicosia area. On those two nights Barbara and I found sleeping virtually impossible. We had repeated cold showers, but before we had dried ourselves off we were perspiring again. In spite of it being against Emergency advice we had our bedroom shutters wide open and slept with nothing on (this was not Emergency advice!) Our overhead fan was going full blast, but it did little to keep us cool, so in desperation we borrowed the children's individual fans and directed them on ourselves. The children seemed little affected and slept right through both nights.

Also at this time another phase of married quarters was under construction at Ayios Nikolaos. One member of the Civilian Wing called Ron Stivey was a union representative on the local Whitley Council, a forum where Official and Staff Side met to discuss matters of mutual interest. The Colonel was the chairman and as a staff side rep Ron had repeatedly requested that workmen should not start work with pneumatic drills at half past three in the morning. This was a sore point with Ron, as his quarter was adjacent to the new development. The Colonel stated that there was absolutely nothing he could do about this matter. The very next morning the usual cacophony erupted at three thirty. Ron slipped on his shorts and sandals and walked to the phone box at the Guard Room and rang the Colonel's number. Eventually a sleepy voice asked what was so urgent at this time of the morning. In reply Ron said he didn't want anything, but he did wonder how the Colonel felt at being roused at this hour as he had just been. There was a tremendous row about this the next day, but a couple of days later the time for starting work on the site was amended to six in the morning.

As we didn't have a car we couldn't take advantage of a holiday in the cool of the Troodos mountains at the British Services leave centre, so we decided to have a few days at the Florida Beach Hotel at Famagusta ,which was within the secure wired-off area of the beach. We had a wonderful relaxing time with lots of snorkelling, and found it amazing to see the vast numbers of different fish there were to view. It was Barbara's first real introduction to snorkelling and she thought it was wonderful.

Stephen and Anne had several trips out in a boat with one of the local Greek Cypriot fishermen. We had to make sure she was well protected from the sun, but they both loved it and had a wonderful time. It seems incredible that even in that time of trouble we were perfectly happy to entrust our children to someone we had only known a few months.

Throughout the summer months the political situation in the Middle East gradually intensified. On the 13th June the last of the British troops left the Canal Zone, a large number of them deployed to Cyprus. On the 23rd June Colonel Nasser was elected President of Egypt. About a month later Britain joined the DSA and withdrew financial help for the Aswan High Dam project. On the 26th July Nasser nationalised the Suez Canal Company. In my opinion Nasser was not a communist or a would-be dictator but a sincere, perhaps misguided, patriot who thought he could finance the Aswan Dam with the revenues from the Suez Canal.

By the end of July we were on an increased state of readiness and as the situation intensified it seemed that anything could happen. At the beginning of October I started a local four-week training course, but as the month progressed it was obvious that things were becoming serious. After only two weeks our course was interrupted and we were told to report to our individual watches the next day. My watch was due to start at eight the next morning. My usual route to work was to walk a few yards along Edinburgh Road then cut through between two quarters past the church, then walk diagonally across the large Parade Square towards our Set Room. On this morning as I came out by the church I gazed upon a square packed with literally hundreds of tanks and armoured vehicles. I couldn't thread my way across - I had to walk around the perimeter, which was peppered with tents occupied by French troops. It was almost impossible to believe that we had heard nothing at all during the night from less than a hundred yards away.

When I came off duty at one we decided to go for a swim, but instead of going to our usual safe beach we decided to go to the Turkish Old City beach, not so salubrious but nearer, and considered very safe. As we approached the beach and looked across Famagusta Bay we saw an armada of warships and transports for almost as far as the eye could see. We didn't stay very long because as we swam we all became covered with black oil, obviously discharged from these ships. We had great difficulty in removing it so we could get dressed again.

From this time on the situation appeared to be deteriorating once again. We were warned to prepare for Egyptian planes bombing Cyprus and we had several soundings of practice air raid sirens. The crisis was reaching alarming proportions when a few days later the Israelis attacked Egypt, the air war commenced and soon after this British and French troops landed at Port Said. Russia then threatened to intervene on Egypt's behalf, and this brought an immediate warning from the USA for Russia to go in at their peril, as the US Sixth Fleet kept within striking distance. Britain and France then had to bow to international pressure from the bulk of the United Nations. A ceasefire was declared and the world breathed a sigh of relief. As a direct result of the Suez fiasco Anthony Eden, the British Prime Minister, resigned. Years later it was revealed (as we all already knew) that the whole sorry episode was a plot hatched by the British, French and Israeli governments, to our eternal discredit.

Christmas in the aftermath of Suez turned out to be a very enjoyable one. The small contingent from our Regiment, which included a couple of our baby sitters, had all returned safely. EOKA activity during the Suez period had been at a very low level. There were now in excess of 30,000 British Forces on the island, but Grivas still managed to elude every search.

Our next-door neighbour, Jim Fraser, had married a Cypriot girl and her family often visited at weekends. One evening while I was trying to have a sleep before going on a night watch I had a very vivid dream that Grivas was hiding next door. As I awoke thinking how audacious this would be, I was perspiring profusely and could hear Greek voices coming from next door. This did become a recurring dream, but I doubt if Grivas was ever in our vicinity.

It is not my intention to catalogue every EOKA incident during the troubles, but a couple of events I remember well. First there was the bomb which was discovered under Governor Harding's bed, placed there by his personal servant, who then vanished. The other was the terrible incident when a team from a Scottish infantry regiment played a football match against a village in the area they patrolled. After the final whistle the soldiers all gathered around the adjacent water tap queuing up for a drink when a bomb went off, killing and maiming several soldiers. The opposing village team, some of whom were obviously involved, had all retreated to a safe distance. Understandably, shortly afterwards the Security Forces rounded up the whole of the male population of the village and a lot of rough treatment was meted out, but the actual culprits were never discovered.

Throughout 1957 our routine rarely altered. Once a week Barbara would go on the special bus with other wives to shop in Famagusta. The rest of our requirements were purchased from the NAAFI store within the Regimental compound. There was the usual round of sporting activities (poor wives!) with an occasional dance or visiting entertainer to break the tedium. Because of the shortage of War Office volunteers, we now had a party of Admiralty volunteers, some of whom had come from Malta. Their arrival caused quite a stir, because on their overseas tours they were entitled to ward room (officer) status, whereas we only had Warrant Officer status. The problem was never satisfactorily resolved. They were not allowed to use the Officer's Mess but did manage to retain their officer status for medical and hospital treatment.

We had also been joined by a contingent of United

States Navy operators, most of whom were very experienced, but they all copied their intercept on typewriters while we still used pencils. They were a pleasant bunch who integrated well and some friendships were struck up which are still in existence.

As our tour drew to a close, we began to consider which way we would travel home, as regulations now allowed civil servants to arrange either their trip to or from their posting within a specified time; ten days was the travelling time allowed for Cyprus. We decided to opt for a trip home on a cargo-passenger ship. The actual passage was arranged by our Admin office and we expected to sail some time in February 1958, when our three years was completed.

February slipped away and our heavy baggage had already gone, as had most of the friends who were due back with us. As March passed and there was still no sign of a ship for us. We were beginning to regret not opting to travel home by air. Then three weeks into March we were told we had passages booked on the MV *Sycamore*, a cargo passenger vessel of the Furness Withy Line which was due to sail from Xeros in Morphou Bay in four days' time. We were "marched out" of our quarter the next morning and moved down to Famagusta for the last few days. I even managed to play in a vital hockey match on our last day and many of our friends came down that night for a farewell drink.

The next morning we actually had a staff car to take us to Xeros. It was quite a long journey to Morphou, and I must admit we had a few qualms about something happening en route, as we were travelling through some rather remote parts of the island. Though our driver was armed, his Sten gun was under his seat and not easily accessible, and it was not unknown for lone vehicles to be ambushed. After an uneventful journey we drew up to the jetty at Xeros just as the ship had completed loading her cargo of iron pyrites. We were welcomed aboard by the Purser, who informed us that we were the last of the passengers and showed us to our impressive adjoining cabins. Just before he left us he warned us to watch that Stephen and Anne did not lock themselves in their wardrobes. Only a few minutes later while we were unpacking, we heard cries coming from the next cabin. Yes, they had locked themselves in as quickly as that.

Within a couple of hours we were on our way and the journey home had begun.

CHAPTER 7

HOMEWARD BOUND

Our fellow passengers included Major Tommy Thompson and his wife Gladys, who had just completed their tour, and a Ewan Morrison and his wife and child, who had just completed a tour as an Admin Officer or something similar at Episkopi. There were also two unaccompanied ladies, Marshe Truman and Marjorie Borlase, who always dined with the Chief Engineer, an archetypal Scot called Macfadyen. At breakfast and lunch we sat at separate tables. The children had their meal at about was four thirty, while we had our evening meal at seven at a table which was enlarged to include most of the passengers plus Captain Kemp.

Our first evening meal was excellent, and in a relatively calm sea we settled down to a good night's sleep. We awoke to a beautiful day, but a rather stiff breeze made the sea rather choppy. After breakfast we went on the upper deck, where the children were enjoying skipping, deck tennis and quoits while Barbara and I took turns relaxing and reading in our deckchairs or playing with the children, thinking this was the life for us.

Suddenly the throb of the ship's engines ceased and within a very short time the *Sycamore* lost way and began to turn broadside into the wind until she came to a full stop. As she slowed her cargo of iron pyrites shifted in the hold and our deck began to slew from side to side. Barbara hung on to the rail at her side, holding Anne. I ran to the centre of the deck to get Stephen, but as I picked him up the deck tilted sideways at an angle of about forty degrees and I was unable to prevent myself careering towards the opposite rail. I managed to turn at the last moment so that my back and not Stephen bore the brunt of crashing into the rail. Moments later as the deck tilted the other way and we went hurtling back towards Barbara and Anne at the opposite rail.

Fortunately at this moment the Chief Officer and the Bosun came striding across the angled deck with amazing alacrity, intercepting us and escorting us all down to our cabins. We were informed that it had been necessary to stop the engines to prevent a major breakdown and it could be several hours before the fault could be rectified. The Purser requested that we all remain in our bunks with our lifejackets under the edge of our mattresses.

After a few minutes of this violent and unpleasant motion Barbara and I had to make several trips to our washbowls to be sick, but the children were remarkably unaffected and were crayoning and drawing in their bunks. As we lay there, both feeling nauseous and with me nursing cracked ribs (so I thought), we both simultaneously voiced the same thought - what would our friends Len and Jean Tovey think if they could see us now? At this we both burst into uncontrollable laughter and I laughed until my ribs ached even more.

In spite of the terrible motion our sickness subsided. Six hours later our engines throbbed into welcome life and the horrible yawing was transformed into a normal roll. As we sat down to a belated evening meal we discovered that all the adult passengers and several of the crew had been sick and more than half the ship's crockery had been smashed as there had been no time to secure it.

A few days later we docked in Algiers and the agents turned up at the quayside with a fresh supply of crockery. We had an interesting day sight-seeing and sailed in the early evening. Less than a month later all hell broke loose in Algiers as the struggle for independence from France began.

A few days later, after we had left Gibraltar and were sailing along the coast of Spain and part of Portugal, the Captain suggested that Barbara and I had a drink with him in his cabin before dinner that evening. He was anticipating bad weather in the Bay of Biscay and as he had already similarly entertained the other passengers he thought if he didn't do it then Barbara might not be feeling up to it later. We had a very entertaining hour that evening, as the Captain was a great raconteur and a very pleasant man to boot.

Two days later, instead of sailing across the Bay, we were heading out into the Atlantic, because the Captain said to have sailed directly across would have made our wallowing without an engine seem like a picnic. We all found this hard to believe, but after all he was the Captain. Throughout the daylight hours most of the upright passengers congregated in the lounge and watched mountainous seas break over our bows. The children remained unaffected and even seemed to be enjoying themselves. Barbara had also acquired her sea legs and didn't turn a hair. Twenty four hours later the weather moderated and we were able to resume a normal course.

A few days later we were sailing through a very foggy English Channel heading for Rotterdam. The Sycamore was scheduled to call at another couple of Continental ports after Rotterdam, so we were asked if we would like to return to the UK by the Hook of Holland to Harwich ferry. This suited us, as we were anxious to be home as soon as possible. When we tied up in Rotterdam there were visits from the Customs, River Police and the ship's agents with our ferry tickets. A couple of hours later we were in a large Dutch taxi which easily accommodated our vast amount of luggage and on our way to the overnight ferry. It was a good overnight crossing and we cleared Customs despite declaring everything but the kitchen sink.

Immigration surprised us by asking us to wait while they phoned someone. A few minutes later an Intelligence Corps Captain strode up and said in an officious voice, "Where the hell have you been? We've been expecting you for days now". I was annoyed and said "I didn't know you cared" or some such flippant remark, and then explained what had happened to us. We were then provided with a rail warrant from Harwich to Cleethorpes via London, and half an hour later we were relaxing on the train and ordering a meal in the dining car.

It was early evening when we arrived at Grimsby Town station and boarded a taxi to Cleethorpes. When we arrived at Barbara's parents there were hugs and kisses all round. Norman was out at a darts match, Ethel looked well and Pamela and John had grown tremendously in the past three years. However Ethel's next request really floored us. Would we mind hanging on for a while, as they were half way through watching a very interesting play on the television? Barbara and I exchanged meaningful glances. It really put things in perspective for us, though in retrospect it was probably just thoughtlessness.

The next few days were spent visiting my parents and family as well as close friends and family on Barbara's side. As we had not been offered any council accommodation in Woodhouse Eaves, it was essential that we found a place to live in the Loughborough area as soon as we could, so after a week at Cleethorpes we set off on our quest, leaving Stephen and Anne at Cleethorpes. We booked into a small hotel-type boarding house on the Leicester Road leading out of Loughborough and systematically visited all the local estate agents for suitable houses. After three days we had seen quite a lot of houses but had found nothing suitable.

On the third day we decided to call back to the first estate agent we had visited, just in case anything new had come on to the market - and there was just one. There were no brochure details available yet, but they did have a key and we could go and have a look if we wanted to. The house was number 221 Beacon Road, a three bed-roomed semi priced at £2000. From the outside it didn't seem very attractive because it hadn't been painted for years, but inside it was very different. The front door opened up into a parquet-floored hall with an oak staircase to two good-sized bedrooms and a third of reasonable dimensions. There was a good sized bathroom next door to a separate toilet. Downstairs there was a decent-sized kitchen and a good-sized living room which opened into the garden via French windows. The inside decor was all excellent, with expensive wallpapers all in good condition.

Though we had never bought a house before, we both rapidly reached the same conclusion - that this was the house for us. It was the estate agent's early closing day, so we couldn't get back to them, but we went straight to the bank and obtained a cheque for £50. The next morning I was waiting outside the estate agent's office before he opened at nine o'clock. They accepted our deposit pending our mortgage application to the Woolwich Building Society being approved. As we were putting down £500 and I was in a secure job, it was going to be a formality. We had a good solicitor, and within four weeks we had completed and were in occupation.

We had already measured up for curtains and carpets, which were going to be supplied by Petchell's of Grimsby, a wholesaler with whom Barbara's father dealt through his shop. They even sent their carpet fitter and his wife over to fit the carpets. Our furniture arrived the following day, and when Norman and Ethel brought Stephen and Anne from Cleethorpes on the Sunday they sat down to dinner with us and marvelled at what we had accomplished in such a short time and how "jammy" we had been at finding such a house.

Someone recommended a decorator, who agreed to burn off and paint the exterior of the house for the sum of £25. This utterly transformed the outside appearance. Heaven knows how he could do the work for that price, even in 1958.

Before we could really get settled in, Stephen and Anne both went down with a severe attack of measles and they were both very ill. Anne was delirious, imagining insects were climbing all over her.

On the work front, at Beaumanor it was business as usual, but I was scheduled for my long-awaited upgrading course at Bletchley Park along with quite a few colleagues who had recently returned from overseas. I travelled to Bletchley with George Fell in his Morris Minor, along with Len Tovey, Jim Southwell and Bryan Taylor. Ralph Cook and Peter Jones were also on this course. We then began six weeks of very intensive study of radio theory and the practical aspects of our specialised work.

When we were half way through our course it was announced that after a major revaluation exercise our grade had been awarded a top rate of over £1000 per annum - a considerable amount in those days. There was a mixture of service departments including War Office, Admiralty, Air Ministry and Foreign Office, about 28 of us in all on this upgrading course. Our two written exams were on the Thursday of our final week. The atmosphere was rather tense as we all realised that there was now even more money at stake in attaining our final two increments.

On the Friday morning we were all assembled in the main hall waiting to hear our results at ten o'clock. after a few minutes we were told to return in another hour as our exam papers were being reviewed to try to squeeze some of us a few extra marks (this was a ludicrous excuse). I have a very clear recall of what happened next. When we reassembled the Officer In Command Bletchley Park, a Captain Kelsall, addressed us and stated that when he called out our names we should shout "yes" and hold our hands up. He then began calling out our names, and as we responded he would announce our marks if we had passed, but not if we had failed. He commenced with quite a few failures on both exam papers, and when he announced Ralph Cook and said "Failed on both", Ralph said clearly and distinctly "Oh my God". When he called out Jim Southwell's results he said "You've passed on both, but only just scraped through". Jim yelled out "I don't care". I think it was just the tension.

When he called out my name I was determined that I wasn't going to put my hand up, as I was there standing right next to him. I just said "yes", but even though he could see and hear me he repeated my name until I yielded and put my hand up. He then said that I had passed with two well-balanced papers, and I heaved a sigh of relief.

Len, George and Brian, as well as Ralph and Pete Jones, all had to return the following Monday to begin another course of intensive study for three weeks, after which they did all get through. When I reported to Beaumanor on the Monday morning, I was asked if I would like to join the TA section on day work. I jumped at the opportunity and joined the printer section, which dealt with radio printer intercept. I soon adapted and found it very interesting work. Our next door neighbours were a Mr and Mrs Redmayne, a very friendly middle-aged couple. He was the secretary of the Loughborough Building Society and they became our lifelong friends, they were wonderful people. They had been in their house since it was built some twenty years previously. They told us that our house had had several tenants during the war including Dan Maskell, the tennis coach and radio commentator.

A few weeks after I started my day duties we all had a dreadful shock with the death of Ralph Cook at the age of 33. He had not long since returned from his upgrading course, which he had eventually passed, and was due to go on a morning shift. Someone called at his house to give him a lift to work, but he indicated from his bedroom window that he would make his own way to work. Then, according to Wink, he just collapsed and died from a massive heart attack. He had never been quite his old self since his course. Wink of course was devastated.

Barbara was now expecting another baby and life was very good. Stephen and Anne were happy at their school and we had regular visits from both sides of our family. The back pay from our arbitration award was well in excess of £200, so we had our kitchen refurbished and bought a Hall's cedarwood conservatory to erect over our side entrance. We hired a builder to erect it and he told us he could have made us a better quality one and erected it for the same price. We had been promising the children a dog for some time and we drove to Gamston Kennels in Nottingham with Barbara's parents and selected a lovely little Corgi bitch we named Cindy. She adapted to us straight away and became a great house dog. After we had acquired Cindy, Norman and Ethel called back in at Gamston on their way home and picked up Mitzi, a Cairn Terrier puppy they had noticed there. A few months later they called once again and picked up Trixie, another Cairn, this time for Bill and Jean.

I took up hockey again and started playing for Loughborough Town second team on Saturdays. Cyprus had been making the headlines again with various incidents, including the murder of Catherine Cutliffe, the wife of a British soldier, in Famagusta in broad daylight. Not surprisingly the volunteer list had virtually dried up, and there were rumours of compulsory tours in the near future.

On July 1st 1959 I was at my desk when the Head of TA, Eddie Bowman, came in and told me Mrs Redmayne had just rung to say we had another daughter and all was well and that she would meet the children and take them to her house for tea. I cleared my desk and a few minutes later was pedalling furiously the five miles back to home. Beverly was a beautiful baby and weighed eight pounds. Apparently while Barbara was upstairs with the midwife Cindy had howled and was quite worried. When Barbara did eventually come downstairs Cindy just lay at her feet the whole time and refused to leave her. When Beverly was outside in the garden in her pram Cindy lay beneath it, and woe betide any stranger who came near.

We often made day excursions by bus or train to Nottingham, Derby or Leicester for shopping and a day out and thanks to what was still a reliable public transport system we didn't miss having a car. Beverly was a super baby. She hardly ever cried and was always so happy.

In a pre-season friendly hockey match I found myself playing centre forward for the second team and I was up against Ron Colomb, the first team centre half, who was a regular county player and had played in trials for the England team. The seconds won by two goals to nil, and I scored both the goals. The first team were rather disgruntled and Ron described me as a "mad bull".

The first game of the season was a needle match between old rivals Loughborough and Leicester Hockey Club, and because they were short I had been selected to play outside right for the first team. I had a nightmare first half against the county fullback, who completely shut me out of the game. I was then moved to centre forward and scored almost immediately. a few minutes later I added a second and we beat the old rivals 2-0.

After this I became the regular first team centre forward. We had a great season playing some of the best teams in the area, and were beaten only twice, I was very pleased with myself, as I was our leading scorer with 38 goals. It was good to play in such a team with players of the calibre of Ron Allen, Ron Colomb and Mike Fentum, who laid lots of my goals on a plate for me. The Scriptures say an end to all good things must come, and it came in the shape of a letter waiting for me one Monday morning . It was a preliminary warning for a compulsory tour of Cyprus in April 1960. As an established civil servant there was no way out. Quite a few of my colleagues had also been warned, including members of the "Gallant 78", who had never stirred from Beaumanor since they arrived from Chatham during the war.

Barbara and I were most unhappy at the thought of a move. The children liked their school, the house was all we could wish for and we were managing well on my salary, though we didn't have a car. But chiefly it was the current uncertainty of the Cyprus situation that made us so reluctant to return. We remembered what a relief it had been when we returned after our last tour no longer having to keep looking over our shoulders, and we didn't relish returning to a similar situation. However we had to be realistic about the situation and pondered about what we should do about the house. Should we try to rent it, or should we sell it? When we asked the Woolwich, they said they wouldn't allow us to rent it out, and according to our solicitor they were quite within their rights to do this. At the same time he advised us to make sure we didn't use the Woolwich again.

We placed the house on the market at a modest £2250 to recoup the money we had spent on the conservatory and the kitchen. there was not a lot of interest shown, probably because mortgages were becoming very difficult to obtain, and we seriously considered leaving it empty. Then in the last few weeks a young couple came along, the husband worked in the bank(no mortgage problems), they fell in love with the house and the sale was provisionally agreed almost straight away.

Fortunately during those last few months the Cyprus situation had improved dramatically and the date for independence had been agreed. This made the prospects of another tour much more inviting, but it was still a compulsory tour and we had no real desire to leave England at this time. The same options were open to us; we could make our own travel arrangements either to or from Cyprus, so we decided to let the War Office transport us once again, leaving us free to decide how we would travel home. We also decided it was time we joined the motoring fraternity and so with the help of a three-month advance of salary we ordered a de luxe export model of the Morris Oxford, to be delivered to us in Cyprus soon after we arrived. The price was £610, duty free of course. I must confess we or rather I, was tempted to go for a luxurious Jaguar saloon priced at less than £1000, but fortunately prudence prevailed.

So on a Saturday in mid April, along with quite a few friends and families, we boarded the troopship *Dilwara* at Southampton. It was a repeat of our embarkation on the *Empire Windrush* ten years previously, with Regimental bands playing and streamers flying as we cast off. The difference was that I was now a married man with a wife and three children commencing a trip we had no desire to make.

Our five-berth cabin was quite pleasant and situated amidships. Next door to us were Dave and Doreen

Mitchell with their baby Linda, who was the same age as Beverly. The sea was quite calm for the first few days of our voyage and Beverly was her usual happy self, as were Stephen and Anne, until they discovered that they were expected to attend school on board ship. This was because there were a lot of Service family children aboard, many of whom were travelling to the Far East and would be shipboard for five or six weeks. The teaching was carried out by Army Education personnel, some of whom were en route to postings, but I think one or two were permanent staff.

Our first port of call was Gibraltar, where we stayed for a day and went on a sight-seeing tour around the Rock in glorious sunshine. We saw the Barbary Apes and the children thought it was great missing school and being able to run around again. A few days later we sailed into the Grand Harbour in Valetta, Malta, but we only stayed a few hours before setting sail for Cyprus.

On the morning of the 30th April we dropped anchor in Famagusta Bay, and once again we came ashore in small tenders. There were several friends waiting to greet us, some of whom had been on the lookout for prospective accommodation for us. In the meantime we were booked in once again at the King George hotel on Famagusta beach.

After lunch we placed Beverly in her push chair and went to view some prospective bungalows. It was an excessively hot day even for Cyprus, and the temperature reached a record 100 degrees Fahrenheit.

Beverly was fine, because she had a sun shade over her pram, but Anne caught the sun even though she had a sun hat and long sleeves. Stephen took it in his stride and was already well tanned from the voyage.

After viewing several places there was one we particularly liked, a new semi-detached bungalow in a place called Scra Street. It was only about fifty yards from the beach and less than a mile from the Golden Sands holiday camp. It only had two bedrooms, but the landlord promised that if we took it he would build us an additional bedroom within a few weeks. We said we would think about it and went back to the hotel to consider our options. There were married quarters still available, but with the situation now normalized we preferred to live in Famagusta.

That afternoon had seen the Gala opening of a new civilian club called The Anchorage, on the beach quite close to our hotel, so went to have a look at it and were quite impressed. It had been the brainchild of quite a few Civilian Wing members and what had been a run down beach bar had been transformed into a popular and thriving club.

That evening at the hotel quite a few friends came over to see us, including our old Cypriot friend Tassos Paralimnitis, our grocer. He told us an incredible tale of how he had been arrested, very roughly treated and detained for several days by the Security Forces soon after Mrs Cutliffe was murdered not very far from his shop in Hermes Street. The next day we went to have another look at the bungalow and agreed with the landlord that we would take it, subject to a satisfactory valuation by the Hirings Officer, to be followed by a further valuation when the third bedroom was completed. A few days later we moved in and the valuation was set at £28 per month furnished.

Very soon after this I was notified that our car had arrived and accompanied by Len Tovey, who lived close by us right on the beach, I went to collect it at the docks. I had just failed my driving test a few days before we left UK so I had to display "L" plates. Not long after this, having had a few hours of intensive clutch control lessons from Les Dowsett on busy, narrow Famagusta streets for two consecutive Saturdays, I had no problems passing my Cyprus driving test.

Work had already started on the extra bedroom, which was a little inconvenient at times but well worth it. When the work was completed and the landlord had provided another bed and furniture, I went to see the Hirings Officer to arrange for a reassessment of the rent. I walked into his office and was peremptorily told to stand and wait. There I stood with the appropriate form in one hand with my other hand in my pocket (a habit Barbara deplores!) The Hirings Officer (a recently retired Colonel) then said to me "Take your hand out of your pocket, it's slovenly and extremely disrespectful!" Of course my hand remained rooted firmly in my pocket and at this stage, his face purple with rage, he screamed at me, "Take your hand out of your pocket!" I still refused to oblige and at this point his assistant intervened and said that I was a civilian. He then said "I don't give a damn, I expect my orders to be obeyed".

About a week later he came to assess the additional room (I was at work) and increased the rent by a miserable £2 per month. I protested to Roy Ward, our Staff Side secretary, whom I had already informed about the hand-in-pocket incident, and Roy promised swift action. Within a couple of weeks the assessment was increased by £5 per month and I received a written apology from the Hirings Officer.

Anne and Bill Cooper came to live next door to us and we couldn't have asked for better neighbours. The Anchorage Club was a great asset and we used it frequently especially during the evenings. Anne attended a dancing class there, and both Stephen and Anne had joined the Saddle Club at Four Mile and were learning to ride. Barbara started taking driving lessons with a local Cypriot driving school. On her second lesson she started off in front of Bill Cooper and myself watching from our respective verandahs. This of course put her under pressure, and she set off with "Kangaroo Petrol" in her tank - Bill and I howled with laughter as she bounced out of view. Despite this she very soon passed her test and became an excellent driver, but with a tendency to speed, especially on the Larnaca straight on the road to Dhekelia.

We soon settled down and really began to enjoy our

life in Cyprus once again. Having the car meant we could now travel around the island and visit places on our days off, which were every fourth day. On what we called our sleeping day off I usually arose after about four hours' sleep, and Barbara would have already prepared a picnic. We also had a home-made tent which Barbara had improvised out of old bed sheets so that Beverly could sleep protected from the sun.

Our favourite destination was Salamis, which was about five miles away on the road to Boghaz. It was a beautiful stretch of beach only a few hundred yards from the ruins of the ancient city of Salamis, the same place where St Paul had preached on his first missionary journey. More often than not we were the sole occupants of the beach. Stephen used to bring his fishing gear and fish for red mullet, which were there in profusion. Sometimes we brought our "kebab machine" (barbecue) with us and we would wrap the fish in tinfoil and grill them freshly caught - they were delicious.

Another favourite haunt was Fig Tree Bay, which in those days was a beautiful secluded beach with one small café, a far cry from today's conglomeration of hotels and restaurants. Anne was an excellent swimmer and Stephen could swim like a fish, and we used to spend hours snorkelling and observing all the different types of fish and other sea life. It was all too easy to forget time as we swam and floated around, and Barbara often admonished us for staying out so long.

At the end of August we went up to the Troodos

mountain resort of Prodrhomos to spend a few days at a very good hotel. It was wonderful to be up in the cool forest air away from the heat of the plains, and our time passed all too quickly. We resolved to have a much longer stay the next time. When we had been in Cyprus six months we decided to bring Cindy out, as the children were really missing her. We made the necessary arrangements and a couple of weeks later we left Anne Cooper babysitting while we travelled to Nicosia Airport. Cindy had travelled in a sealed dog container, and we had to wait for a Cyprus Government vet to come along and check her out after unsealing. We were amazed when Cindy waddled out - she had put on an enormous amount of weight, but she was overjoyed to see us. It was after midnight when we arrived back in Famagusta and the children were all asleep, but Cindy seemed to know just where they were. She jumped on each bed in turn and licked them all into wakefulness, and they all went wild with each other. Half an hour later they were all fast asleep, including Cindy in her bed outside their bedrooms.

Cindy and Beverly became inseparable, and wherever Beverly went in the house or garden Cindy was always following close behind.

In February 1961 Barbara's mother came out for a six-week holiday, and from the moment of her arrival she thoroughly enjoyed herself. In those six weeks we travelled over three thousand miles and visited several places on the island which we hadn't visited before.

Ethel was very impressed with everything, but in particular Bellapaix and St Hilarion. When we escorted her to the departure lounge at Nicosia airport, she impressed on us what a wonderful holiday it had been. A couple of hours previously we had watched amazed as she had tucked into a lavish farewell meze at Charlie's Bar and still found room for the special dessert they insisted on giving her "on the house".

My interest in *Exodus* was rekindled when Otto Preminger turned up in Famagusta with a host of stars to shoot footage for this epic film. The stars included Paul Newman, Peter Lawford, Eva Marie Saint, Sal Mineo, Olivia Hussey and a host of other well known names, who frequented the local hotels and beaches for several weeks. Preminger's idea was that shooting the film at the actual locations specified in the book would add realism to the film. Lots of scenes were shot at Karalaos Camp area, Kyrenia and also on the beach at Famagusta. Les Dowsett produced some great camera shots of various stars on location.

Roy Porter, a friend of ours, asked if we could do him a big favour and go with him to Nicosia to buy a new car. It was a Mercedes 190, and I remember he paid for it in cash and it was £1038. I had the pleasure of driving it back to Famagusta, as Roy had only just started having driving lessons, Barbara following on behind in our car. For the next few weeks I drove the car quite a lot until Roy passed his test, and it truly was a pleasure to drive.

One day Beverly had a horrific accident on a swing in Len and Jean's garden. The swing hit her in the mouth and she was obviously in great pain. Fortunately the Medical Officer was just paying a visit next door to us and he examined her straight away. There were no teeth visible and the doctor thought she might have swallowed them, but he didn't think it would harm her. He didn't think her jaw was broken, but we should contact him if we were worried. Later that evening her mouth began to bleed and her chin swelled up so much that it looked as if she had a tyre under it. We rang the doctor and were told we must take her to BMH Dekhelia straight away. We arrived just after midnight. After she had been examined we had to leave her alone and in pain among people she didn't know - looking back it seems almost barbaric. We visited her every day for the next five days but we could only watch her from a distance as their policy was no parental contact with young children in hospital. It really was heartbreaking.

When we brought her home she looked terrible, with a huge black and blue swelling hanging down under her chin, but all her teeth were now visible and appeared undamaged. I remember Gerald and Linda Cooper staring at her and Linda asking her mother whether Beverly would ever look pretty again.

We managed to find accommodation in Famagusta for our friends the Braithwaites, the Quirks and the Lowes, who were all due to arrive very shortly. At the end of that summer I developed hay fever, which became so bad I was prescribed large doses of Piriton and bed rest for several days. (Forty years later it is still an intermittent problem for me). George Quirk had an obsession with horses and was intent on obtaining one to be ridden by himself and his daughters Jacqui and Carol. Sheila, his wife, was not so keen, but didn't put obstacles in his way. On our days off we would often be scouring the island for a suitable horse. One day out on the Pan Handle (Rizo Carpasso area) we found what he was looking for in the shape of a fine-looking gelding whom he christened Prince Hal.

I must admit that George's enthusiasm was infectious, and I too was almost bitten. Both Barbara and I began to spend a lot of time at the Four Mile Regimental Saddle Club. Anne had really taken to riding, and though she was very small she was by now a very competent rider and was often allocated the biggest horses because of her ability. Stephen, however, had decided that riding was not for him, after being unhorsed a few times in the course of his first few lessons.

George asked me if I would go with him to the Turkish farrier in the Old City to get Hal some new shoes. I had a troublesome boil on the back of my thigh and was holding Hal while he was being shod. He was very lively and backed me into a nearby open cesspit manhole (there were quite a few of . these in the Turkish quarter). My leg went down into the pit and the boil was scraped along the edge and burst - it was agonising.

George helped me out and was concerned because he thought I had broken my leg. Once the pain had subsided I was more worried about any infection I might have picked up. Fortunately there wasn't any and it soon healed.

One night after completing an evening shift I drove into Famagusta on my way home and turned into the street by the water tower at Stavros. Coming towards me in the distance I saw a single bright light in front of me and I watched it waver and then vanish. I switched my headlights to main beam and as I approached I saw a motor cycle and a body in the middle of the road. I pulled to the side of the road and saw a man unconscious and bleeding. There was a Cypriot taxi office on the next block and I shouted loudly for someone to call an ambulance and to come and give assistance. A couple of Cypriots came over, bringing a blanket to cover him, and told me they had called for an ambulance and the police. The motor cyclist smelt strongly of brandy and as he came round he seemed to be very drunk. The Cypriot police arrived at the same time as the ambulance and I told them briefly what I had seen. They said they would come round and see me for a full statement the next day.

When they came to our house they said it was necessary for me to go to the main police station to make a statement, and naively I agreed. Barbara was suspicious and said something was wrong, but I poured scorn on the idea. When I arrived at the main police station I was shown into a room with the two constables who had brought me and an inspector, and I then dictated my statement which the inspector then read back to me. He then said are you sure that this is the truth and I said something like don't be ridiculous of course it is . The inspector then said "I'm afraid we already know you James Ryan, you have been in trouble with the police before and what is more it was you who caused the accident. We have already had a statement from the victim in hospital".

I was flabbergasted, but asked to make a phone call to Matt Dillon, who was our Senior Admin Officer at Four Mile Point. He advised me to say nothing more until the Sovereign Base Area solicitor arrived, but that he would let Barbara know that I was being delayed. Half an hour later the solicitor arrived. He was a Cypriot, but he immediately assessed the situation and suggested that two things were going on. Firstly the new Republic of Cyprus police force was flexing its muscles against their old Colonial masters, and secondly the Cypriot motorcyclist was trying it on in an attempt to get compensation and damages from me. He then said a few sharp words in Greek to the policemen and shortly afterwards they took me home. He turned out to be absolutely right, and I received an apology from the police. A few months later I had to appear in court to give evidence against the motor cyclist, who was fined £250 or given the option of prison for three months. I suppose the moral of the story is that you should be careful next time you attempt to play a good Samaritan.

We had started to make tentative plans for our trip home and decided we would travel from Cyprus to Marseilles by ship and then have a leisurely overland drive through France with lots of stopovers. We were friendly with Savvas Savvides, who was the local agent for the Israeli Zim Lines, which had a regular passenger service between Israel, Cyprus, Italy and France. Savvas drove us to Limassol one afternoon when the Zim Line flagship the *Jerusalem* was in port, and we had a conducted tour. We were impressed and decided to book on the ship.

The powers that be decreed that any Radio Officer who had not passed their upgrading must attend the final upgrade exam at Bletchley Park and that there would be no exceptions, irrespective of where you happened to be serving at the time. In Cyprus we had a few colleagues who came into this category and among them was our old friend Jim Murray, whose skills had long been exploited by the War Office while they still continued to pay him at two increments below the maximum salary. Another one was Lobby Dunne, a likeable rogue with Romany blood in him. A few weeks later we were all shocked to hear that he had been killed driving a hired car from Bletchley to Preston one weekend. Ironically Jim did pass his upgrading exam and later transferred to the Linguist Grade and served most of the rest of his career in Cyprus, becoming a very senior grade linguist.

Another happening in this eventful year was that the Dowsett twins were promoted and returned to Beaumanor. Gerald did appear before the promotion board but Les was promoted in "absentia" without a board, most likely as a reward for spending six months on detached duty in Kuwait. The twins still argue about which one was responsible for the other's promotion (they were both worthy candidates).

Our friend Bernard Braithwaite was also further promoted, which meant the family had to return to England after less than a year in Cyprus. Edith was not very pleased.

In the summer of 1962 we had a great holiday at the Naafi holiday camp at Troodos. It was wonderful to be in the cool mountain air. The regimental band of the Black Watch was in residence and we had band concerts every day and marvellous music for dancing every evening. There were plenty of activities for the children, and Anne brought her riding gear and rode every day. While Anne galloped ahead on Tarzan, her hired horse, Stephen was usually to be found trotting some distance behind on Mary, his hired donkey. Now when we think of Anne galloping along those narrow mountain tracks, often at breakneck speed, we realise we were not being responsible parents and her guardian angel must have been in close attendance.

The Gary Powers U2 incident in May 1960 placed us on a very high state of alert at work, but the situation gradually cooled down. When Bill and Anne Cooper returned to England, George and Barbara Lowes, with their children Elizabeth and Robert, took over their bungalow, so we had more super neighbours. We often played beach sports together and George and I often played tennis and hockey. One day George and I were invited to play for the Cyprus Combined Services team against a touring Services team. George was a great player and had played County hockey for Leicestershire. He played at centre half and I had expected to play centre forward but was asked to play left half. The Regimental Parade Ground at Four Mile was black asphalt and the ball always came through hard and true. I didn't put a foot wrong and was amazed how well I was playing in this unaccustomed position.

With only a few minutes left and the score at two each I was going flat out with the ball and came an awful cropper. I put my right hand out to save myself and the parade ground made an awful mess of it and I couldn't finish the game.

Barbara was watching the match and drove me to the Medical Centre for some first aid. She had to do all the driving for the next few weeks until my hand had healed sufficiently to allow me to drive again.

Our next period of tension was the Cuban Missile crisis, a very nervous time for us, as indeed it must have been for anyone who was aware of how dire the situation had become. We immediately went on to a three-watch system which meant compulsory overtime working round the clock. As a result of a lot of praying was done throughout the world. Thanks to President Kennedy's tough stance Khrushchev backed down, but it was a hair-raising time.

Shortly after this we had had another shock. I had just got up to go to the toilet at about half past three in the morning when there was a tremendous outbreak of howling, which seemed to be coming from every dog for miles around. This went on for at least a minute, then there was an eerie silence for about another minute, followed by what felt like an express train approaching a level crossing. As Barbara joined me the ground began to shake and objects on shelves began to fall down. I'm afraid that the thought uppermost in my mind was that some fool had pushed the nuclear button and this was it. As it happens it was merely an earthquake, which measured 5.8 on the Richter scale. Lots of people came out on to the streets, especially the locals, who were expecting more aftershocks but they didn't materialise. There was quite a lot of structural damage, including a huge crack in the recently-completed British Military Hospital, but there were only two casualties on the island. One was a schoolmaster in Paphos who jumped out of a second floor window and the other was our very own J T C Purdie, who was working a night shift at Four Mile. When the tremor started he told everyone around to stay calm, but as the tremors gathered strength he changed his message to "Get outside quickly and run for your life". He dashed outside and jumped off a very high balcony, breaking his leg in several places. In typical Purdie fashion he then developed thrombosis and had an extended stay in BMH.

The last part of our tour seemed to be rapidly slipping away and we were busy deciding just where our stopovers in France would be. Since my parade ground fall my hand had healed well, but every so often while I was driving I had a sharp stabbing pain in it as I manipulated the steering wheel. After an investigation at BMH they decided that it was scar tissue which had formed on a nerve ending. A small minor op soon snipped the offending tissue away and I had no more problems afterwards.

According to the news Europe was now in the grip of an exceptionally bitter winter, brought home to us as we heard week after week of the number of football fixtures cancelled through frost and snow. We continued to enjoy our normal quota of winter sunshine, except for an unusual happening. February 1st 1963 was the day when the Civilian Wing were playing a challenge match against our regimental football team, which had beaten every Service team on the island. Our team included Jim Peddie (one of our hierarchy, who had organised the game), Joe Moffitt and Peter Woolley (playing wing half instead of goal). We also included in our team an outstanding young footballer called Elgin Smith, who had recently joined us from Beaumanor. Just as we were about to kick off the skies darkened and two minutes later we were in the thick of a blizzard which lasted for about ten minutes, and it was another half hour before the snow had melted enough for the game to commence. We then proceeded to run rings round our illustrious young opponents to the tune of four goals to one. It was a major upset, and as yours truly scored two goals it was indeed a game to remember.

In March we discovered that Barbara was pregnant again and we were both very pleased, as a couple of times previously on this tour Barbara had been disappointed when she thought she was, then found she wasn't. We had been seriously considering adopting two more children when we returned to the UK as we wanted more children.

CHAPTER 8

A SLOW BOAT TO ENGLAND

During April we were busy with packing cases for our heavy baggage and manipulating suitcases to see which ones would fit best into the cavernous boot of our Morris Oxford. We had also purchased a large sheet of tarpaulin to cover the cases due to travel on the roof rack. Barbara has a flair for packing (praise the Lord!) and the packing cases were nailed down and as many suitcases that could be packed in advance were packed and lined up in our bedrooms. Then we had further trauma, as Barbara thought she was losing the baby and the MO ordered immediate bed rest for several days. He also decreed that we couldn't travel home by sea unless the ship carried a doctor. I checked and was assured that the *Jerusalem* carried a doctor and medical staff, so we felt more relaxed about the situation.

It was very difficult for Barbara to rest in those last couple of weeks with a thousand and one things to do. When our departure date arrived every space in the car had been utilised and the cases we would need on the voyage carried on the roof rack ready for easy access. We had an uneventful drive from Famagusta to Limassol and boarded the *Jerusalem* with the minimum of fuss, and our family cabin was quite up to expectations. A few minutes later we watched with some trepidation as our car was hoisted aboard. Our fears were not without foundation, as a few minutes later another car in the process of being loaded was dropped into the harbour, an absolute disaster for the owner, who was just about to start a voyage.

It amazed us that the ship carried quite a number of steerage passengers travelling without sleeping accommodation. By far the largest proportion of the passengers were Jews from Israel on a Mediterranean cruise. Our first stop was to be Naples and the night before we were told that there would be plenty of buses at the quayside to take us sight seeing. As we docked and the gangway was lowered there was an unholy mad surge and the young and frail were thrust aside as they dashed for the buses. I have never seen Barbara so angry, and she lashed out at some of the culprits.

En route to Herculaneum and Pompeii we passed through some of the worst slums in Naples. The sights in Pompeii brought home to us how sudden and devastating it must have been for the inhabitants in AD 79 when Vesuvius erupted and people and animals in those two towns were literally turned to stone by a wall of lava and suffocating dust. It was as if time had stood still for almost two thousand years.

When we returned to the ship the children had their tea and the ship sailed almost straight away. We were heading for Marseilles across the Bay of Lyons. The sea was beginning to get rather choppy and Barbara was beginning to feel queasy and said she wouldn't bother going to dinner, so I said I would bring her a plain biscuit and a drink of lemonade before I went to dinner. As I was changing the ship began to pitch violently and I began to feel sick myself, so Barbara didn't get her biscuit and lemonade. I pushed lifejackets under the sides of the children's bunks to wedge them in and then did the same with ours, between staggering away to be sick a couple of times. A quick glimpse through our porthole revealed mountainous seas washing over the decks and also over our car, which was clearly visible, along with several others. The children slept like tops, completely unperturbed, while we had a terrible night, especially Barbara, being pregnant as well.

The next morning the sea had calmed considerably and our car was still visible on deck. The children were clamouring for their breakfasts, so I had to accompany them down to the dining room and watch them eat. I can still remember the runny eggs on Anne's plate. I must admit that after a cup of tea and some toast I began to feel a little better. Instead of the usual crowded dining room there were probably less than forty people. I couldn't help overhearing animated conversations between Jews who had escaped the Holocaust and hadn't seen each other since fleeing from some ghetto in occupied Europe twenty years previously. I was reluctant to leave the table with so many interesting stories being exchanged.

When we returned to our cabin Barbara, who we had left "resting", had just completed packing our cases, though she was still feeling ill and surviving on lemonade and arrowroot biscuits. Her reason for not doing as she was told was that she considered me incapable of packing properly, and we had to get a move on because we were due to dock in Marseilles in the early evening.

Shortly afterwards our cabin steward came in and we told her we had almost rung for her during the night. She replied that we would have been wasting our time because three quarters of the crew were sick!

After we had docked and our car was unloaded we were very relieved that it started first time after seeing those heavy seas washing over it. Our next problem was negotiating the journey from the docks to the hotel. It was dark and I was driving on the right for the first time and trying to follow the directions we had received from the hotel. We were very fortunate and found the hotel without too much trouble. It was pleasant but old-fashioned, with a large open lift to the upper floors. We slept soundly and after an excellent continental breakfast I took the car to a nearby car wash to get rid of all the salt encrusted on it. I then returned to pay our hotel bill, load up our roof rack and start our journey from the south of France to the north.

So on a beautiful Sunday morning in May we climbed up out of Marseilles and looked down on a magnificent view of the sea and the coast as we headed into Provence. Our first stop was Avignon, where we viewed the famous bridge featured in the song. A few hours later we stopped for a meal in Orange. In the café we saw several posters advertising bullfights, which still went on in France at that time. Orange itself was a very interesting place, with lots of Roman remains and antiquities. Then it was on to Montelimar, where we sampled the famous nougat before we carried on to Valence, where we had booked in at a hotel for the night. The hotel was excellent for both accommodation and food and we would have liked to stay a little longer. We decided that from now on we would buy food in the local shops and picnic en route.

Our next stop was to be Nevers via Clermont Ferrand. This was really a little too far for one day, but we had to push on because we had booked a hotel in Nevers. This hotel turned out to be equally good, but unfortunately Barbara's condition was still spoiling her enjoyment of French cuisine. The children seemed to be enjoying our travels, as we made frequent stops to relieve the tedium of travel and they loved the picnic aspect of it all.

As we came to the outskirts of Paris we approached our first major roundabout and found it horrendous, with traffic hurtling past at breakneck speeds on both sides of us every time the traffic lights changed. I made an instant decision not to continue to the centre but to find a country route to our hotel at Pont sur Le Marne, a picturesque little town about fifteen miles from Paris. The hotel of our choice turned out to be a very unusual establishment. It was teeming with NATO personnel, civilians and officers of various nations, with men and women coming and going at all times of the day and night. On both the days we were there the owner and his wife and children piled into their big Citroen estate car at about ten in the morning and didn't return until about nine in the evening. The evening meal wasn't served until ten o'clock, far too late for our children. We had great difficulty finding a shop to buy something suitable to feed them on our first night.

The meal served to us on both nights was absolutely wonderful, but I must admit I was a little suspicious when I overheard snatches of Russian coming from the next table. During the day we caught a train to Paris and visited the usual tourist attractions but used taxis for transport. We had been advised that reasonable meals could be obtained from the railway stations, and on both days we had good lunches at the Gare Du Nord station. While we were there Stephen and I went to the toilet in the station and afterwards discovered our camera was missing. We went back straight away but there was no sign of it. Because we omitted to report it to the police we were unable to claim on our insurance.

Our next destination was a place called Montreuil, which had been the headquarters of the British

Expeditionary Force during the First World War. Our hotel was a former Rothschild château and we had a beautifully-appointed family annexe. The town itself was a pretty, engaging place filled with mementos, statues etc of the BEF leaders who had been stationed there nearly fifty years before, and the local population were extremely friendly.

Now we were in northern France the weather had changed and it was cloudy skies, rain and cold winds, in marked contrast to the weather we had experienced all the way from the south. In spite of the weather we had a very relaxing couple of days there until we embarked on the Boulogne to Dover ferry. It was a slightly choppy crossing and to our surprise Stephen and Anne sat in the ferry lounge looking distinctly green about the gills, strange considering the rough seas they had encountered on the *Jerusalem* and not turned a hair.

Waiting and waving to us from the dockside at Dover were Norma, Barbara's sister, and Royston, her husband of only a few months, whom we had yet to meet. After Customs and Immigration, plus the inevitable interrogation from an Intelligence Corps officer concerned with where we had been all this time, we drove through and met Norma and Royston. We then followed their car along the coast road to Eastbourne where they now lived. We had a lovely meal and did a lot of catching up for a few hours. Their bungalow was too small for them to put us up, but Royston, who was now working for Eastbourne Council as a Local Government Officer, had found us a good recommended bed and breakfast for Saturday night.

After a good breakfast we set off for Tenterden in Kent, where we had arranged to have lunch with our old friend Graham Offen and his wife Isabelle. Graham had served in the "I" Corps in Cyprus on our first tour; he had attended our wedding and we were close friends. He was an excellent all-round sportsman but particularly outstanding at cricket. He was a very fast, accurate bowler who had been offered terms with Kent but had decided against it. Isabelle had cooked us a wonderful meal, which we thoroughly enjoyed, and it was great to talk about old times with Graham and to hear how he had met Isabelle while he was working in the Channel Isles.

Later we set off on our journey to Cleethorpes, via London. We picked up the newly-completed M1 motorway as we headed north. There was relatively little traffic and we made good time until we picked up the A46 near Leicester, which took us all the way to Cleethorpes. When we arrived it was about nine thirty in the evening and after greeting everyone I can still remember what an age it took to unload the car. Barbara really had utilised every iota of space. I

We were faced with our usual scenario on return from a tour. Once again we had to set off as soon as possible to find a new home in the Loughborough area. Our requirement now was a four-bedroomed house, and Mr and Mrs Redmayne had been on the lookout for something suitable for the past couple of months. A few days later Barbara and I travelled down to view a house in Quorn which was only about a mile and a half from Beaumanor. It had great potential. It needed some renovation and redecorating but was modestly priced at £3500. A major drawback was that it was right opposite a farm. In the end we decided not to have it, mainly because of the pervading smell of farmyard manure which drifted across.

We continued our search in other areas, but there didn't seem to be any four-bedroomed houses available other than the new ones which were being built on a couple of sites on the outskirts of Loughborough. We decided to take the plunge and go for a new house on the Davis Estate, which was off the Nanpantan Road going out of Loughborough. We were informed that it would be ready for occupation in six to eight weeks. The price was £4990, rather more than we had anticipated for one extra bedroom, and in the meanwhile we had to find somewhere to live until the house was ready. We found accommodation in the village of Kegworth with a widower, a pleasant man called Mr Perkins who had a lovely friendly sheepdog. Stephen and Anne had stayed with Jean and Bill and attended the same school as William and Janet, while Beverly came with us to Kegworth.

Over the next few weeks we were constant visitors to the building site and built up a good rapport with the site foreman and some of the workers, in particular the joiners. As a result our house was the first one in the row to be completed, and it also included a few innovations in our kitchen, diner and lounge which were the envy of people who moved in to Priory Road later. Thanks to our solicitor friend Michael Lewis we managed to move in before legal completion and took up residence in early August.

We had our husband and wife team over from Petchells to fit our carpets, and soon after this I brought Bill over to help with laying out the garden paths and erecting fences. I had a few days' leave, and with Bill supervising I worked harder manually than ever in my life before. The amount of concrete I mixed for paths and fence posts was never ending, and Bill took great delight in seeing my soft hands become hard and calloused. If only we had hired a concrete mixer!

Within ten days our fences were up, our paths laid, a vegetable plot dug and lawn turves laid. It really looked a treat and was greatly satisfying for us both. Unfortunately I was scheduled for an eight-week course at Bletchley Park at the beginning of September, just the time when the children would be starting at new schools, Stephen at Garendon Comprehensive and Anne at Mountfields Junior. During the first week of my course I travelled with John Mortby, who lived on the Jelson Estate on the other side of the Nanpantan Road. This meant that Barbara could have the car to take them to school. The first weekend I came home we bought Stephen a bicycle, as Garendon was almost two miles away, and Mountfields was only a reasonable walk away from us.

The view from the rear of our house was superb. We had a large hedge across the bottom of the garden, there was a small stream the other side of the hedge and then we had an uninterrupted view of green fields all the way to the woods at Nanpantan.

We remembered what Mr Bennett the builder had said about building us a conservatory and contacted him about it. He was as good as his word, and in a very short time he and his sole employee George had laid the foundations and erected and painted a fair-sized conservatory. This turned out to be a great boon to us, as the children could play in it on wet days, clothes could be dried in it and on a narrow piece of staging I erected we had excellent crops of early tomatoes. The total cost of this magnificent edifice was £250. You really did get value for your money in those days.

Our course at Bletchley was conducted by Tom Methven and was specially for Beaumanor people, namely John Mortby, Pete Bateman, Tom Creber, Gordon Heasman, Bob Stephens and myself. We were generally a happy bunch and attained good marks, but there was an awful lot of needle between Bob Stephens and Gordon Heasman, which I presume must have originated many years previously, as they were both members of the "Gallant 78".

When we returned to Beaumanor a special set position had been installed to allow us to use and develop the special skills we had so recently acquired. The plan was that quite a few people on each watch would attend similar Bletchley courses, but very few were. On my watch I was the only one and consequently spent almost the next two years on the position. I didn't grumble, as it was experience which was valuable and it was interesting work.

On the 5th December 1963 our daughter Louise was born at home. She was another beautiful baby. I was with Barbara when she was born, and it was an unforgettable but very moving experience.

It was about this time that the piano arrived. Barbara's mother had arranged for one to be delivered as no one played it at her house and she knew that Barbara played a little and that we intended that Anne would start to take lessons. When it was in situ in the lounge Barbara sat down to play to see if it needed tuning. It sounded awful, and when we raised the back lid lots of moths flew out. When the piano tuner arrived he discovered that the felts were riddled with moths and grubs and it needed a complete new set of felts. This cost us £20, a lot of money in those days, and money we could ill afford with Christmas at hand. Still it was a lovely piano and Anne went on to do very well with her lessons and her playing.

We had been warned by our union during our last year in Cyprus that integration of all the three services performing our type of work was in the pipeline and that GCHQ would be co-ordinating our joint efforts. This was largely due to Lord Mountbatten's reorganisation plans as Chief of Defence Staff. The official announcement when it arrived early in 1964 came as no surprise to us. The document also went on to state that there would be no station closures as a result of this integration. We could then rest easy in our beds - or so we thought! We were also informed that we could now volunteer for service abroad at any other Service stations, so my name was now on the volunteer list for Cyprus, Hong Kong, Mauritius and Ascension Island.

A few weeks after we had moved in at Priory Road, Barbara's parents came over for a few days and Norman cut back considerably the hedge at the bottom of our garden, which gained us several feet of vegetable plot. The plot produced all kinds of super vegetables, probably because it was virgin soil. The lettuce we grew was Webb's Wonderful, a forerunner of the modern Iceberg lettuce, and for several weeks I took boxes of them to work for free to anyone who wanted them. The flowers were also large and prolific - we had never seen anything like it. I can recall several times when Barbara was up very early in the morning feeding Louise she would call me to come quickly and survey the wildlife at the bottom of our garden. We had all sorts including partridges, pheasants, water voles and even foxes. It was not surprising then that on several occasions we saw the Quorn Hunt in full cry in the adjoining fields.

It was about this time that I decided to apply for a TUC English Correspondence Course. This was supposedly the equivalent of "A" level and consisted of a mixture of grammar, literature and essays. I enjoyed it and received good markings from my tutor, especially for my essays. At the end of the course, when I received my certificate, I was asked if I would like to go to Ruskin College Oxford for two years subject to me providing a couple of essays for Ruskin to assess. My tutor was sure I would have no problems and that leave of absence would be arranged with the Civil Service. I was flattered, but had no hesitation in refusing. It was bad enough going to Bletchley for weeks or months, but to go off to Oxford for two years was out of the question with our family commitments.

Less than a year after the "no station closures" announcement I was on duty on an afternoon shift when our Duty Watch Officer, Andy Plowman, came into the set room and dropped a notice for circulation to all staff on the supervisor's desk. He then beat a hasty retreat, went down the corridor and locked himself in his office. Beaumanor at that time was considered to be the most disciplined station in the whole organisation and was run with an almost military routine, so no one left their set positions without permission. As the notice was passed from set position to set position, within a very short time large numbers of people were walking around and everyone knew exactly what was in the notice before they had read it for themselves.

The notice stated that Beaumanor would be run down and closed within four years. Transfers to other

UK stations would be on Public Interest terms and they would try to give people their first choice of UK station. If however an overseas tour intervened they would try to relocate everyone at their first choice station on return to UK. The set room was a hubbub of noise and very little work was being done. Dire threats were being issued against the establishment concerning what would happen if certain people were forced to move against their will. Normally senior staff visited the set rooms at regular intervals during the day, but for the rest of that day there wasn't a single appearance.

During the next few weeks, as the dust began to settle, most people had begun to accept the inevitability of a move, and there was a rush of volunteers for Cyprus, Malta and Hong Kong. We decided to opt for an overseas tour before moving to a fresh UK station. Volunteers were required for a new station shortly to be opened on Ascension Island in the South Atlantic and we placed our names on that list along with Cyprus, Mauritius and Hong Kong and then sat back and waited to see which came first.

Stephen was making good progress at Garendon, while Anne had passed her eleven plus and was set to transfer from Mountfields to Loughborough College Grammar School, which was very close to Garendon. We bought Anne a cycle to ride to school, sometimes but not always accompanied by Stephen. Beverly was attending the infant school in Outwoods Drive with her friend Linda Mitchell and seemed happy there. Our next door neighbours were Peter and Enid Coles. Peter was a Lecturer at Loughborough College and they had three children, Mark, Richard and Belinda. They were great neighbours, never intrusive but always there if you needed them.

I resumed my association with Loughborough Town Hockey Club and though these days I rarely made the first team I enjoyed myself in the second team alongside old friends Gerald Dowsett, Freddie Smith and Tom Atkinson.

One day at work Slap Reedman approached me and asked if I would be interested in a change of work. As I had spent a long period on the job I was doing I said I would be interested. I was then told that the job was ultra secret and I must be further vetted to see if I passed the security criteria. A couple of weeks later I was informed I had been approved and that my name had been added to a special "Codeword" list. I would be starting the next day doubling up with people who were already working on the task. Among the select few working on this job were Tom Creber, Jim Southwell and Bob Venters.

We were in a small room between the main set room and the TA section. The door carried a large notice saying "Strictly No Admittance". A ridiculous anomaly was that the Duty Officer, who was in charge of all the set rooms, didn't know what we were covering and was not allowed into the room. Our intercept material was collected by a special courier each day and transported by road. I found the work extremely interesting, but there was one major drawback - the shift rotas were produced by Slap on a weekly basis. There were no night shifts, but we often had to work late and sometimes began as early as six in the morning. Often you didn't know until the day before which shifts you were working for the next seven days. This made family outings, and I must confess my hockey, very difficult, so after only six weeks I requested a return to normal shift working. I gave my reasons and after about three months a replacement was found and I returned to normal duties.

We then discovered that Barbara was pregnant again and would be due about the end of July. Though we were pleased, we realised that life was going to be rather hectic and expensive during the next few years, so an overseas posting would help to alleviate the expense.

When we lived in Beacon Road we had attended Emmanuel Anglican Church whenever we could and that was where Beverly was baptised, but we now found it easier to attend a church at the end of Nanpantan Road on the outskirts of town. The services were usually conducted by one of the curates from Emmanuel. It was a beautiful little church and the children used to go to Sunday School, even when shifts prevented us from attending. It seemed that Beaumanor was now fairly calm after the shock of the impending closure and the chief interest of the majority of staff was seeing whether they had obtained their first choice of station, whether it be UK or an overseas posting.

On Saturday July 31st Richard was born, yet another beautiful baby. For the first three months he was very demanding and cried quite a lot, and Barbara really had her hands full with a new baby, Louise, only nineteen months old, and a husband and three other children to feed too. Stephen and Anne always helped with the chores, cleaning shoes and bathing the younger ones. Our abiding memory of" that time was that almost every night at five o'clock or very soon after Louise used to grab her teddy and say "bed", quite often before she'd had her bath.

About six months later we had notification that we had been selected for the new station on Ascension Island, but the drawback was that there were only primary school facilities available on the island. We made preliminary arrangements for Stephen and Anne to board at Loughborough College Grammar School. They didn't seem to mind as our tour was only going to be for eighteen months with an option to stay on for another eighteen, and they would be flying out to us at Easter, Christmas and for the summer holidays.

We were then informed that there would be a delay of at least six months before our accommodation was completed and we then had problems on the boarding school front, so we decided to forgo our trip to the South Atlantic.

The Braithwaites set off for another tour in Cyprus, taking Janet and Catherine with them. They were close friends and we missed them. They were also Louise's godparents, and although we were now quite a large family we were always made welcome at their house in Woodhouse Eaves. Catherine used to love mothering our two youngest.

About six months after they departed I went to work on an afternoon shift and my Duty Officer Andy Plowman called me into his office and asked me if I had heard the news about Catherine. When I said no, he told me "I'm afraid she's dead". Our whole family were absolutely devastated - it seemed unbelievable. It appears that she had returned home from school complaining of a headache and suddenly became unconscious. They dashed her to BMH but she died shortly afterwards, just sixteen years old. We wrote to them straight away but it was about six weeks before we heard from Bernard. It appeared that the cause of death was a congenital aneurism. Edith blamed the Cyprus climate and said she hadn't wanted to go on another tour. She of course blamed Bernard and we didn't think things were ever quite the same between them again.

I was still having problems with my hay fever and my doctor recommended that I made a trip to the Birmingham Allergy Centre for a thorough testing. These tests revealed that I was allergic to moulds (garden), pollen and household dust, but they said they could make up the appropriate prescription for a series of injections over a four month period and they forecast that my symptoms would gradually disappear. I thought I had nothing to lose, and agreed to have the injections.

My old friend Slap contacted me at work and asked me if I would like to go to Hong Kong to work as a special analyst. If I agreed, this would necessitate a four and a half month course at Cheltenham. I expressed my interest and after discussing it with Barbara we agreed that it was a good opportunity, but of course she wasn't very happy at the thought of me being away from home for such a long time. Somehow, whenever I was away on a course, something always seemed to happen, and when I was needed I was never there. The children were quite excited at the prospect and we knew that there was a good standard of education available in the Colony. My course was scheduled to begin the first week in February 1967 and we were due to fly out to Hong Kong in July.

I started out at five in the morning on a dark and frosty winter's morn and reached Cheltenham at about seven thirty, where I checked in at the Askham Court Hotel, where I had stayed on previous visits to GCHQ. It was a small but very well run hotel which provided good accommodation and food. It was also only about fifteen minutes walk from Oakley, which meant it was unnecessary to become involved in the daily traffic crawl in and out of GCHQ. There were three fellow members, Reg Barwick, Archie Cockburn and Brian Ainley. Reg was a Welshman who had spent many years as a Radio Officer on a trawler sailing out of Hull, but before the service merger he had worked for the Foreign Office and lived in Cheltenham.

Archie had also been a Radio Officer but in the Merchant Navy, and was a Scot from Cupar, another Foreign Office man. Brian hailed from Hull and was also a ship's Radio Officer prior to joining the Admiralty at Scarborough. They were both in their late twenties. Our course tutor was Charlie Fenton, a pleasant though rather strait-laced man who rarely showed a sense of humour. As the course began I experienced a few qualms that the others with their Radio College backgrounds might leave me behind on the technical and theory aspects of the course, but it turned out that we were all good students and passed the various stages of the course with good marks.

As spring approached and the weather improved, I often used to go home on a Wednesday afternoon and return early on Thursday morning in time for a quick breakfast at the hotel before going to my course, and I always managed to arrive in time for our nine o'clock start. There was however one Thursday morning in May when I ran into thick fog when I was only a few miles from Cheltenham. I was hopelessly lost and finally ground to a halt, wondering where on earth I had left the main road, as I was now on a minor road. Then almost miraculously a breeze materialised, and a few minutes later the sun broke through. I discovered I was right in the centre of the beautiful Cotswold village of Bourton on the Water with the river running through the village. I soon found my way back to the main road and made it back in time for breakfast.

May progressed and we were preparing for our final exams when clouds began to appear on our horizons. Civil unrest in Hong Kong, which had been sparked off by a small rise in the fares on the cross harbour Star Ferries, was appearing all too often on our television screens. We began to wonder if our tour would be cancelled, but we were assured that we would definitely be going as scheduled because there were four analysts waiting to be relieved by us.

We all passed with excellent marks and returned to our home stations to await our movement orders. Barbara had just taken delivery of packing cases for our heavy baggage to be forwarded by sea. At the same time we had a memo from our admin office stating that we must take advantage of our large accompanying baggage allowance, so we went out and bought a couple of large aluminium trunks. That meant that along with all our suitcases we had what could only be described as a colossal amount of baggage to travel with us by air.

Our house was on the market, as we knew we would certainly not be returning to Beaumanor. This made it hard work for Barbara, combining leaving preparations with always having to be reasonably tidy to show potential buyers around the house.

There was still intermittent rioting and unrest in Hong Kong, but nearer to home we were much more concerned with the ever-worsening situation in the Middle East. The Israelis had taken the Arab world by surprise as they swept through Gaza across the Sinai

Peninsula, a cunning strategy which after overcoming initial resistance from the Egyptians continued right through to Suez. This became known as the Six Day War and brought the Superpowers to the brink once again. I began to wonder if our tour would be cancelled after all.

A couple of days later our movement orders arrived. We were to travel from RAF Brize Norton in Oxfordshire in mid July. That very same night on the news we watched a Japanese airliner crash into the harbour in Hong Kong as it attempted to land at Kai Tak airport; fortunately no lives were lost. Our house was virtually sold to a family moving from the London area who thought it was a snip at the asking price of £5250; this was the price we had insisted on though the estate agent had told us we couldn't expect to sell it quickly if we exceeded £4990.

Peter Coles, our neighbour, kindly offered to drive our car to Felixstowe to go by sea. We then hired a large estate car to enable us to go to Cleethorpes to say our goodbyes, stay a few days and then drive down to Brize Norton, where the hire company would collect the car.

CHAPTER 9

HONG KONG

Our new venture began early on a summer's morning. We left Cleethorpes early to enable us to have a leisurely drive down to Brize Norton. We certainly couldn't have driven at excessive speeds with the amount of luggage and the number of passengers we were carrying.

It was early evening when we arrived and reported for the necessary booking in and pre-flight formalities. We were then directed to our on-site overnight accommodation, which was excellent. We were booked for a five in the morning call as we were scheduled for an early take off which somehow dragged on until ten o'clock.

As we finally boarded our aircraft, a VC10, we were impressed with the amount of passenger room and the new safety feature recently adopted of rear facing seats. The pilots and crew were all RAF personnel, as were the stewardesses. Our flight was timed to last eighteen hours, so our friendly GP had suggested that Richard and Louise take a mild sedative when we were a few hours into our flight. Instead of having a calming influence it seemed to have the opposite effect, and as we came in to land at our first stop, Bahrain in the Persian Gulf, they seemed almost hyperactive. It was midnight Bahrain time as we touched down and as we alighted it was as if a blast of hot air was being directed straight at us. It was hard to believe that it could be so hot in the middle of the night.

It was a two-hour stopover, fortunately in air conditioning, and we enjoyed a meal, exercised the children then boarded the aircraft again. This time we were headed for Gan, a tiny island in the Indian Ocean. The children settled down and slept for quite a while on this stage and somehow our navigator seemed to find his way to Gan without any problems and we made a smooth landing. The facilities at Gan were rather primitive and there was no air conditioning, so we were pleased that it was only a short stay before we took off again. There were 148 passengers on our VC10, a mix of service and civilians, including Reg, Archie and Brian with their families. There were also quite a few other civilians from other UK stations all bound for Little Sai Wan. This was a new situation for us as we were accustomed to knowing all our fellow War Office travellers on trips abroad.

On the last stage Barbara and I had quite a long conversation with one of our stewardesses, which didn't exactly lift our spirits. She had been to Hong Kong quite a few times recently and in her opinion we would be wasting our time bothering to unpack our heavy baggage as the British would be leaving Hong Kong within six months.

Shortly after this conversation the red warning light came on for everyone to fasten their seat belts, as we were expected to encounter turbulence. Apparently we were coming under the influence of a typhoon which was expected to make landfall within a hundred miles of Hong Kong. Sure enough we began to experience quite a lot of turbulence. Beverly felt ill, so I moved into the seat next to her and was fully occupied ministering and assisting with the sick bags. The others didn't seem too bothered about it.

As we came in to land at Hong Kong I felt most uncomfortable at how close we seemed to the tops of the tenement flats as we landed at Kai Tak in Kowloon (Seven Dragons), part of the New Territories ceded to Britain until 1997. Our aircraft taxied to within a short distance of the terminal buildings, but we were then informed that Typhoon signal no 6 was hoisted and there was a torrential rainstorm in progress, so we must wait for it to ease before we could leave the aircraft.

About fifteen minutes later the rain eased and we were able to enter the terminal building and see the friendly faces of John Mortby and Joe Moffitt waiting to greet us. The Sai Wan admin officer, who was also waiting to meet everyone, was appalled when he saw the amount of luggage the Ryan family had brought. I politely informed him that we were only acting on instructions from our UK admin, so perhaps they should liaise.

Our accommodation had been reserved at the Sunning House Hotel, which was located in the Causeway Bay district on Hong Kong (Fragrant Harbour) Island. It was arranged that Stephen, Richard and I would travel in Joe Moffitt's car and Barbara and the girls would travel with John Mortby. The normal route from Kai Tak was along Nathan Road, Kowloon's main thoroughfare, but we had to make several diversions on the way to the car ferry because of bomb scares. We were told that the usual method of depositing bombs on the busy roads was through a hole specially made in the car floors, often in a red cardboard box. They often turned out to be hoaxes, but they still caused traffic chaos until the Bomb Disposal Unit attended to them.

We were of course not used to the hot and sticky humidity we were now experiencing, so when we arrived at our hotel we were looking forward to a shower and a change of clothes, but we were disappointed. There was a serious water shortage in Hong Kong and supply was restricted to four hours every four days and it wasn't due again for another three days. We had to make do with buckets of water carried up to our rooms and poured into our baths by the hotel staff. This then was our introduction to Hong Kong - an imminent typhoon, bombs and a chronic water shortage. We wondered what would come next!

Fortunately the typhoon veered away from the Colony overnight and we were able to go with John Mortby and view a few possible flats he had lined up for us. There were quite a few which were about to be or had already been vacated by Americans and other nationals who were pulling out, and our stewardess' forebodings certainly seemed to have some substance.

We decided on a flat in Stanley, a new block only three stories high known as Reef Court and only about a hundred yards from where John and Jose Mortby lived with their three children Michael, Stephen and Teresa. We spent a fortnight in the hotel and during this time we had to make arrangements to hire furniture and make preliminary visits to the children's schools. Stephen and Anne were to attend St George's Army Children's School in Kowloon while Beverly was to attend the Junior Army Children's School at Stanley Fort.

During our hotel stay it seemed to us that police cars and ambulances with sirens blaring were constantly speeding past the entrance to the hotel, and we used to peruse the South China Morning Post every morning to see just what incidents had been happening in Causeway Bay. My introduction to our workplace CSOS (Composite Signals Organisation Station), Little Sai Wan, which was on the north east of the island about six miles from Stanley, was quite a cultural shock for someone like me who was used to the fairly rigid service discipline of War Office stations. There was an extremely relaxed atmosphere about the whole station. It had previously been the domain of the Air Ministry, but was now becoming a mixture of Air Ministry, Admiralty, War Office and Foreign Office personnel, now integrated into GCHQ. To add spice to the variety, we had a contingent of RAAF (Royal Australian Air Force) personnel and even a small group of Australian Army men, a veritable hotchpotch.

The section we were assigned to was under the direct control of an RAAF Flight Lieutenant named Kingsley Porter. Nominally in charge of the GCHQ analysts in the section was Jack Bentley, an ex-Admiralty supervisor. Archie and I were assigned to a very busy part of the section where it was all go, whereas Reg and Brian were assigned to less active areas. It was interesting work and we buckled to and began to enjoy it. Our on-the-job mentors were Jim Winks and Tam Morrison, both Scots, very experienced and they taught us well.

At our introductory briefing the first thing that was impressed upon us were the procedures should we receive word that the People's Liberation Army had crossed the border to restore Hong Kong to China. All secret files and documents were to be burnt or destroyed immediately. The Governor, Sir David Trench, had an aircraft on permanent standby at Kai Tak to whisk him and his family to safety should the balloon go up. I'm not sure what would have happened to the rank and file!

The children started school and adapted well considering it was a new school in a new environment. A major problem for Barbara at first was washing, as we were still rationed to four hours every fourth day, so during that time the washing machine was going non stop and before the water went off every bath and utensil in the flat which would hold water was filled to the brim. Everyone had high hopes that on the first of October China would open up the sluices and allow water to flow into the Colony again as per their long-standing annual agreement for which they were paid handsomely. China was however in the middle of the Great Proletarian Cultural Revolution and nothing was certain.

On the first of October the water supply was resumed and we all breathed a sigh of relief. Though there was still quite a bit of Communist agitation in some parts of the Colony, things seemed generally calmer. The Ryan family were managing quite well in Reef Court and though we only had three bedrooms, as we didn't have an *amah* (maidservant), Stephen elected to use her quarters, which consisted of a small bedroom and a toilet which was situated just inside the back entrance to our flat. We had two other bathrooms, so there was rarely a problem.

When there were mosquitoes about, Stephen used to grab the Flit gun and spray his room vigorously, then go in and close the door to work at his homework and listen to his music, which always had to be a combined effort. Nowadays when we read about the toxicity of the old DDT Flit type preparations, we wonder how he survived.

Stanley lies at the start of a small peninsula which juts out into the South China Sea and the road from Stanley to the Fort gradually climbs for about a mile until you reach a plateau, an area known as Stanley Fort. The junior school is there and quite a few married quarters occupied by the regiment and their families who happen to be on a tour of duty at the time. When we arrived it was the Duke of Wellington's Light Infantry, renowned for their fighting and sporting prowess and in particular rugby football. This was not surprising since Major Mike Campbell Lamerton of British Lions fame was one of their star players. The area also had a beautiful green sports field and a swimming pool, and the Garrison church and the medical centre were also in the same area. Reef Court was on Stanley Main Street and only a few minutes' walk from the market. We had been warned that the smell took some getting used to, but you could buy practically anything there and it was absolutely true, meat, fish, fruit, vegetables, materials, clothes etc all at very reasonable prices. It was true however that the stench and the local habit of spitting were very disconcerting.

Locating places in downtown Hong Kong was quite difficult at first, as was finding where you had parked the car when every street looked alike. Barbara was usually very observant and steered us in the right direction.

John and Jose had introduced us to the Luk Wok Hotel in Wanchai during our first few days in HK, made famous in the film *The World of Suzie Wong* starring William Holden. The food and drink were first class, with a cabaret for good measure, and the prices were unbelievably cheap.

I started playing tennis and football again and sometimes played with a friend called Harry Forrester during our lunch break. It became very embarrassing when Kingsley Porter began asking me to play tennis at any time of the day. He would clear it with Jack Bentley first, but I was only too aware that Jack didn't like it, and understandably so. When Kingsley was around I used to forgo my break so that I could play with a clear conscience if asked.

There were four other RAAF men in our section including a Flying Officer, a Sergeant Alan Oldacres-Dear and a Corporal Hoppy White. They were a very gregarious bunch and always arranging parties and social functions which we were expected to attend. Their Commanding Officer, Squadron Leader Sandy Baxter, lived next door to us in Reef Court with his three children.

All in all we were very much involved with the Australians. The RAAF organised a raffle in aid of a well known Hong Kong charity for a prize of a brand new automatic Morris 1100. The tickets were HK$100 each and I bought one of the first ones sold, number 6. A couple of weeks later Kingsley rang me in the office to tell me that I had won the car, but the bad news was that I had to proceed to Ariel House straight away and buy all the people assembled there a drink. I was most happy to do this, even though it more than doubled the price of my ticket.

That same evening we had been invited to a party

at John and Jose's and as we arrived their front door was festooned with coloured lights flashing on and off proclaiming "Lucky Jim". We enjoyed a very convivial evening, but what I didn't know was that my drinks were being laced and before the evening was over John Mortby and Joe Moffitt had to help Barbara to get me home. I was quite alert and can remember everything, but I had no control whatsoever over my legs.

To say that Barbara was displeased with me was the understatement of 1967. As I was being assisted up the stairs to our flat I remember her hissing, "Don't you dare let the children hear you or see you like this!"

I awoke next morning feeling like death warmed up and tried to turn over, but Barbara soon reminded me that it was the first weekend I was working alone in my section. The whole station knew I had won a car and most of them would soon know about my performance at the party, which meant there was no option but to go into work. I'll never know how I managed to open the combination lock on our section door.

When I went down to the set room I hoped that there would not be a lot of work for me to analyse, but of course there was a load. I carried the work up to my section, where it took me a full hour to make a start. Fortunately I didn't have anything difficult to analyse and managed to struggle through them all. By the afternoon, after a cup of coffee and a turkey sandwich, I began to feel much better.

While we had been very fortunate to win a car it did

present us with problems. Our seven-year-old Morris Oxford, which had only recently arrived from UK, was much bigger than the prize car, so it was much more suited to our family requirements. Another snag was that if we disposed of the Oxford during our first year the Government would claim back from us the cost of shipping the car to HK. We decided to advertise the prize car in the South China Morning Post and at HK$10,000 the phone never stopped ringing. The money was placed in a savings account to be used to help to purchase a new car at the end of our tour.

It really did seem that with the resumption of the water supply from China things were slowly beginning to return to normal in the Colony. In all probability the Chinese Government had realised that China's foreign exchange earnings in trade and tourism were grinding to an all-time low, which was making things very difficult for their economy, and the trend had to be reversed.

As a family we were all beginning to enjoy our new way of life. School was presenting no problems, although discipline at St Georges was quite strict - as a Service school it needed to be. Persistent misbehaviour could result in both parents and family terminating their tour and returning to UK. This was impressed on both parents and pupils when they entered the school. While we were there a family we knew was sent home because one of their children was caught with drugs at school.

The cost of living was relatively cheap for most things that were produced in the Colony, like clothes, dairy products, bread biscuits and a wondrous assortment of delicious cakes of all kinds. At the other side of the scale, imported goods were very expensive, especially chocolate. Whenever we went shopping in HK, sometimes late in the evening, there were always bustling crowds thronging the pavements. The people of HK set great store by education, as was evident by the number of children of varying ages sitting by their parents' vending stalls diligently doing their homework impervious to the hustle and bustle which was going on around them.

There were several English-style department stores including Wing On's and Lane Crawfords, both in the Central district while Causeway Bay boasted its own unique Japanese store called Daimaru's. Dotted around the various districts of HK and Kowloon were the Communist China Products department stores, which sold a myriad of products of China, some of which were amazingly good value, so we often shopped there. The downside of shopping in China Products establishments was the stony-faced countenances of the shop assistants, both male and female. I doubt if they were all ardent communists, but no doubt they were acting on party line orders.

As the tour progressed we settled into a pleasant round combining work and recreation. Barbara and I socialised quite a bit and went to functions at all the famous hotels, including the Mandarin and the Peninsula. At weekends we usually went to Sai Wan for a meal at Ariel House. The Reclamation was a large area of grassy land which had been reclaimed from the sea and provided a football and cricket pitch as well as a tennis court. There were two more tennis courts at the other side of the camp site. Beverly, Louise and Richard loved their Sai Wan trips at weekends, but Stephen and Anne usually stayed at home to complete homework or followed their own pursuits. In typical teenage fashion the state of the flat when we returned home often left a lot to be desired.

My first trip into the New Territories was to play in a football match against the Gurkha Regiment which patrolled and guarded the Chinese border. Little Sai Wan had turned out a fairly strong team, which included Phil Webb, Charlie Darker and Jim Winks and a newcomer to HR, a Clerical Officer who had recently arrived called Ron Speakman. He had the reputation of being an outstanding goalkeeper in the local Cheltenham leagues.

We played well from the start and were soon a goal up and for most of the first half we were well on top. The first time the Gurkhas came into our penalty area a slow, innocuous-looking shot went straight past our goalkeeper and it was one all. After this, every time the opposition came anywhere near our goal they scored, and we finally lost by eight goals to one. We were all disappointed and rather annoyed with the people who had lauded Ron's goalkeeping prowess. Little did we know until a few months later that he had begun to develop multiple sclerosis.

There were two beaches available to Stanley residents, one at Stanley Beach, which was only a few yards from the Main Street, and St Stephen's beach, which was a little further away on the road to Stanley Fort. This was a much cleaner beach and usually attracted far more locals and expatriates.

There was another beach in Stanley known as Tweed Bay, which was kept in immaculate condition by some of the inmates of Stanley Prison. The prison had been built by the British in 1937 and was then ironically used by the Japanese to house the British civilian prisoners who were interned when they invaded HK in World War Two. The Allied POWs were interned at a camp in Argyle Street in Kowloon. Honorary membership of the Stanley Prison Officers' Club was open to British expatriates provided you were proposed and seconded by a couple of serving Prison Officers. It was an excellent club which ran quite a few well-organised functions and included lawn bowls and tennis as well as the attraction of a beach which was always clean, so family membership was well worthwhile.

One day Barbara and I spent several hours looking around Stanley Military Cemetery, which was just the other side of Wong Ma Kok Road not far from St Stephen's beach. Some of the inscriptions on the gravestones went back to the second half of the 1800s, when the British first occupied HK. It was a very moving experience reading the inscriptions, so many of them young children and babies and sometimes whole families. Usually cholera was the main cause of death. It was surprising to us that so many wives and children accompanied their husbands in those days.

There were many British and Canadian troops killed and wounded in a forlorn attempt to prevent the all-conquering Japanese taking HK. It was hard to believe that only twenty-two years previously the Japanese were still occupying the Colony. We did meet a few people who had been interned at Stanley and had now returned to their homes in the affluent Peak area.

A must for all visitors to HK is a visit to Victoria Peak, which is over 1300 feet above sea level and when not shrouded in mist affords breathtaking views of the harbour, Kowloon and the New Territories. At night it can be even more spectacular, with a brilliant display of multi-coloured lights stretching as far as the eye can see.

At the beginning of April our Admin Office always issued a directive warning people of the advent of the typhoon season, advising us to have good stocks of tinned foods, flour, biscuits and candles in case power supplies were interrupted . Our only experience of a Typhoon so far had been the near miss when we arrived in the Colony.

The word typhoon is Chinese for "big wind" and Signal No. 1 is hoisted at the Royal Observatory and at various vantage points in the Colony especially in the harbour area, when a tropical storm is within 500 miles of the Colony. These signals can increase up to nine or ten. When signal No. 8 is announced all offices , shops, schools and businesses close, though public transport is maintained for as long as possible to allow people to travel home. There are constant updates on television and radio as to how close the storm is. When Signal No. 9 is hoisted it means winds are expected to increase in strength significantly and Signal No. 10 means hurricane force winds are imminent.

One day in late July I was at work when Signal No. 8 was announced, which meant everyone had to leave the building and set off for home as quickly as possible except for those who were among the skeleton staff chosen to remain behind. On this day I was travelling back to Stanley with my friend Peter, who lived just opposite us in Stanley. When he drew up at the entrance to Reef Court I opened the car door and jumped out. I then had to hold on to his door for dear life to prevent it being blown off its hinges. I then spent several minutes trying to close the door so that he could move off. I eventually succeeded, but the force of the wind was awesome.

It transpired that during the half hour it had taken us to travel home Signals 9 and 10 had been hoisted and we were in the middle of a full-blown typhoon. The children were quite excited and called me to look through our verandah window at a stout eucalyptus tree outside our flat which was bending almost double in the wind. Stephen and Anne insisted that it was just about to blow over. I had just finished ridiculing the idea when there was an almighty crack as it snapped off almost at ground level. I then made sure everyone was staying away from the large plate glass windows of our verandah, which could be seen bowing in and out under the tremendous pressure. Another manifestation of the typhoon was the movement of the water in the toilet pans, which swished to and fro at times, almost splashing over the tops of the seats.

Early in the evening the torrential rain and the winds gradually eased and about half an hour later the sky was blue. When we opened the door and looked out there was no wind at all, just an almost eerie silence. A few minutes later it was announced on the television that the eye of the typhoon was now stationary over the Stanley Peninsula, but they warned that the winds would soon freshen and become hurricane force again. This forecast was exactly what did happen before it headed inland towards China and was eventually downgraded to a mere tropical storm. We had another two days of high winds and heavy rain before cleaning up could begin in the Colony. Fortunately there were only a few lives lost.

One of the perks we enjoyed in HK were an additional five days' public holidays, in accordance with local customs, which included two days for the Chinese Lunar New Year. This is the time when traditionally gifts of money are given in red envelopes to people such as the postman, the caretaker (who also cleaned your car every day) and of course the shop assistants at your regular grocery store. Ching Ming was another such holiday when families visited the graves of their ancestors to clean the graves and leave food and wine for the spirits, while incense and paper money were burned for the dead.

Our second year was not to be blighted by the all-too-common water shortages, as this was the year when the Plover Cove Reservoir came into service. This was the result of a brilliant idea by a British engineer who thought why not build a dam across the mouth of a bay in the New Territories only a few miles from the Chinese mainland. The sea water was pumped out of the bay and the reservoir was allowed to fill with fresh water, most of which came from China.

We had already come to know and respect the local Chinese and found them honest, conscientious and very hard working. They loved children and nothing was too much trouble for shopkeepers and stallholders. I had come to know quite a few local Chinese through playing for Little Sai Wan in the local tennis leagues. Sometimes Barbara came to watch with Louise and Richard, and they always provided delicious cold drinks and refreshments during and after matches.

I played in our second team along with Jim Statham, Phil Webb, Ian Cummings, Geoff Wells and Wilf Lyth, and during that season Jim and I played as the No. 1 pair and were undefeated throughout the season.

I do clearly recall the match when we nearly came unstuck. It was against the Chinese Recreation Club's No. 1 pair and we won a marathon hard-fought match.

Talking together in the club after the match it transpired that the elder one was in his mid seventies and had been singles champion of Shanghai in 1928 and his partner was only in his fifties. Shanghai was a major European and United States enclave before the Second World War, tennis was one of their major sports and was played to a high standard.

Sometimes at weekends we would pack a picnic or take a barbecue and head for the New Territories via the car ferry. There were some lovely beaches and beauty spots and in contrast to HK there were usually very few people around. If we were going to a Stanley beach at a weekend or on a public holiday, Stephen always wanted to know which beach we were going to, just to make sure that he and his friends went to a different beach where we wouldn't be likely to cramp his style.

It was common at this time to find the bodies of refugees washed up on the various beaches of the New Territories or HK. Quite often they had been eaten or mauled by sharks. It didn't say much for the Chinese Communist regime when people were willing to risk their lives swimming across the shark-infested Mirs Bay to try to take up a new life in the decadent, Westernised Hong Kong. If the harbour police picked anyone up swimming they were returned straight away to the authorities at the Chinese border. This was the same fate meted out to anyone caught by the Gurkhas at the border.

One day Barbara and I took Louise and Richard to Tweed Bay for a swim and as we approached the beach we saw a large notice saying "Sharks Sighted". The lifeguard told us that several had been seen in the bay and no one was allowed to go in and swim. We stayed on a while to let the children play in the sand. As we were leaving a young American couple came along and viewed the notice and asked us if it was a joke. When we assured them it wasn't, they beat a hasty retreat.

Another time at Stanley Beach Barbara had taken Louise and Richard and they were just paddling near the edge of the water when she saw the lifeguard shouting and gesticulating for them to come out of the water. When she looked she saw a couple of black menacing dorsal fins swimming up and down less than fifty yards away. The lifeguard wouldn't even let the children paddle near the edge. It made us both very aware and alert afterwards.

The perpetual greenery of HK was very attractive to us in comparison to the rather arid landscape of Cyprus, which lasted for eight months of the year. The flora included more than seventy species of orchid, and there were violets, honeysuckle and Flame of the Forest Trees, a wonderful sight.

Our flat was often the meeting place for Stephen and his school friends, in particular Mark Harland, Mike Davis and Ben Cromarty. They used to congregate for long sessions of Bridge, especially when a near-miss typhoon had given them an extra day off school. Stephen and his friends were very fashion conscious, as were most of the young HK population, and they took great pleasure in having the latest trends in trousers, shirts etc made to measure for them at a particular tailor in Temple Street Kowloon, not too far away from their school. The prices were incredibly low and we even had Richard measured for a suit before we came home. When he went for a fitting the tailor brought lots of the nearby shopkeepers in to have a look, and Richard quite enjoyed being the centre of attention.

When we were approximately half way through our tour I was offered an extra year's extension, but we turned it down because we thought it might have an adverse affect on Stephen and Anne's education. Afterwards we wondered if we had made the right choice, as we were all thoroughly enjoying Hong Kong life. We had also made our application choice of station for when we returned to UK, picking Scarborough, Cheadle or Taunton in that order, and we sat back to see which we would be assigned to.

By this time we were very close friends with Kingsley and Heather Porter, and Kingsley was trying to persuade us how much we would love life in Australia, not just for a visit but to live there permanently. He told us that through his contacts with DSD Melbourne (Australia's version of GCHQ) he had already ascertained that they would guarantee me a job, but first of all I must resign at the end of my tour. This was necessary because there was an agreement between them that they would not poach personnel from each other, so I had to resign first and allow GCHQ to ship us to Melbourne, which was an entitlement. My pension and lump sum would be frozen and I would commence new terms with DSD. It was a big decision and we thought about it long and hard, but in the end decided against it. Barbara's main reason against the move was that we had left our families in the UK expecting us to return after three years, and it would have been unfair to go from HK to live in Australia on a permanent basis. I quite fancied a new life down under but only if we were all in total agreement, and I was a little unhappy that I had nothing in writing from DSD. So for the third time in my life Australia had beckoned but it just wasn't to be.

We attended the Garrison Church at Stanley Fort on a fairly regular basis and along with Anne, Beverly and a few more young people I began to attend confirmation classes run by the local Anglican padre. He was a pleasant enough man, but was always complaining about the state the church had been left in by the Roman Catholic worshippers, as it was a shared church. I'm sure the fact that the padre was a staunch Ulsterman must have coloured his protestations about the Catholics.

At this stage I must confess that my reasons for wanting to be confirmed were not really the right ones. First I wanted to please Barbara, and second I always felt excluded when Barbara went up to the altar rail for communion.

The day arrived and we were all duly confirmed at the Garrison Church by the Bishop of Hong Kong. It was a beautiful day but very windy, especially up at Stanley Fort. It wasn't a very spiritual occasion for me, but it was a day I'll always remember, being confirmed at the same time as two of our daughters. The Anglican padre who succeeded the Ulsterman was John Williams, a native of Wales, who was different again. We became very friendly with his wife and family and he and I used to play tennis together at the Stanley Club.

It was about this time when the name of Jackie Pullinger first came to our notice, because of the following she appeared to be attracting among the teenagers at some of the Colony's most prestigious schools. There were quite a few critical letters in the *South China Morning Post* because some of the young people had been "speaking in tongues". No mention was made of the wonderful work she was performing with the drug addicts, especially her work within Kowloon's walled city.

The UK Radio grades in HK were represented by two unions, the Civil Service Union (CSU) and the Association of Government Supervisors and Radio Officers (AGSRO). Roy Ward was the local chairman of the CSU and Jack Hart the secretary. Nationally both unions had decided they had to do something to refute an outrageous statement which had been made by an Official Side GCHQ representative during pay negotiations. He was a very senior official called Ray Frawley, who some twenty years later was to be lauded in the notorious book *Spycatcher* as one of the

Department's brighter boys. At this meeting he had stated that the clerical grades provided the frequencies and the callsigns for intercepts, and a trained monkey could perform the job of a Radio Officer. This caused bitter resentment, and both unions agreed on a joint action to be taken at selected stations throughout the world. At the arranged time the action, or perhaps we should say inaction, commenced. Officially the unions called this action a "Work To Rule". Sets were tuned to the predicted frequencies and in the majority of cases there was no activity audible at all, because usually it was necessary to search a little on either side of the frequency predicted by the Clerical Grades.

After a few days alarm bells began to ring at GCHQ and the Unions agreed to suspend their action pending negotiations. The offer was then made that from now on Radio Officers would be equated to Executive Officers. There was a lot of antipathy towards this offer, because most Radio Grades had no wish to be associated with Clerical Grades. In HK a joint union meeting was arranged at the China Fleet Club and in an impassioned speech, Roy Ward convinced most people that it would be sheer folly to reject such an offer. He pointed out that we would no longer need to negotiate our pay because we would receive the same award as the Executive Grade, but at the same time we would always be well ahead of them by virtue of our Shift Disturbance Allowance. Furthermore it would ensure our Officer status. Thus our link with the

Executive Officers was established, and it has been very good for the Radio Grades.

The time arrived when decisions had to be made about how we were going to travel back to the UK, and we had three options. The first was to let the department arrange our return, which would most likely be by RAF VC10. The second was to allow the department to book us on a suitable cargo-passenger ship heading for home about the time our tour expired. The third option was the enormously attractive one of staying on an extra couple of months and returning on the luxury P&O liner *Canberra*, which would be travelling via Singapore, Australia and Acapulco - a six-week dream holiday.

The vast majority of our party opted for the dream trip and thought we were mad to turn down such an opportunity. It was very tempting, but it would have meant that after the long summer vacation in Hong Kong the children would have been away from school an extra six weeks, and we thought this was too long a gap, particularly for Stephen and Anne, who would both probably be involved in "A" Levels. We finally decided to request a curtailment of our tour by four to six weeks to allow us time to arrive in UK and settle the children to begin school at the start of the autumn term.

By this time we had heard that we had been allocated Cheadle in Staffordshire, our second choice. The Braithwaites were already living there and would be looking out for suitable houses for us to view on our return. The Morris Oxford had been a good and faithful servant which had never let us down, that is until one day we were heading for Central via Repulse Bay when we broke down. I went to a phone box and rang the Shell Garage in Stanley, which used to service it. About twenty minutes later the old Chinese mechanic drew up, lifted up the bonnet and asked me to try to start it. When there was no response he said straight away "It's your petrol pump".

When the car had been new in Cyprus I had experienced petrol pump trouble on three occasions, and the main agent's solution each time had been to fit a brand new pump. This old genius took the pump out, stripped it down, cleaned it and replaced it, all in the space of about fifteen minutes. The car started first time and was still going strong when we left HK. The charge for him coming out to me and doing the job was HK$25. or about two pounds sterling.

Richard had now started school, so we now had Beverly, Louise and Richard at Stanley Fort and Stephen and Anne at St Georges and there seemed to be an awful lot of school functions to attend. At a sports day at Stanley Fort I was persuaded to enter the fathers' race, which was on an age handicap basis, so as a forty plus I had about ten yards start over some of the young backmarkers. With the tape in sight I thought I was winning in fine style, only to be overtaken in the last few yards by a young army Dad who thundered past me wearing a pair of heavy ammunition boots - so much for handicaps.

Richard had just started to swim and was quite fearless. He used to jump off a raft into deep water, which didn't matter so much when the older ones were with him but he wasn't supposed to swim to the raft on his own. His favourite ploy was to pester Barbara while she was reading her book on the beach. The next time she looked up he'd be there standing up on the raft and he always used to insist that his mother had said he could swim out.

The department offered us a trip home on a cargo-passenger ship in early July, but agreed that before we accepted we could look over the ship and our quarters the next time she called in at HK in late April. The ship was called the MV *Spaarnekerk* and was owned by the giant Dutch Nedlloyd Line. As we approached her in a small launch she was riding at anchor, and she looked pretty big. We were quite impressed with the ship and with our accommodation and accepted our booking.

The last few months were beginning to fly past and there seemed to be so much to do. It was necessary to obtain quotes from local contractors to pack and ship our heavy baggage. Because we already had a piano at home we decided to sell the modern Yamaha piano we had bought for Anne to continue her lessons. It I was advertised in the South China Morning Post for HK$2000 - we had paid five hundred dollars more for it three years previously. The piano was sold just a few minutes after the advert appeared and as with car we had sold, the phone didn't stop ringing about it for days.

We also had to decide on a new car to be purchased mainly with the money and accrued interest from the sale of the prize car. Our final choice was a large Ford estate with automatic transmission, to be picked up when we arrived in the UK. The HK Ford dealer allowed us HK$3500 for our Morris Oxford, which after ten years and 90, 000 miles on the clock still had the original paintwork with little or no rust. The agent told us that such vehicles were much sought after in HK to be used as "Pak pais" (illegal taxis).

Stephen had produced excellent "O" Level results the previous year and was now half way through his "A" Levels. We had managed to find a college in Leek which had promised him a place and was using the same examining board. Anne's "O" Level results turned out to be very good too, with "A" grades in Latin and French, and we had arranged for her to start her "A" Levels at Cheadle Grammar School. This meant it was vital that we found a suitable house within reasonable distance of both places. The HK we were about to leave was very different to the way it had been when we arrived. As the probability of a Chinese takeover had diminished, lots of American and European businesses had returned to the Colony. Rents were beginning to soar and there was a building and construction boom which included the commencement of a Cross Harbour Tunnel to link HK Island with Kowloon, and thanks to the normalisation of relations with China and the Plover Cove scheme there was now a plentiful all-year-round supply of water.

After a few farewell parties it was time to pack our suitcases and prepare to depart. It was sad to be leaving some of our Australian friends, knowing we would probably never see them again. Even among the local admin office and Ariel House staff there were quite a few we had come to know as friends. One in particular was Lee Man, a superb waiter who also doubled as the camp barber.

We booked into the Excelsior Hotel in Kowloon for what we thought would be our last three days, but we had not reckoned with the vagaries of the HK weather during the typhoon season. There was a nasty typhoon directly in the path of our ship as she was heading from Japan to HK, so in the end we had a week's stay in the hotel. The accommodation was first class, but it was inundated with American servicemen on rest and recreation leave from Vietnam. They were often accompanied by lots of local girlfriends, and there were often late-night parties. Most days we had our breakfasts in the YMCA, and we took our main evening meal in the Viking Restaurant, which provided a super carvery-type buffet with a wonderful range of both savouries and desserts.

Our ship finally arrived and was berthed at the Ocean Terminal in Kowloon. After we had embarked and settled in we had a sumptuous meal and our old friends Jack and Iris Hart came aboard to have a few drinks and to see us off. They were in a very happy state by the time they went ashore! Fortunately they were taking a taxi home.

Early next morning we cast off from the Ocean Terminal and about half an hour later we sailed past Little Sai Wan and our voyage home had begun. Homeward bound again. The crew of the *Spaarnekerk* consisted mostly of Dutch officers and a Chinese deck crew. Two of the officers had their wives accompanying them. The deck was well and truly laden with container cargo, including four small cabin cruisers secured to the deck with chains. Adjacent to these boats was the ship's swimming pool. This was a small canvas affair with the times for use shared between passengers and crew. It was rarely used by the crew, but it was a pleasant diversion for us during hot weather.

Some passengers had disembarked in Hong Kong leaving only one passenger aboard with us, a Mrs Pearson, who was probably 1nher sixties. During the Second World War she had been living in Bali and had enjoyed a very adventurous life there. She had worked in the local Resistance against the Japanese and had become the concubine of one of the rulers of Bali. All this had been related in a biographical account called *Revolt in Paradise*. The book had sold well and she had already sold the film rights to Hollywood, but we have never heard of the film being made.

As we sailed through the South China Sea heading for Singapore, our evenings were usually spent in the lounge, either reading or playing Scrabble with Mrs Pearson. Stephen and Anne were always eager to play. By a strange coincidence there was an autographed copy of her book in the ship's library, which I didn't read until after she had disembarked in Singapore. A pity really, for there were lots of questions I would have like to ask her about the book and life at that time.

We were scheduled to spend three days in Singapore and we went ashore for the first time in a launch, just our family and Mrs Pearson, who was leaving the ship to travel on to Bali. As we approached the landing stage Stephen and I just managed to prevent her from falling into the water between the launch and the pier. She was rather tipsy at the time, something we had noticed a few times before on the ship.

Singapore was immensely beautiful and immaculate to our eyes, especially after the squalor of some parts of Hong Kong. This was in no small measure due to their almost Draconian laws regarding litter and spitting. There were strictly enforced penalties for offenders of either a $1,000 fine or six months in jail. It certainly worked!

We spent two days sightseeing when we visited the usual tourist attractions including the Raffles Hotel, the Tiger Balm Gardens and the magnificent Botanical Gardens. Stephen and Anne were very much at odds with us during our stay in Singapore because we would not allow them to buy food or ice cream from any of the numerous vendors. In retrospect we believe we went rather "over the top", but our actions were influenced by a sad event which had occurred only about three months previously. One of our colleagues was returning home with his family on a ship similar to the one we were travelling on. The ship had docked in Thailand for a couple of days and the family had gone ashore and bought some food at a vendor's stall. They returned to the ship and continued their journey, and a few hours afterwards their children a boy of five and an older girl were very ill. Shortly afterwards the boy died and was buried at sea. He was barely five years old and had been in the same class as Richard at Stanley Fort school. His sister made a good recovery. It was difficult to try and imagine the agony of that family continuing the journey home without their little boy, or the heartache of the grandparents looking forward to seeing him after three years.

In the early hours of the morning, just before we left Singapore, I had to get up to go to the toilet. Before I climbed back into bed I glanced through our porthole curtains just as a sampan drew up out of the mist and stopped at the side of our ship. A crew member who I later found out was the bosun leaned over and picked up what appeared to be a large canvas bag, which was passed to another crew member. To this day I am convinced that this was a consignment of drugs. I considered informing Customs when we docked in Holland, but my nerve failed me at the last moment.

We had been joined at Singapore by a Scot with his Eurasian wife and their children, a girl and a boy. They had also just completed a three-year tour but were heading for Holland to visit the wife's relations. At first they kept themselves very much to themselves, but they became quite friendly during the latter part of the voyage.

After leaving Singapore we sailed through the Straits of Malacca and were impressed with the beautiful scenery on either side of us. Some of the islands looked like tropical paradises. Just as we entered the Indian Ocean a large school of porpoises appeared in front of the ship and cavorted around us for several miles. At this point we knew we had the best part of another four weeks of shipboard life, but we had really begun to relax and enjoy it.

During our time aboard we had to be very careful with Louise and protect her from the sun as much as possible as she came out in lots of what looked like blisters, and though she didn't complain a lot we knew she wasn't her normal self. When we had only been in Hong Kong a few months Louise was having problems with a urinary tract infection which, according to the doctor in Hong Kong, had been precipitated by not having antibiotics after a bout of chickenpox not long before we left England. She had suffered intermittently throughout our stay and we had been supplied with sufficient medication to see her through the voyage. What we hadn't realised was that these blister-like lesions were a side effect of the strong antibiotics.

Our shipboard routine as we sailed south west across the Indian Ocean was pleasantly varied. We played lots of table tennis on deck, along with other deck sports, plus plenty of swimming in our canvas pool. There was plenty of reading material in the ship's library and all these activities were interspersed with wonderful menus of every type imaginable.

Travelling across a vast ocean makes one realise just how small and insignificant we humans are. The only life we saw was a small Indian fishing vessel, on our sixth day. As we headed towards Cape Town we must have skirted the Seychelles, because we received wonderful reception from their two commercial radio stations for at least two days. A few days after this we began to pick up other South African stations as we proceeded ever closer to Cape Town.

Because our schedule was already two days behind schedule after the typhoon delay, we were informed in advance that we would not be docking at Cape Town. We were all bitterly disappointed, but there was nothing we could do about it. The ship was running short on soft drinks and a few other items, so the local agent had arranged that a pilot launch would come out to us and bring what was required along with mail for the crew.

As Table Mountain came into view the weather began to deteriorate and we were warned to expect very rough seas, which duly materialised as we reached the area where the Indian and Atlantic Oceans merge. Then we began to appreciate why sailors in previous centuries had named it the "Cape of Good Hope".

We were all looking out towards Cape Town, trying to spot the launch which was supposed to be approaching us. A few minutes later we saw a small boat come up on the crest of a huge wave and then almost immediately disappear as it dipped into the next trough. Stephen and I were sharing a pair of binoculars at the same time as we were recording the events on our cine camera.

As the launch came closer and tried to come alongside we failed to see how any transfer could take place with these huge rolling waves. The Chief Officer was standing by our side on the deck and was in communication with the launch by radio. After two abortive attempts he decided they would have one more try before abandoning the effort. This time it was successful and the large canvas holdall was winched aboard and we continued our journey round the Cape.

Table Mountain and Cape Town slowly faded into the distance and the seas slowly began to subside. Barbara had felt a little queasy in the rough seas, but no one else had any problems. So began a pleasant cruise heading north along the West Coast of Africa.

During our trip we had observed one of the crew cutting other crew members' hair out on the deck. Stephen's hair was blond and long, very fashionable at the time, but he needed it trimming. One of the ship's officers assured us that the barber cut all the officers' hair too and they all looked very well groomed. Stephen went along and sat in the barber's chair. After he had been in the chair a few minutes, Barbara and I went to have a look to see how things were progressing. We were appalled as we watched the barber put the finishing touches to what could only be described as a basin crop. We fled to our cabin, locked the door and dissolved into hysterical laughter on our beds. Five minutes later Stephen was banging on our cabin door, demanding that we open up and view the atrocities which had been perpetrated on his hair.

Before dinner that evening we managed to have a word with the Chief Officer and cautioned him that if he or any of his fellow officers made any comment about Stephen's hair at dinner we would never forgive them. Stephen had told us that he would not be coming down for dinner that evening, but in the end his love of food prevailed and he appeared. Fortunately no one said a word.

About a week later we were just a few miles off Dakar when the ship's engines suddenly stopped and a strong sense of "deja vu" overtook us as the *Spaarnekerk* gradually lost way, just as the *Sycamore* had on our way home from Cyprus some twelve years previously. Fortunately this time the Atlantic was almost a millpond. The purser came along and informed us that it had been necessary to stop the engines immediately to prevent irreparable damage taking place and that it would take several hours to fix. He then suggested that Stephen and I might like to do a spot of deep sea fishing, and provided us with a couple of long lines, some lead weights, hooks and some large pieces of meat from the galley.

This was right up Stephen's alley, being a keen

fisherman, so we baited our hooks and cast out from the stern of the ship. Two hours later we hadn't had a single bite, and all of a sudden the ship's engines began and the ship started to move. We had great difficulty reeling in our lines as the ship gathered speed, and we both had burns on our palms trying to reel in as fast as possible.

We decided to have our farewell celebration dinner as we crossed the Bay of Biscay, even though the voyage still had two or three days to go. Ours had been a trip which had produced so many wonderful meals. Our farewell dinner surpassed all the previous ones, with all sorts of wonderful dishes and champagne in abundance. Beverly normally had her evening meal early with Richard and Louise, but this night we allowed her to stay up and dress up and have her meal with us, which she thought was wonderful!

Soon after this we all went up on deck to the sound of sirens and foghorns blaring as one of the *Spaarnekerk*'s sister ships passed within a hundred yards of us, on her way to the Far East.

Two days later we were threading our way through the busy English Channel and heading for Antwerp in Belgium. It was good to be ashore again after such a long spell at sea. Antwerp appeared to be a mixture of the old European World and the new modern trends, and we spent an interesting day just browsing around. Then it was back on board for the last part of our shipboard journey.

This was just a short run back to the sea and then a

little further up the coast to Rotterdam. Because the Captain had told us it might be another fortnight before the ship docked in the UK, passages had been arranged for us on the overnight ferry from the Hook of Holland to Hull. This was very convenient for us, because it meant we had only a short journey from Hull to Cleethorpes.

Very soon we were saying our goodbyes to the crew members we had come to know quite well in the past few weeks, then it was two taxis for us and our luggage as we headed for the overnight ferry. The ferry was called the *Norlander* and the accommodation was excellent, but Barbara was rather disconcerted that we appeared to be right down in the bowels of the ship in a cabin without a porthole, which didn't help her claustrophobia. The ship did however have a first-class air conditioning system, which helped to alleviate her closed-in feeling.

We all had a good night's sleep and after a good breakfast it was time to dock at Hull. As we docked my mind went back to the time 23 years before when I had embarked on a rather nauseous journey from Hull to Cuxhaven. Hull to Cleethorpes was the shortest of any homecoming trip so far, a mere hour and a half via the Humber ferry and then the train from New Holland to Cleethorpes.

It was good to be back in England and see our families and friends once again. One of the first things we had to do was arrange for Louise to see a doctor, who told us that her blister lesions were an adverse reaction to her antibiotics. According to her path lab tests they had still not succeeded in clearing up her infection. A different type was prescribed, and after a few weeks she was given a clean bill of health. We were warned however to be always on the alert for a return of the problem.

Once again it was necessary to visit our new station as soon as possible to find a suitable house. Stephen had a temporary job helping out at a local holiday camp run by my brother-in-law Peter Munnings and his wife, my sister Thora. Anne had managed to find a holiday job at one of the local fish processing factories. Beverly, Louise and Richard went to stay with John (Barbara's brother) and his wife Beverly who lived on the outskirts of Leicester. The children loved Bev and John and their young daughter Emma and were happy to go with them.

We now had a new Ford estate car and were experiencing no problems with the joys of automatic transmission, a particular boon when in heavy traffic. It was arranged that we should stay with Bernard and Edith, who lived in Blythe Bridge, a village about four miles away from our new station at Cheadle in Staffordshire. It was the first time we had seen them since the death of Catherine in Cyprus some four years before, and it was obvious that the loss had profoundly affected them both, but especially Edith.

After looking at lots of houses we decided to make an offer on a house which had been up for auction a few weeks before but had been withdrawn when it had failed to reach its reserve price of £8,000. We then returned to Cleethorpes to await developments. Two days later the estate agent rang us to say that if we increased our offer by another £250 the house was ours, and we agreed straight away. Thanks to our friendly solicitor Michael Lewis we completed within four weeks, and another new era in our lives began.

The site of my new workplace was Woodhead Hall, Cheadle, a country mansion very similar to Beaumanor, the difference being that our work now took place in rooms specially adapted or built on to the house itself, whereas at Beaumanor our work was conducted in a series of outbuildings. There was already a sprinkling of ex-Beaumanor staff at Cheadle, some of whom had remained at Loughborough until the actual operational closing of the station, leaving behind our old friend Frank Cameron to oversee the handing over of the property to the new owners, Leicestershire education Authority.

The bulk of the station personnel at Cheadle were ex-Air Ministry staff. Les and Ina Dowsett lived at Alton, only a couple of miles away, while Gerald and Mary lived in Blythe Bridge, only a short distance from our house in Orchard Rise. Gerald was on the same watch as me, so we shared cars travelling to and from work.

We had bought a second-hand scooter for Stephen to travel to and from college at Leek, but there was a school bus to enable Anne to travel to and from school in Cheadle. Beverly had started at Blythe Bridge High

School and Louise and Richard attended Marsh Primary, which was very close to Beverly's school. At first Richard didn't take to his new school, though, he had been very happy during his first few months at his infant school in Hong Kong. During the first couple of weeks he was often allowed to go into Louise's class and sit next to her, and after a while he seemed to be much happier.

We had promised that as soon as we were settled in our house we would let the children have a puppy, and we decided that this time we would have a Cairn Terrier, who we named Mandy. She was the smallest in the litter but looked so appealing that we were all unanimous in our choice. By the time we reached home with her she seemed to have already bonded with the children in the back of the car.

When we had only been in Blythe Bridge about six weeks, a minor disaster occurred. I had just dropped the children off at school and was returning home on the A50, which in those days ran through the village main street. I had to pull up when the line of traffic in front of me halted. As I did so there was a horrible crunch in the back of the car and I was shunted almost into the car in front of me. I jumped out in a furious mood, to be confronted by a young policeman, who kept saying repeatedly "I'm so sorry sir but my brakes failed and I can see that your estate is brand new too!"

I was so disarmed by his obvious genuine contrition that I offered to run him into Hanley, as his car was a virtual write off and he was due to appear in court as a witness in less than an hour. He refused my offer, as we were just opposite the Blythe Bridge police station, and they said transport would be provided to get him there in time. The insurance side was quickly settled because we both had the same insurance company.

There was quite an interesting range of cover at Cheadle, which called for various operating skills and expertise. Most of the ex-Beaumanor people were extremely versatile and so were very welcome additions to a station whose own people were generally not so versatile. The OIC (Officer in Charge) was called McLennon, known as Mac, and he was an unusual character for a high-ranking civil servant. Normal procedure on transfer to a new station was for an interview within the first few days with the OIC, who introduced himself and gave a station brief and welcome to the newcomers. Mac never adhered to this procedure and a few months after I joined the station it backfired on him. A party of high-ranking GCHQ visitors were on a conducted tour around the various set rooms accompanied by Mac, Ron Hart (Senior Operations Officer) and our own Bernard Braithwaite, who was now Operations Officer. They came into a set room which was being supervised by our own Les Dowsett, who by this time had been at Cheadle for about nine months. Ron and Bernard were explaining the intricacies of the operational side while Mac tagged along at the rear of the party. Les said to Mac, "Don't I know you?" There was no reply from Mac. A couple of minutes later Les said, "I definitely know you!" Mac then hissed back at him, "For Christ's sake shut up man! I'm your OIC." The whole station reverberated with laughter over this incident.

Stoke on Trent in 1970 was not a very prepossessing area, although a clean up had begun in some parts. There were now quite a few smokeless zones and lots of the pottery kilns had converted to electricity, but pottery and coal mining remained the main local industries. The locals were a generous, warm-hearted and friendly lot, though with a tendency to want to know everyone's business. We had lots of visitors that first year from both our families and they were all impressed with our new abode and all it had to offer, which made it so ideal for a family such as ours. There were two garages, one integral and the other adjoining a large concrete area at the side of the house in front of the garden. Between the integral garage and the utility room was a built-on large dog kennel in which Mandy was quite happy to sleep at night. There was a small study between the lounge and the dining room, just big enough to hold a single bed, so Stephen claimed this room as his own (shades of his Amah's room in HK.) This left four upstairs bedrooms for the rest of us, and it was easy to double up when we had visitors.

Our first winter produced quite a lot of snow, with the first heavy fall as early as Boxing Day. Situated as we were at the top of Orchard Rise, it was sometimes difficult garaging the car coming up the slope at night, but the children loved the snow, as did Mandy. A greenhouse had been purchased and erected. We lined it with polythene, put in a small heater and started off quite a few seed trays, including tomatoes, cucumbers and various annuals. It was a good summer and we had a bumper crop of tomatoes and cucumbers, plus plenty of annuals to plant out in the garden.

Bill was now very much an invalid with chronic emphysema, and hadn't worked for several years other than a short spell as a deckchair attendant on the sea front at Cleethorpes. This made life very difficult for Jean with two teenage children and her home help job as her only source of income. When Bill deteriorated he was admitted to hospital in Sheffield and we travelled several times from Blythe Bridge to see him. He was always remarkably cheerful and was trying to smoke whenever he had the opportunity, strictly against doctor's orders. Within a few weeks he was dead.

Only about six months later Jean met Norman at a dancing class, which she was attending to try and start living a little again. Very soon afterwards they married. Norman and Ethel were not very happy about it, but it was Jean's life and she was well old enough to make her own decisions. In fact it was to prove a very wise choice.

Stephen's ex-Hong Kong friend came over from Scarborough and persuaded him that food technology was the up-and-coming career to follow, and together they applied for Reading University. Unfortunately

Mark didn't manage the necessary "A" Levels, which meant that Stephen went alone on a course he wasn't too sure about. While he was awaiting his "A" Level results, he went down to Kent with some college friends, fruit picking. He returned six weeks later looking very lean and tanned, and from the way he ate on his return it seemed as if he hadn't eaten for six weeks.

Norman and Ethel visited us from time to time, usually coinciding with a race meeting at nearby Uttoxeter. Norman loved his day out at the races and was soon well known in our local pubs, enjoying his darts and dominoes. We decided that Mandy should have just one litter of pups, so we took her to a dog breeder in Biddulph to have her mated. She produced just two pups, a dog we named Bruno and a bitch we named Suzy. They were beautiful pups and raising them was made relatively easy with the aid of our large indoor kennel which we could open out into the garden. The children were heartbroken when the pups were weaned and had to go. Bruno was sold, but Suzy had won Norman's heart, so we were happy to let him have her – that way we wouldn't really lose touch with her.

We hadn't been to Grimsby more than a few months when word came that Norman had seen my mother, and that she looked terrible. a couple of weeks later we went over, and were appalled at her appearance and loss of weight. Mum told me she had visited the doctor a couple of times and he had said it was sciatica. I asked Thora to see that Mum went for a thorough check-up and she went with her very soon after. The next thing we knew Mum had been admitted to hospital, but no one seemed to know what was wrong. I phoned the hospital and managed to speak to the doctor who was dealing with her. He told me that they had discovered that Mum had a massive stone in one of her kidneys but they were hopeful that if the other one was unaffected she would be able to live a normal life after it was removed.

We went to see her in hospital the next day, and though she looked awful she told us she was now feeling much better because she had been convinced she was suffering from cancer. I arranged leave so that we could go and see her as soon as she had had her operation, but only two days later I was called to the office at work to speak to Barbara. I knew it was serious as she never phoned me at work. Apparently my brother Terry had phoned to say that Mum had been operated on but there were serious complications, and it was now touch and go.

It took me about half an hour to get home, and I had only just arrived when Terry phoned again in great distress. He had just seen Mum and told me there was no way she could survive. He was right. We were told that Mum had died on the operating table. In her frail and weakened condition she just wasn't strong enough. Ironically, when the stone was removed her other kidney was fine.

We were all very naturally upset, but for me the realisation didn't really sink in until the day of her funeral. During the church service, as the 23rd psalm to the tune Crimond began, it hit me that my beloved Mum was gone for ever, and I cried as I have never cried in my life before. I was utterly devastated and bereft. I was aware that the rest of our family were feeling the same way too and I was grateful that I had Barbara by my side.

This was a black time for me and I didn't think of turning to the Lord for comfort. We used to attend St Peter's Church at Forsbrook intermittently when I had a clear Sunday, but it was typical of some Anglican churches and we were not made to feel particularly welcome during our infrequent visits. Richard and Louise had now transferred to a new primary school which had just opened in Grindley Lane, only about five minutes' walk from our house. This was great for us, as it meant we no longer had to negotiate the dreaded A50 to take them to school. One day we had a call from school to say that Richard had fallen in the school playground and it seemed serious. Were we available to take him to hospital?

It was obvious to us on arrival that he had broken his arm, and every little bump in the road made him cry out with pain while we were taking him to the hospital. As he was in a lot of pain he was attended to straight away and was soon taken to theatre. Some time later the doctor came to see us to inform us that it was a bad break and they had been unable to set it properly as they couldn't keep him under the anaesthetic any longer. We were assured that he would be kept comfortable and free from pain and advised to return the next morning.

When we arrived the next day he had already been to theatre and was sitting up in bed looking quite cheerful and boasting that he had been sick no fewer than 26 times. The next few weeks were purgatory, trying to stop Richard indulging in any activities which could put his arm at risk. When the plaster was removed his arm was quite misshapen, and the specialist said it would probably never regain its old shape - but he was wrong and eventually it did.

Only about three months after my mum had died, Barbara's mum came to stay with us for a few days, leaving Norman back in Cleethorpes running his shop. John (Barbara's brother) was working for Sainsbury's as a produce display manager and travelling around various branches. This particular day he was at a branch near us and had arranged to call and pick Ethel up from our house and take her to spend a few days with them at Long Buckby. Norma and Royston also now lived in the same village with their children Tina and Tracy, so with Emma and Jason there too it meant she could see both families.

Ethel had only been there a few days when news came that Norman had suffered a stroke and she had to return home immediately. A few days later when Barbara and I visited him in hospital he managed to tell us, in spite of his badly affected speech, what a great day he had enjoyed before it happened, playing lawn bowls in the afternoon, going home and cooking himself a big fry-up before going to his club in the evening for a drink and a game of snooker and darts.

Just three weeks after his stroke, Norman was dead. Though we were half prepared, knowing it was a critical time, we were all very sad and down when it did happen. Norman was much loved by his family, friends and customers. He had a great rapport with his grandchildren and in particular with Richard. They always had jokes to tell each other.

Norman's demise brought an immediate problem about what to do about the shop, which was a going concern. Jean and Pamela ran it for a short while on a half-day basis. I took a few days' leave and helped out for a while, but after a few weeks we decided to close it down until it could be sold.

In September 1972 there was a call for volunteers to attend a linguist course, subject to passing an aptitude test at Cheltenham. There were two courses available, a twelve-month one and a four-month one. Both Les Dowsett and I were interested in the long course, probably because we had regaled him on the delights of Hong Kong. Our old friend Phil Webb, who had only just returned from HK as a short course linguist, fancied another spell, this time as a long course man. We three travelled together in my car to Cheltenham. I missed the turn off the M6 at Junction 8 and this put another hour on our journey. We had all booked in to the same hotel for the night so that we would be refreshed ready for our test the next morning. I remember Phil took us to a Chinese restaurant he knew, where we had a fabulous meal at a very reasonable price.

About a week later we had our test results. Phil was accepted for the long course, but Les and I were offered the short course, which we declined. In my case it was because I knew I would be returning to Hong Kong fairly soon because of my position on the "Overseas List", but Les was now far more interested in his old love, Cyprus.

Because of computerisation another prerequisite for Radio Officers going to HK was the necessity to be accomplished keyboard operators. This involved another six-week course at Bletchley Park to ascertain typing and special morse skills. I found the course relatively easy, but for some people it was quite stressful. It was especially so for my colleague, who travelled with me to and from Bletchley every weekend. He was very upset when he failed to reach the standard required and his posting was subsequently cancelled.

Anne had enrolled for an interpreter/translator course at Solihull, a two-year course with a mid-course six weeks in France. We managed to find her what we thought were reasonable lodgings with a middle-aged lady though Anne and her friend eventually moved into a flat together.

At the end of Stephen's first year at university he was having problems with one part of his course, mainly because he hadn't taken Physics up to "A" level standard. His tutors were convinced that he could make up the shortfall before Christmas and allowed him to commence his second year studies.

After Norman died Ethel decided that she couldn't cope with a puppy, so we brought Suzy back and found her a home with Les and Ina in Alton. It was about this time that we were informed that we were scheduled to return to Hong Kong in June 1973. We had reservations about going, but decided we would be better able to support Stephen and Anne's education if we went and that the other children would be receiving good schooling in HK. Ethel insisted that we should go, and said she was hoping to come out and visit us as she had done in Cyprus.

One weekend Stephen brought a girl called Pamela Beardsley over to see us. She was at a teacher training college near him and they seemed very suited and wrapped up in each other. Pam came to stay with us over the Christmas period and she and Anne took temporary jobs at Kwik Save to earn some money for Christmas.

Stephen found that he hadn't managed to pass the part he had failed after all, so it seemed best that he left university. He managed to find a temporary job in Southampton and travelled back most weekends to see Pam, staying overnight with university friends. Barbara and I didn't think Pam was very good for Stephen's studies, but it was obvious to us that they were very serious about each other.

CHAPTER 10

HONG KONG – SECOND INNINGS

As Easter approached we were beginning to make tentative arrangements for our next trip abroad. Stephen and Pam had both applied to join the Hong Kong Police, but were not accepted. Pam only had one term before she completed her teacher training, and Stephen was still working at Southampton.

Our preparations, heavy baggage etc were almost complete by the end of May when things began to go wrong. My dad and my mum's sister Aunt Ethel were staying with us when Barbara began feeling unwell. She was in such severe pain I had to call our GP, Dr Toh, to visit her. He thought it was probably a kidney problem and prescribed some painkillers and some other appropriate medication. He also advocated drinking lots of liquids. The pain was acute but intermittent, and Barbara had great difficulty in putting on a brave face to say goodbye to Dad and Aunt Ethel when I took them to the station.

That same night I had to call the doctor out again, but once more, by the time the doctor arrived the acute writhing in agony had subsided. After a few days of this our doctor said that the next time it occurred we should take her straight to Accident and Emergency at North Staffs Hospital, because otherwise it could take a couple of weeks or more for him to obtain a referral to see a specialist.

Very soon after this Barbara was in so much pain I drove her to hospital in her nightie, dressing gown and slippers, and she was admitted immediately for observation and a series of tests. Some few days later it was established that she had a kidney stone. They hoped surgery would not be necessary, and that provided she continued to drink the copious amounts of water and other approved liquids she should pass the stone naturally. Her liquid input and output were measured meticulously, but since she had been admitted the intense pain had not returned.

Then on a Friday evening when I had just returned from visiting Barbara, the phone rang and it was Stephen. I immediately sensed that something was amiss and asked him what was wrong. He replied in a choked voice, "It's Pam, she's dead!"

It seemed unbelievable, and I didn't know what to say to try and comfort him. It seemed that Pam had been on a recreational study looking for fossils at Beachy Head while awaiting the results of her teacher training exams. It wasn't clear whether Pam or her friend went over the edge first as it crumbled, but one tried to save the other and they both went over. Pam's friend landed on top of her and sustained only minor injuries, but Pam was dead. The local police had met Stephen at the bus station as he arrived from Southampton and told him the terrible news, and it was only a few minutes after this that he rang me. I remember trotting out to him a useless cliché about God helping him to get over this terrible tragedy, and he replied, "What God?"

The next morning I had the task of going to the hospital and telling Barbara the news. Barbara said that as soon as I entered the ward she knew something was very wrong by the look on my face. She thought it was bad news about her latest test results and had great difficulty in taking in what I had to say. Her first concern was for Pam's parents and Stephen. Unfortunately relations between Pam and her parents had been at a low ebb for some time, for reasons which entirely defeated us to try and understand.

The following Monday Barbara was allowed home for complete bed rest and with instructions to carry on drinking enormous quantities of liquids, including pearl barley water, which I prepared in our old pressure cooker and decanted into jugs, adding a little squash to flavour it. The hospital also insisted that her output be closely monitored to see if and when the stone was passed. A week later Barbara passed her stone without a lot of discomfort and it ultimately finished up with a collection of similar objects in Dr Toh's surgery.

The next day Stephen arrived home. He had left his job and hitch-hiked home ready to go to Pam's funeral in her home village near Derby. After the funeral he came home and shut himself in his room, eating very little, just lying on his bed listening to records. This went on for several days.

During this time he opened a new toothbrush by biting open the cellophane wrapper and in doing so bit the inside of his mouth. It soon developed into a terrible mouth infection, so I took him to see our dentist, Charles Toh (the son of our doctor), who immediately referred him to his father, who prescribed antibiotics and what we presumed were tranquillisers, which we had to keep and give him the prescribed dose. After a few days his infection cleared up and he was able to start eating again and became less withdrawn.

Pam's death had affected us all, including Bev, Louise and Richard, but particularly Anne, who had received a letter from Pam posted on the day she died. Back at work I was asked to let them know immediately Barbara was cleared to travel and complete a three-year tour in Hong Kong.

Then there was yet another turn of events. I was called into Admin and told that because of the chronic housing shortage in the colony it might well be necessary to spend several months in a hotel before suitable accommodation became available. Because of this I was given the option of postponing our tour until the situation improved. When I conveyed this news to

Barbara I fully expected her to say we should postpone, but I was wrong. Even though she was still recovering from her kidney problems, she considered that with our heavy baggage already packed we were in limbo, so the sooner we departed the better.

By this time Stephen had recovered enough to take the Civil Service entrance exam for Executive Officers. Unfortunately he stipulated that the only branch he was interested in was GCHQ Cheltenham. As we needed to know as soon as possible in view of our impending departure, I managed through the good offices of our OIC to ascertain that Stephen had not been successful because of his GCHQ-only proviso. Stephen then said that what he would really like to do was to apply for teacher training, to which we readily agreed. He had no problems finding a suitable college to start in September.

When Barbara saw the consultant he pronounced her fit to travel and to complete a three-year tour, assuring us that if there should be any further trouble there were plenty of good kidney men in Hong Kong. I had no sooner informed our admin office that Barbara was fit than we had a phone call telling us we were booked on a flight in two weeks' time.

The next few days were really hectic, with so many last-minute arrangements to be made. Richard and Louise were quite looking forward to returning, but Beverly was very much against the move, as it meant leaving her school and friends, plus in particular a boyfriend. At fourteen she was at a very vulnerable age, but she accepted that the die was cast and we had to go. We decided to rent our house unfurnished to a tenant recommended by one of our local estate agents, namely Louis Taylor, a decision we were later to regret.

Jean and Norman had offered to take Mandy as a companion to their Cairn, Trixie, while we were abroad. Les and Ina had offered to give Stephen a home for a few weeks, and he was then going to stay with one of his old friends from Hong Kong, Mike Davis in Cardiff, until the term began at teacher training. We felt terrible when we left him with Les and Ina just before we departed for our last visit to say our goodbyes at Grimsby and Cleethorpes, but we were committed to going and life had to go on. It was just as hard saying farewell to Barbara's mum and my dad, knowing they had both just been bereaved.

In what seemed no time at all we were on our way to Brize Norton, this time in our own estate car, as I had found a firm who were only too happy to collect my car and ship it out to Hong Kong. After the usual RAF Transport Command formalities we were shown to our overnight accommodation and after an early breakfast we were aboard our VC10 and winging our way towards HK once again. Our first stop was to be Akrotiri in Cyprus, where we hoped to see John and Jose Mortby for a brief encounter. Because of shift problems they couldn't make it, but they called us on the phone and we had a good chat before we took off again.

Our next stop was Diego Garcia, an even tinier island than Gan. This was a British Protectorate but was jointly leased by US. Forces. After only a short stay we were airborne once again, with Hong Kong as our next scheduled stop. On this trip we only had Beverly, Louise and Richard with us, and at first they were taking the trip in their stride. While we were flying over Vietnam, however, we began to encounter turbulence, and Beverly began to feel very sick, so I moved into the seat next to her. I was always uneasy overflying Vietnam, and though we were in an international air corridor, looking down and seeing the flashes from the opposing Vietnam and US artillery didn't help.

As we flew in over the harbour at Hong Kong, the burnt-out wreck of the QE2 was clearly visible. Once again the high-rise tenement flats of Kowloon appeared to be almost touching our landing wheels as we dropped down to the Kai Tak runway. On this arrival there were no friendly faces we knew waiting to greet us, just an admin rep with some official transport to the Sunning House Hotel.

History was however repeating itself, as typhoon signals were hoisted and it was forecast that there could well be a direct hit on the Colony within the next 48 hours. The next morning I listened on the local radio for any weather news but didn't hear anything, so I went downstairs and waited outside the hotel with John Wood (another recent arrival) for our official transport. It was blowing quite hard with intermittent torrential rain.

After waiting about half an hour we were just about to call it a day and go back inside when a car drew up and someone shouted at us to get in. This was my introduction to Jock Kane, later to become infamous for his whistle blowing book and TV interviews on Little Sai Wan.

When we arrived at the station the police on the gate told us that the admin offices were all closed and that there was only a skeleton staff on duty because the typhoon was really battering HK and we had missed the radio announcements telling everyone to stay indoors and not to travel. We were then marooned in Ariel House until early evening, when conditions eased, and we were given official transport back to Sunning House.

Regardless of the forecast of a long stay in the hotel, we were determined to find accommodation as soon as possible, so most of my time away from work was spent checking out any possible flats, which had to be within our rent allowance but. which appeared to be generous but was not adequate for most decent flats. The allowance was supposed to be increased, but no one was quite sure just when this would be. Just a couple of weeks into our hotel stay we found a beautiful flat in mid levels (about half way up to the Peak area). It had magnificent views of the harbour and the landlord was happy to lease it to us for three years at a rent only slightly higher than the current maximum allowance - we agreed that we would pay the extra out of our own pockets.

The procedure was that the Lands Officer would inspect the flat and make sure the rent was reasonable, but after a week he hadn't been to inspect it and the flat was snapped up by someone else. It was galling, because we now faced the prospect of several months in the hotel.

One day Barbara and I were viewing a new block of flats which were almost completed on a site on Wongneichong Gap Road. Some of them were almost ready for occupation. The site foreman directed us to a lift and indicated that there were several flats to view on the fourth floor. It was early evening and most of the workers had finished for the day. Much against Barbara's better judgement (she hates confined spaces) we got into the lift along with a Chinese workman who pressed the button for the fourth floor. The lift stopped at the fourth, but the door refused to open. There was no alarm button and there was nothing we could do, so we pressed the button to return us to the ground floor, where once again the door refused to open.

By this time Barbara was really distressed and the site of her recent kidney stone was giving her excruciating pain. I was trying to calm her. We tried several floors, but the lift door just wouldn't activate, and we had now been in the lift for about half an hour. The local workman was as helpless as we were, and the language barrier didn't help.

Just when we were beginning to despair, someone called the lift up to the fifth floor, and this time the door opened to a group of workmen just finishing for the day. We quickly got out and our fellow prisoner explained in Cantonese about the lift door. We then all walked down the stairs - no one would risk the lift!

Barbara had several days of discomfort after that incident and of course she will have nothing to do with lifts to this day.

After only six weeks in the hotel we managed to find a suitable flat also in Wongneichong Gap Road, overlooking the racecourse at Happy Valley with views across the harbour to Kai Tak airport. It was in a small two-storey block of eight flats and we were on the second floor. It was built on the old colonial style, not particularly luxuriously appointed but with two bathrooms, three toilets, a good sized lounge and three fairly large bedrooms, so it suited us fine. Once we had unpacked our heavy baggage and installed our hired furniture, Barbara soon had it looking like our home. Furthermore we had moved in just in time for the start of the new school term.

There had been quite a lot going on in HK during our three-year absence, the most notable event being probably the completion of the Cross Harbour Tunnel which entered the harbour close to the China Fleet Club and emerged in Kowloon, not far from the Peninsula hotel. It was a great time-saver for a modest amount toll. It also meant that children attending St George's School remained on their buses all the way to school, cutting their travelling time by a considerable amount.

Work had also begun on the Mass Transit Railway System, a massive project which would help to alleviate the problems of local people travelling in and around the Colony but in particular to and from their work. Thanks to a very hard-working fundraising committee at Little Sai Wan, a new swimming pool had been built next to Ariel House, adding to the other attractions of tennis, football and cricket played on the beautiful big grassed reclamation area. Our children were particularly impressed with the swimming pool and made frequent trips during our stay in the hotel.

Another phenomenon was the advent of the Public Light Buses, a wonderful, readily available source of additional public transport which would stop and pick up or drop off passengers at any point on their route. They carried a maximum of twelve passengers, no standing passengers were permitted and the fares were incredibly low, especially during off peak periods. Within a few weeks of arriving back in HK I was Shanghai'd (pardon the pun) into taking over as secretary of the LSW Dolphins Swimming Club, a very thriving and popular concern with about a hundred members with ages ranging from five to 16 years. There were regular training sessions three times a week run by Jack Rose and Peter Woolley, another old friend from Cyprus. Peter's son Paul had recently won the HK 15 and under 100 metres freestyle and was an all-round swimmer of great potential, as was Alan Wood, the son of John Wood. There were quite a number of up and coming young swimmers in the club, which seemed to augur well for future competitive galas.

Barbara and I had decided we would both take up golf on this tour, but instead Barbara thought she would like to give tennis a try, though she had never played the game before and some people thought that the age of forty was rather late to start. I spent as much time as I could with her just knocking the balls back and forth, but she spent many hours alone on the court with a bucket of balls practising her serve. All this dedication paid off, as after a couple of months we were able to have a reasonable game of mixed doubles at the Stanley Club with our old friends Charles and Amy Ginn. Barbara was a fast learner and soon we were beating our opponents on a regular basis and Barbara was able to graduate to club tennis at LSW.

Anne came out to us for Christmas and looked really well, plumper than we had ever seen her. She told us she had enjoyed her summer in France but that she had stayed on a few weeks longer after she met some people from an evangelical group and had been going door to door selling bibles. This had improved her French far more than her studies at the French College.

It was wonderful weather that Christmas and when we picnicked at Big Wave Bay the temperature was 29 degrees. unfortunately Anne had not put enough sun oil on and with her pale skin and colouring was very uncomfortable for the next few days.

In January 1974 I was working an evening shift

when the Duty Officer informed me that a signal had just arrived saying that my father had passed away. This was on the Tuesday and they were trying to arrange a flight home for me for the funeral on the Friday. I was naturally upset, but it wasn't anything like the scale of emotion my mother's death had triggered off.

There was no flight available for me until the Friday, which would have meant missing the funeral, so after a long talk to my sister Thora on the phone we decided that it just wasn't worth all that travelling and that she would arrange for Stephen and Anne to represent us on the day.

Dad had recently slipped on the ice and had broken ribs and a fractured pelvis, but he had made an excellent recovery for someone in their eightieth year. Only a few days before we had received two letters from him in which he said all was well and that he wasn't being morbid but he was just looking forward to joining mum. Early in 74 I was asked to join a PRO (TA) Section headed by an Australian Squadron Leader, John Gavey, with a mixed staff of Australian Air Force and GCHQ personnel which included Denis Compton EO and Bill Smith CO, both from Cheltenham. There were also two other Radio Officers, namely John Stuckey, a pleasant young man from Taunton and fiery but with a heart of gold, and Jack McCoull, ex Beaumanor, a good all-round sportsman and a golfing fanatic who spent most of his spare time at the Royal Hong Kong Golf Club at Fanling in the New Territories.

My work was extremely interesting and covered an area for which I was solely responsible, and I enjoyed it. There was just one drawback - when I wasn't there the work wasn't done, so after weekends or leave I had to work doubly hard to catch up.

There were advantages. John Gavey was a good Head of Section to work for and during school holidays he had no objection to me arranging my hours around the Dolphins' swimming training, in which I had now become very involved. Beverly, Louise and Richard were all excellent swimmers and were improving all the time. As a result of my contacts with other swimming clubs and arranging galas and matches I found myself serving on the HK Age Group Committee, arranging competitions open to all the youth of HK. I was also Chairman of the LSW Tennis Club and played league tennis for the first team.

Barbara had really acquired the tennis bug and spent every spare moment improving her game. When she beat Anne Amery in the first round of our club championships I felt she had arrived in our small tennis sphere. Most of our weekends and holidays were now spent at LSW , usually playing tennis or swimming or swimming training. The children had developed their own circle of friends and most of them spent their days off in the same pursuits.

On Sundays we always attended the Garrison Church at Stanley Fort before going on to our recreation at LSW . There was always of good food on offer at Ariel House Restaurant and the children had our permission to sign their Ariel House chits (bills) using our bar number. At the end of each month we received our account with all the signed chits returned, and it was surprising how many bar snacks and chocolate bars had been purchased for friends.

One Saturday morning we were shopping in Stanley. It was the day of the seasonal opening of the swimming pool, and we were heading there after we had completed our shopping. We were walking along Main Street when we spotted Bob Davis and his wife (Stephen's friend Mike's parents). We waved a greeting to each other and then noticed another man who looked very familiar walking along a few paces behind them. He gave us a big beaming smile. Barbara said she thought she recognised him and asked me who it was. I said it must be someone we knew from a previous tour who had just returned to HK.

A couple of hours later we were at the poolside when it was announced that a surprise celebrity would open the season for us with the first dip. There standing at the edge of the pool was the person we had seen in Stanley. He entered the water with a bit of a belly flop and as he came up for air he gasped, "It's bloody cold!" It was dear old Leslie Crowther. No wonder we thought he looked familiar. He was in HK for a few days, staying with the Davies, who had showbiz connections. We sat at adjacent tables in the restaurant afterwards and were treated to a constant flow of witty asides - he really was a very funny man.

In the summer of 74 we were all very concerned when the Turks invaded Cyprus and Famagusta was bombed. Many of us had friends serving on the island, and though everyone was eventually evacuated safely they had lots of harrowing tales to tell about the period leading up to the evacuation.

Anne came out for her last entitlement flight. She had taken her exams and was awaiting the results. Her friend Jane was marrying a young man in the Christian Fellowship with whom she had become involved since her trip to France. Anne told us they would have liked her to marry someone else in the group (I believe he was called Mario), the twin of the one who was marrying Jane, but Anne told us she wasn't interested. Looking back it was significant that at that time she was still making her own decisions. I was often being called on to officiate at swimming events during my working week but as it was done through the "old boy" network after a phone call to our very enlightened OIC, George Hopkins, I never had to forfeit any leave on these occasions.

Another amusing incident happened one lunchtime when I walked into the bar at Ariel House. Sitting there all alone was someone I immediately recognised as Frank Sharples, a colleague I had known quite well on my first tour. I went up to him and shook hands and said, "I didn't know you were back Frank!" He laughed and said, "Neither did I, because I'm not Frank, I'm Reg!" Then it dawned on me it was Reg Varney of "On the Buses" fame. It was quite embarrassing, but there was an amazing resemblance - they could have been identical twins. Reg told me that he had just arrived from Sydney, where he had appeared on an all-star bill to mark the official opening of the Sydney Opera House. He wanted to spend a few days in Hong Kong but had been having great difficulty obtaining decent hotel accommodation, due to a tourist overflow. He had rung the Davises, who had managed to get him a room at the hotel in Kowloon where Mrs Davis worked. He had come up with Bob Davis to have a look at LSW and Bob had already informed him about his "doppelganger".

Life was very good for us all in HK. Louise and Richard were thoroughly enjoying their schooling, sport and swimming. Bev used to do some fantastic times in training, but could never seem to replicate them in competition. This did change one evening, when we went over to Kowloon to compete against a visiting team from the Philippines. She swam as if it was a training session and left the opposition standing.

LSW Dolphins' greatest triumph came in the 1975 HK age group championships open to the whole of the Colony. Paul Woolley came first in the 100m Breast, Back, Butterfly and Freestyle and was part of our winning freestyle relay team, along with Alan Wood, Chris Wild and Carl Ginn. We also had several second and third places that day, but Paul was superb

LSW had an excellent cricket team which competed

in the Colony League, quite a high standard. Our team was made up of a mixture of Aussies and Brits, plus a Cathay Pacific pilot, a very prolific opening bat who played whenever he was in the Colony. There was one memorable match played at LSW versus the Indian Recreation Club, which had included Farokh Engineer, the Indian Test wicketkeeper, who was staying with friends. LSW did very well and bowled out the opposition for a mere 60 runs. Then much to our surprise Engineer came on and opened the bowling. He was virtually unplayable and finished with bowling figures of something like seven wickets for 18 runs and we were all out for less than 40. How we wished he'd played as wicket keeper instead!

Another interesting cricket event took place when HKCC's ground in Chater Road was the scene of a special match between a team of Australian past and present greats and a team selected from the best HK cricketers. This was to commemorate the closure of Chater Road ground, where so many international teams en route to Australia or England would stop for a couple of days to stretch their legs and play a match against the best of the local cricketers. The ground, a veritable green oasis in the central district of HK, was an extremely valuable piece or real estate valued at many millions, so it wasn't surprising that they had decided to move to a new ground quite near to where we lived in Wong Neichong Road. There was massive publicity for this event and the Aussies were bringing with them a lot of veteran Test players who had been invited, including our own Harold Larwood.

Through the good offices of the large Aussie contingent who worked at LSW, a it had been arranged for the visiting party to have a day at LSW. The idea was that they would be picked up at their hotel in Central to board a couple of traditional Chinese junks and sail round the island to LSW. Unfortunately fate intervened in the guise of a strong wind and a very choppy sea, and before they were only halfway some of the passengers were so ill it was decided to land the passengers at Repulse Bay and continue to LSW by taxi. Harold Larwood was one of the veterans who felt so ill that they had to return to their hotel by taxi, so I never did meet the man who was probably the best bowler England ever had, the hero of the 1932 Body Line tour, so fast and yet so accurate. He was vilified for the type of bowling he produced on that tour, but he was only bowling to his captain Douglas Jardine's orders.

When the rest of the party arrived at LSW there were all sorts of food and drinks laid on for them. They included Richie Benaud, Bobby Simpson and Ken Archer, who told some wonderful stories and anecdotes of matches they had been involved in. Ken Archer said that Frank Tyson on the 1952 tour was so awesome and fast that the wicket keeper had to retreat at least ten yards in order to catch the balls the batsmen couldn't deal with.

One morning I was driving to work through very

heavy rain, deposited on the colony by a nearby tropical storm which hadn't managed to attain typhoon status but had caused considerable disruption, with mud slides and minor floods. My car radio confirmed that the route I was taking through North Point, then Chaiwan, was probably my best option, as these roads were still clear. A few minutes later, as I was about to drive through Chaiwan, the radio warned of floods on the main road. Almost immediately I was driving through about three feet of water. There was no way I could turn back, so I tried to keep my revs constant and pulled in as close behind a moving tramcar as I safely could, saying prayers for deliverance. For the next few hundred yards I travelled in the tramcar's wake, until we reached higher ground and I heaved a sigh of relief that I had not stalled my engine. The rains eased later in the day and my journey home was uneventful.

We discovered that Anne was not looking for employment in her newly-qualified secretarial role but was working unpaid in her Fellowship Christian Bookshop, and we began to feel a little concerned. We asked her if she would like to come out to us for Christmas, and she said she would love to if we could arrange it. There was a special Christmas flight arranged by Forces Welfare, which we were entitled to use, so we booked her a return flight. Imagine our surprise when a couple of weeks before the flight we had a phone call from her saying she had changed her mind and that she had spoken with her heart and not her head and was it possible for us to get our money back?

This call was not a normal conversation, and background whispers and prompts were clearly audible. It was almost as if they had read our minds, as we had already decided to ask her to stay in Hong Kong for the rest of our tour and look for a job. We had already contacted the Hong Kong and Shanghai Bank and they had told us that with her qualifications they would be pleased to find her employment subject to a satisfactory interview. We realised that there was very little we could do about it, especially while we were still in Hong Kong.

After many phone calls we managed to transfer Anne's flight to Stephen, which meant he wouldn't have to hang around hoping for an Indulgence flight. Stephen looked well and was obviously enjoying his teacher training. He arrived with most of his luggage filled with ballast and a list of items he was going to purchase for his friends, as well as a list of his own.

In the lead up to Christmas I had been involved in rehearsals for an old-time music hall show which was being produced and directed by George Budd, the senior technician at LSW. I was talked into it by Peter and Kath Buckby, old friends of ours from War Office days, but instead of helping out in the chorus I found myself playing several different roles. The show ran for five nights to full houses of about 300 people. I must admit I did enjoy it, but Bev, Louise and Richard were rather embarrassed when I played a smarmy character in a Victorian Soirée sketch. To give it the authentic atmosphere drinks were served to the audience in their seats, not really a good idea (I thought). The night Stephen went to see the show he laughed so much at one sketch that he knocked Joan Ainley's drink into her lap. Fortunately she took it in good part.

Despite the disappointment of Anne not being with us we had a very enjoyable family Christmas, and Stephen went back to college with such a load of purchases we don't know how he managed to go through customs without being stopped. Over the Christmas and New Year period the weather was wonderful. We had arranged to go on a junk trip and picnic and barbecue at one of the many small islands in the Hong Kong waters. Richard had brought along one of his friends, a boy called Graham, and Louise had brought her friend Wendy Wilson. Also aboard were Graham Mountford, his wife Francis, Graham's parents who were visiting and our friend Charlie Ginn and his son Carl. Amy Ginn had left them and returned to the UK well over a year previously, and there seemed to be irreconcilable differences.

All was well as we sailed along in the lee of the Stanley peninsula, and we had an excellent view of the new quarters specially built for our CSOS personnel and called Pendragon. As we moved out into the open water things soon began to change. We met a stiff breeze and the sea became very choppy. Bev of course was the first one to be affected, and I had to escort her down below to the toilet.

After about half an hour of this quite a few of us

were feeling queasy, including Barbara. This was about the time when Richard and his friend Graham decided they were hungry and started eating corned beef sandwiches with tomato sauce oozing out of them. This was the last straw for Barbara and she relinquished all responsibility for the children. Though Richard and Graham were running around the boat in high spirits, she concentrated on keeping as still as possible and not being sick.

It was decided that in view of the choppy waters we would head for the nearest small island, and we soon found one with a lovely stretch of sandy beach not far from Repulse Bay. After a few hours of swimming, sunbathing and picnicking, we reluctantly boarded the junk once again. Fortunately the wind had eased and we had a relatively smooth trip back to Stanley.

We did notice on our outing that Charlie and Francis placed their beach mats close to each other, but next to us, though we didn't think much about it at the time. We often made up a mixed doubles foursome with them (Graham didn't play tennis) as we often did with Phil and Anne Webb. One day Charlie confided in me that Francis, who lived in the same block of flats, often came to him with home made cakes. He was wondering how best to handle it, as he was afraid people might talk. I tried to reassure him that it was probably just a friendly gesture, knowing they didn't have a woman in the house. Little did we know that our innocent involvement would rebound on us later.

After her O Levels Bev decided she didn't want to stay on in Hong Kong and do A Levels, but she found a place on a two-year NNEB course in Stoke on Trent College. It was her decision. There was accommodation near and we knew the Braithwaites were on hand for any emergencies, so knowing we would be back in England in less than a year, we reluctantly agreed.

About that time we received a letter from William Evison (our nephew, Jean's son) informing us that he was shortly to marry Pat and they planned a Far East honeymoon tour commencing in Hong Kong and were hoping to stay with us for a couple of weeks before moving on for a grand tour. William was a teacher and Pat a secretary, and her parents ran a pub in Birmingham. Quite a lot of the family attended the wedding in Birmingham, including our Anne, and even before William and Pat arrived in HK we heard from Jean and Barbara's mother that Anne had turned up looking rather strained and not very well turned out, so our sleeping anxieties became active again, although we realized there was very little we could do.

When we met Pat and William at Kai Tak airport, Pat seemed a lovely girl and William looked as tall and handsome as ever. They were immediately impressed by HK, beginning with the drive from the airport through Kowloon along Nathan Road and to our flat via the Harbour Tunnel. They stayed with us for about six weeks, during which they visited places in Hong Kong and the New Territories which we hadn't been to see ourselves. They made themselves at home at LSW, and William, though not a tennis player, compensated with his height and agility on court and made a good doubles partner for anyone in our club tennis.

He asked if I could arrange for him to have a game of football with the LSW team, the Swans. In his first game for them I came over to the pitch during my lunch break, and as I approached I could hear someone exhorting the rest of the team to do this that or the other, shouting first names to them all. Yes it was William. He didn't really know any of them and the match had only been on for about twenty minutes. He was an excellent player and commanded respect from the other players, so no one seemed to take umbrage at his instructions even though he wasn't the team captain and had only met them all a few minutes before the match commenced.

The last game he played in before he left was at the Hong Kong stadium against a Hong Kong FC select team versus the Swans, who though very superior could only manage a solitary 1-0 victory, thanks to William's outstanding play. They were all asking if William was staying in the colony. At the age of 47 this was my last competitive game of football, and I only played in the second half. Louise and Richard were both impressed with William, but the thing that really amazed them was his ability to consume three Big Macs at one session - unfortunately Macdonalds had now arrived in Hong Kong.

There were always plenty of activities for them at Little Sai Wan. Apart from the swimming there was coaching in golf and football, while our club tennis coaching for juniors was undertaken by Jock Kane. Richard was still at Victoria Junior School, but Louise was now at St George's, along with quite a few of her friends, including Wendy Wilson. They had been good friends throughout the tour, since we had been in the hotel together. They were both in the Dolphins and both excellent all round swimmers, Wendy being particularly good at breast stroke.

In our last tennis club championships I drew Peter King in the first round and he beat me convincingly, but I did go on to win the men's plate without dropping a set. Phil Webb beat our Aussie friend Brian Wolfe in the men's singles final and Sue Smith beat Anne Webb in the ladies' singles final. In the last match of the day Barbara and Anne Webb beat Sue Smith and Maureen McCoull, with Barbara as the dominant partner while Anne was recovering from her unexpected defeat in the singles. Barbara and Anne won in straight sets. Barbara was really thrilled.

Bev and Stephen came out to us for Christmas 1975. Bev was on a scheduled BA Flight paid for by the Department, as she was still in full-time education, but Stephen managed another indulgence flight with the RAF. Bev was so terribly sick en route that she was allowed to remain on the aircraft during a scheduled stop in Bombay when all the other passengers had to disembark. She looked awful when we met her, but recovered and was her old self by the next day.

We were sad and concerned about Anne, but we still managed a good family Christmas. The last few months of our tour were simply flying past, and in no time at all we were confirming details of our trip home with the department and the HK travel agent who was arranging our trip. We were scheduled to leave HK in mid July, spend three days in Singapore, then fly to Zurich, spend another three days sightseeing, then by coach on to Basle for a leisurely five-day cruise along the Rhine to Rotterdam, then by overnight ferry to Hull. It sounded great, and we were all looking forward to it.

We had a series of misfortunes with the letting of our house in the UK. The original tenants had left after 12 months owing six months' rent with two members of the family serving prison sentences - so much for tenants vetted and recommended by our letting agent. Later on we let it to a colleague who was returning home from HK and needed temporary accommodation while they looked around to buy a permanent residence. They stayed for six months and we had agreed on a nominal rent of £40 a month. Unfortunately my colleague had a phobia about gas and was convinced that there was a leak, so he called out the gas board to investigate. They took up part of the drive near the garage and found absolutely nothing, which meant we had to foot the bill. Then to cap it all he complained about the electrics and called out the electricity board, who obligingly renewed part of the upstairs wiring and of course charged us, this in a house which was only seven years old. Les Dowsett, who was looking after the house for us, was absolutely furious, but could do nothing about it.

During our last year Barbara was summoned for jury service for a trial concerning the biggest jewellery robbery ever committed in Hong Kong, and it was expected to last several days. She was busy organizing our heavy baggage for shipping home and was going to miss an important tennis match. Then the rest of the jury thought she would make an ideal foreman, but she managed to extricate herself from that onerous position.

After only one day the accused, who was wearing some of the items he had stolen, changed his plea to guilty. After the judge had pronounced sentence the jeweller and his family lined up and all bowed to the jury, though really they had done nothing.

Shortly before we left HK we had a pleasing letter from Anne saying how she was looking forward to our return and that she would be coming along to help us put the house to rights again, so we thought things were looking up. For our last couple of weeks we had booked into the Lee Garden Hotel, a new luxury hotel in Hysan Avenue just opposite our old Sunning House Hotel. Our stay coincided with the 1976 Miss World competition and there were lots of celebrities around, along with the contestants staying in the hotel. Richard was quite pleased and a little embarrassed when several contestants came around and said how cute and adorable he was and one of them gave him a big kiss, possibly for the benefit of the numerous photographers.

After several farewell parties given by our tennis and swimming club friends, we left Kai Tak airport on a Cathay Pacific Jumbo Jet heading for Singapore. We remained impressed with Singapore, which looked as clean as ever, in marked contrast to so many areas in Hong Kong. We stayed at a first class hotel with a swimming pool and spent a relaxing three days before boarding a Singapore Airlines 727 with Colombo scheduled as our next stop. We were very impressed with Singapore Airlines, as they provided a high degree of cosseting for all passengers.

As we approached Sri Lanka we realized that we seemed to be an age circling Colombo Airport and were informed by the Captain that the delay was due to a fire which was raging at the airport. As we looked down we could see the smoke and flames. It was decided that we should divert to Bombay, so we sincerely hoped we had enough fuel to reach there. We duly landed at Bombay but were confined to the aircraft. The cleaners came aboard and the aircraft was refuelled, and some two hours later we were airborne again heading for Dubai.

A couple of hours after leaving Bombay we noticed two worried-looking stewardesses coming along the gangway checking all the hand luggage in the overhead racks. What we didn't know was that our pilot had been tipped off by radio that there was reason to believe that we might have had a bomb placed aboard during our brief stop at Bombay (where else!) It was probably considered not to alarm the passengers by informing them of this. Then followed a tense period when two stewardesses and one of the pilots progressed up and down the cabin searching every luggage rack and bags at passengers' feet. It seems they had been told that an explosive device might have been placed on board at our Bombay stop. The tension broke, or perhaps I should say was heightened, when a young man sitting near us suddenly ran up and down the aisle shouting "There's a bomb on board, I know there's a bomb on board!". He was quickly grabbed by a couple of crew members who were still examining hand luggage, and they forcibly returned him to his seat and informed him that he was being ridiculous and that he was frightening the children.

When order had been restored a lady who had been sitting near the panic merchant came over to our seats and said "I am a Jew, as is that young man who caused such a disturbance. I must apologize, I am ashamed of his behaviour."

As we approached Dubai our stewardess warned us that we had been ordered to land on the outskirts of the landing area, away from any other aircraft. As we came to a halt after a rather bumpy landing she said the ground staff had been ordered to bring the landing gangway to us as soon as possible, but after about five minutes nothing had happened. Then the air conditioning went off and the lights followed. At the same time all the passengers' emergency oxygen masks had been released and fell at our feet. Poor Barbara's claustrophobia kicked in, but she managed to keep it under control for Richard and Louise's sake. Fortunately the emergency lights then came on and we heard our stewardess say the captain had ordered that if the landing gangway was not attached to us within the next five minutes they would activate the emergency chutes and we would all have to slide down (something they are loathe to do because it can cause minor injuries to passengers).

At last the cabin door was opened and we were told to be prepared to disembark, but the first class passengers had to go first! We were relieved to be on the ground again, until we discovered we were in the desert about a couple of miles away from the main terminal building. As we left our mini bus transport we filed into the entrance and were informed that every passenger had to be body searched. There were lines of armed guards who had to frisk you and check as you raised your arms. Barbara did lighten the situation a little. She was in such a daze that she raised her arms and went to a male guard to be searched, even though he smiled and directed her to one of his female counterparts.

Dubai Airport in 1976 was a huge glass (Perspex) building with no air conditioning and a very poor restaurant and toilet facilities. It became hotter and hotter as the sun rose in the sky. We were then summoned over the public address system to go outside and identify our luggage, which was in a huge pile outside the building. When we had identified and selected our luggage there remained one medium-sized bag standing there all alone, and people began to back away just in case, for every one was a little nervous in view of what had transpired. A few minutes later a man came hurrying out to us saying how sorry he was but he had been in the toilets and hadn't heard the announcement, which had been repeated several times. It was amazing how we had all been so pleased to leave our aircraft when we landed at Dubai that we couldn't wait to return to the haven of the Singapore Airlines air conditioning and cosseting.

The rest of our flight was smooth and uneventful and Zurich Airport was such a contrast to Dubai. Our hotel was excellent and much to Louise's and Richard's liking too, so we looked forward to three days of relaxing and sightseeing. We must have been relaxed, because next morning Louise and Richard rose early and went out exploring while we were still catching up on sleep. We thoroughly enjoyed Zurich, a wonderful clean city with an excellent public transport system, lovely parks, a zoo and a lake.

Our three days soon passed and we were soon boarding a coach to take us to Basle, where we would join our Rhine Steamer. It was a fascinating trip along the Rhine with several stops at places of interest and a running commentary as we sailed past other places of interest. The children enjoyed Rudesheim, especially going up in a cable car over the vineyards. Our cabin was all you could wish for and the food was excellent, but it wasn't usually to the children's liking and when we stopped at Cologne and were about to look over the cathedral, all they wanted to do was get a big Mac at the Macdonalds close by.

We reached Rotterdam bang on schedule and went by taxi to pick up the overnight ferry to Hull. Barbara was most unhappy because once again our cabin was well below the waterline and her claustrophobia is never far away, but the air conditioning helped and we all had a good night's sleep before we docked at Hull. Yes there was someone there to meet me, but as we were on time and they had our itinerary it was just a formality. There remained a relatively short journey across the Humber by ferry, which gave us the opportunity to marvel at the magnificent Humber Bridge, which was just nearing completion, and then a short train ride from New Holland to Grimsby.

CHAPTER 11

FAMILY MATTERS

After a short visit to Grimsby to see Barbara's mother and Jean and Norman, we were swiftly on our way to Blythe Bridge to put our house to rights and see about any redecoration that might be needed. Bernard had had the worst parts done, so Orchard Rise looked very reasonable considering the previous tenants. We did however have a nasty shock in the form of a letter waiting for us from Anne, in which she stated that she had changed her mind about coming to help us put the house shipshape again because our way of life was 'all wrong'. She then proceeded to vilify us. We were black and she was white, and she added a little aside that I had refused to go to a Billy Graham meeting with her.

We knew she was in the grip of a cult which at that time was thriving in Birmingham. This cult was originally called the Children of God, but after a lot of bad publicity in the press following an exorcism which had taken place in Leeds when someone had died they renamed themselves Christian Fellowship. Apparently they had done some good work in the Birmingham area with drug addicts, but the Bishop of Birmingham was concerned about reports of their splitting up families, with many young people leaving their homes and being alienated from their families. Anne said we could visit her if we wanted to but she couldn't come to us.

We sought advice from various sources about what we could do. My brother Tom, who lived in Birmingham, was quite willing to arrange to kidnap her and bring her home, but we decided that in her mental state that might be dangerous. We consulted MPs, church ministers etc, but couldn't get any real help. The cult was obviously US based and lured lots of young people from their families. They bought up run-down houses and renovated them using the skills and energies of their converts, and they had several such houses in the Birmingham area.

As Anne had said we could visit her, we did so, several times. She had been moved into a house run by the leader of the Birmingham Fellowship, who was absent on a visit to the USA the first time we went to see her. We were surprised to see how Anne was dressed, looking very down at heel, and we could see quite a few of the clothes we had sent her from Hong Kong being worn by other members of the group. We tried to go out with her for a walk, but we always had to be accompanied by at least one group member.

The next time we went the cult leader, Martin, was there, having just returned from a trip to the USA. He was dressed in a kaftan and the girls were all gathered round him stroking his gown and his legs, telling him how much they had missed him and how good it was to have him back with them. I knew he came from Nottingham and that his mother lived there, so I asked him why they were splitting up families in the manner they did and when he visited his mother. His reply was that he visited his mother when the Lord told him to. There seemed to be very little we could do at that time, and we drove home feeling very despondent.

In November we went to Cheltenham to visit our friends Tony and Anne Marie Butt to see a bonfire and firework display and to play a few games of tennis, weather permitting. This was the weekend Anne and a few of her friends from the group chose to pay us an unexpected visit. Because Anne still had a key, they were able to enter look around and make themselves tea or coffee. While they were there my brother Tom rang to see what the situation was regarding Anne. When she answered the phone, Tom said "I bet your mum and dad were pleased to see you". She told him we weren't at home and they had only gone because God told her to. Tom's snappy rejoinder was "It's a pity God didn't tell you they weren't there today".

Things seemed to be improving when Anne asked if she could come home for Christmas and bring a couple of friends with her. We agreed and looked forward to it. When they arrived the two girls were very pleasant and said they were looking forward to watching films on TV, which was not allowed at their own house unless it was a special film vetted by one of the elders of the group. Anne had been moved into a different house and now seemed more like her old self. We had an enjoyable Christmas and told them they could come again anytime.

1977 was an eventful year. A few months into the year we had a phone call from a man who introduced himself as the Reverend Roy Callow. He said he was worried about Anne as she had just spent £200 on a 'primal therapy' session and had become convinced that her mother hadn't wanted her and had tried to abort her. I assured him that this was all arrant nonsense. We thought at the time he was a well-meaning cleric who was concerned about Anne's state of mind. How wrong that turned out to be. In fact he was a former elder of the cult. He was later to revert to his birth name of Kevin Lawlor and become our son-in-law, and he was definitely not a reverend in any church.

On completion of her nursery nurse's course Beverly was having difficulty in finding a job and eventually resorted to looking for vacancies in the *Lady* magazine. I took her down to London for several interviews. She seemed to interview well, and the last couple we saw sent her husband, Mr Kaye, after us just as we were pulling away, saying the job was hers if she wanted it. She accepted it there and then.

Louise had a similar experience. After completing her 'O' levels she enrolled on a secretarial course, but we were in the middle of a recession. She then obtained a Youth Opportunities vacancy in the office of Staffordshire Potteries and was hopeful of being retained after six months, but the firm was already cutting back and there were no vacancies. So she then resorted to the *Lady* magazine as her sister had done and I took her down to Loughton in Essex for an interview with a Mr and Mrs Alter. They liked her and she accepted the job of a nanny looking after their two young children. It was hard work, but she was treated quite well and while she was with them she went on holidays with them to Cyprus and Barbados. By a coincidence both the Kayes and the Alters were Jewish.

On my own job front I was making progress. I was given a temporary promotion and I was still enjoying my work. Bev gave birth to our first grandchild, Daniel, and Barbara's mother often came to visit us.

I was helping with the youngsters at Draycott Tennis Club and Barbara and I often played mixed doubles. Richard, though small in stature, was becoming a very good tennis player, as was Louise. Though she had a very laid-back style she always seemed to amaze her opponent by getting to the ball when it seemed she had left it too late.

Stephen brought home a young lady he had met at teacher training called Sarah Partridge and it seemed obvious that they were serious about each other.
Paul Woolley, our outstanding young swimmer in Hong Kong, was now in the Royal Navy in the submarine service and had renewed his acquaintance with Beverly. They seemed smitten with each other.

When the time came for Richard to take his 'O' levels, we were pleasantly surprised that he achieved C grades in all the main subjects, as he had definitely not been putting the work in he should have done. The recession was still in force and he took a youth opportunities position at Russell Hobbs, whose factory was only a few minutes' walk from our house. He was doing very well and hoped to be given a proper job with the company, but was unlucky.

I went on another promotion board and was promoted to SRO the job I had been doing off and on for quite a while. My previous temporary promotion did stand me in good stead, because instead of five years it only took me two years to reach the top of my pay scale. Soon after this I volunteered to go on detachment to Scarborough to help supervise a big NATO exercise in the North Sea area, with the object of seeing how good their communication security was. I had about a hundred personnel from the Army, RAF and Navy, and to add to the pot a group of US reservists, most of whom were ex Vietnam veterans. Our own service personnel were experienced and needed very little instruction, but the US personnel, which included several women, were rusty and needed more attention. I was the first supervisor on the first shift, and without doubt it was the most demanding task I had taken on in my career so far. I was quite pleased to see my relief, Ben Bolton, also from our station, come in to relieve me at 10 pm. Ben and I were in the same bed and breakfast in Scarborough, and when we were off duty we sometimes explored the locality and visited friends who were stationed there.

After three weeks, on the successful conclusion of the exercise, we returned to Cheadle. About a year into my promotion I was asked if I would like to move out of the set room and join the so called 'hierarchy' upstairs as Assistant Operations Officer. This meant I would be going on a five-day week instead of shift work and sharing an office with the Operations Officer, accompanying him round the set rooms every morning, checking on what had been happening operationally and preparing a report which I had to phone through to Cheltenham every day, after it had been meticulously checked by the OIC, who at this time was Ken Roberts. As part of my duties was conducting visitors round the station it was deemed that I ought to go to Cheltenham on a public speaking course, which it lasted three weeks - I found it very enjoyable.

We had a party of Cheltenham visitors about once a month, and one of the first parties I had to conduct round the station was one with our old friend Graham Mountford in charge. They were a wide miscellany of grades and Graham was a Higher Executive Officer. When we had a chance to talk I asked him how Francis and the children were. He turned on me quite savagely and said, "Come off it Jim, you know Francis has left me and set up home in Scarborough with Charlie Gin". I was amazed, as Barbara and I knew absolutely nothing about it, but I'm sure Graham didn't believe me.

CHAPTER 11

In May 1981 Beverly and Paul were married and Stephen and Sarah tied the knot the following April. By this time the cult group had broken up, thanks to some intervention by the Bishop of Birmingham, and Anne was now living in a flat in Birmingham. Louise decided she had done enough nannying and was looking for another job. She had moved in with her sister Anne, who was now engaged to Roy Callow, otherwise known as Kevin Lawlor. The Callows were his adopted parents, but he had now found his birth relatives. Anne warned us we mustn't slip up when we met the Callows. While Paul was actually under the polar icecap in HMS *Conqueror* when his daughter Gemma was born, his submarine later found fame - or notoriety - by sinking the Argentine cruiser the *General Belgrano* in the Falklands. Fortunately Paul had only just left and was by this time serving at NATO HQ. When he left the Navy he applied for and was accepted in the Staffordshire police, and after completing his training was told that it was now police policy that new recruits should occupy police married quarters as soon as possible. This meant they would have to sell their very nice little terrace house in Stanton Road and move into a police house in Biddulph Moor. This was a beautiful spot in summer. but could be extremely cold in winter.

They had by this time acquired a St Bernard dog called Heidi, and we often called in to find them all huddled together with Heidi on the sofa during cold spells. It cost them a fortune in fuel bills and they were pleased when they were allowed to leave and the police house was put up for sale.

In early 1983 Barbara was a little concerned about a lump in her breast. After a few visits to the hospital we were informed that it was cancer. Subsequently she had a mastectomy and her ovaries were removed. This was a big shock to me and the family because Barbara was indestructible and rarely ailed from anything. My employers were very good, and the OIC, Ken Roberts, said I could go and visit her and have as much time off as I needed. We had started to attend St Peter's church in Caverswall. Barbara was put on the prayer list and we just prayed for a good recovery.

When she came home she was obviously feeling low, so I suggested we went away somewhere for a complete rest for a few days. We decided to go to the Cotswolds and stayed at a lovely hotel called the Bear near Stroud. On the way to Stroud we called in and had a look around Cheltenham. Barbara had been to Cheltenham and stayed a few days while I was on a course and I knew she liked the place. I was surprised when she said she would like to live there, but I said I would see if it could be arranged. Through my almost daily contact with Cheltenham I asked Ron Hood, who arranged postings and movements, if it was possible for me to be posted to HQ. To my amazement he said "Say the word and I can post you to Taunton, Scarborough or Cheltenham, take your pick"

The next day the OIC called me in and said he had

heard I was leaving, and that he would have arranged it if I had asked. He went on to say "It's a pity, because you are on the next promotion board and I expected you to get through".

The family were all amazed at our decision to move, but it was what Barbara wanted and she needed a change of environment. We decided to spend three days in Cheltenham looking at what was available on the housing market. We saw quite a few houses, all pricey and none of them what we where looking for. We were surprised at the way some houses had been left for viewing with unmade beds and dirty pots.

On our third day we thought we would have one more try and rang round to see if anything new had appeared on the market. We were told one had just come on the market in Flecker's Drive, Hatherley, and thought it would not do any harm to have a look We were pleasantly surprised and shook hands with the owner, Colin Taylor, an EO who worked at GCHQ, and the deal was sealed as far as we were concerned. There were a few things that needed altering, but we thought it would be ideal for us.

The next few months were quite hectic with so many things to organize and arrange. Richard was adamant that he didn't want to come to Cheltenham with us as he was hoping that when his Youth Opportunities placement finished he would be taken on by Russell Hobbs. Our house had to be put on the market and in case it didn't sell at first I had to go and see my bank manager, who I had known for many years, to arrange a bridging loan. GCHQ were amazed at the preferential rate he was offering, but he thought he was helping me to make the move.

Anne and Kevin planned to marry in August, which was when we planned to move, so that was a further complication.

One of the things we planned to rectify in our new house was the area below the large front window, which was wood and in need of some remedial work. We contacted a reputable double glazing firm and they replaced the wood with brick, double-glazed the window and placed a hardwood skirting board round the whole of the lounge. It was an amazing transformation, and when we left practically every house in the drive had copied our improvement.

While Louise was staying with her sister Anne in Birmingham she met a young man named Ian Lock, and he was another person who was to impinge on our lives in the years ahead.

Quite a few people came to view our house, but we had no offers, so we decided to leave it empty with our friends Veronica and Peter Green keeping their eye on it and arranging to show any viewers around. We were unhappy about leaving Richard, but he had made arrangements to live with a friend in Fenton and we knew Beverly and Paul would be looking in on him from time to time just to make sure he was on the straight and narrow.

We had arranged for the wedding reception at a hotel

in Birmingham. As well as our side of the family there were Mr and Mrs Callow, Kevin's adoptive parents, and a whole host of recently-discovered brothers and sisters and families who naturally called him Kevin. with Mr and Mrs Callow calling him Roy this raised a few problems at times. Some of the Lawlor family were very nice but there were one or two who were quite belligerent, probably because they had been drinking.

Richard, who had only recently passed his driving test, drove us back from Birmingham to Stoke and negotiated Spaghetti Junction and the intricacies of that congested area with ease - we were quite impressed.

By the end of August we were installed in Fleckers Drive and the very next day they began work on the front window and the brickwork. The work was finished the next morning, and we were very pleased with the results.

I started my new job at Oakley the first week in September. It was quite a culture shock for me because instead of supervising anything from 30-50 men I was in charge of a watch which consisted of four men, and there seemed to be little for me to do. After only a few months I decided to apply for a vacancy I knew was coming up at Benhall on the other side of Cheltenham. I was provisionally offered the job subject to passing a six-week course at Bude in Cornwall on satellite communications. I was a little concerned, because I was now the wrong side of fifty and I knew of several people who had failed the written exam at the end of the course.

Early in January, along with a colleague who wanted

a lift, I set off on a Sunday afternoon to Bude. The weather didn't look very promising and before long we were driving through snow, but fortunately the roads remained clear and we found our way to our small hotel just after ten o'clock. Next morning we found our way to CSOS Bude and commenced our first day of an intensive course, designed, I thought, to weed out the weak links. I drove home on Friday afternoon knowing that quite a bit of revision would be required if I hoped to keep up with the bright sparks (mostly young men) who were my classmates.

The world of satellite communication was new and fascinating to me, and even though it was hard going at times I was beginning to enjoy it. There was one fairly heavy snowfall when we had to walk to the station, but nothing too extreme. Going up to the top of one of the huge satellite dishes and gazing out into the Atlantic ocean was quite an experience.

During our last week we had written exams on the Wednesday and Thursday and were due to assemble on the Friday morning to hear our marks and see whether we had passed or not. On the Friday morning fate intervened when a group of demonstrators using wire cutters broke into the station. There was a high state of alert and we were ordered to go back to our hotels and head for home. Our exam results would be forwarded to our station on the following Monday.

When I arrived at Benhall on the Monday morning I was pleased to hear that I had passed with good marks, so I could take up my new position on my watch and begin to learn the intricacies of the job, which was an entirely new field as far as I was concerned. I had a strong contingent of experienced operators on my watch and during my first few months they helped me enormously.

One of the first things I did when we were settled was to apply for an allotment, and after only a few months I was informed that there was a plot available only five minutes away from our house, so of course I accepted. It had never been worked for years and the ground was full of weeds and as hard as iron, but I enjoyed the challenge. After about a month of hard graft I ordered a load of manure from a local farmer and spread it all around, then dug it well in and left it a while.

Stephen and Sarah now lived about twelve miles away in Cirencester, and they informed us that they were expecting a baby and were hoping that Barbara would be willing to help out so that Sarah would be able to go back to teaching a few months after the baby was born. Barbara was only too pleased to agree. Louise had moved in with us almost straight away and managed to obtain a job with the Cheltenham and Gloucester Building Society.

A few months later we were pleased to welcome Richard back to the fold. He managed to secure a job with Gloucestershire County Council on the environmental side, doing mostly outside work trimming hedges, dry stone walling etc. He loved it and was learning new skills. Barbara seemed to have a fresh outlook and was really enjoying her new life. We all joined the Civil Service Tennis Club and became very active members, especially Richard. I often organized social evenings for my watch members, usually skittles nights or something similar.

Early in my career at Benhall we had a new OIC, my old friend Ron Hood, though later on I was to doubt that friendship. He had lots of new ideas, one of which was a meeting every couple of months which he chaired, with a representative from each of the four watches plus the watch supervisors. For my sins I was elected to take the minutes of each meeting, quite an onerous task. The OIC monitored the minutes and usually deleted anything he didn't like.

Completing ACRs, an annual task, was very responsible, time-consuming work. Making comments on the way the team carried out their tasks and their suitability for promotion was something I was very meticulous about. During my stay at Benhall I succeeded in recommending at least five men for promotion and I was pleased that my recommendations were acted upon. More on this subject later.

Our allotment was now a thriving concern. Our potato crop usually lasted us for several months and Barbara blanched and placed in the freezer enough green beans to last until the following year. Our plot, though it had been neglected, had a couple of Pershore plum trees and some lovely cultivated blackberries, while curly kale, cauliflowers and cabbages grew in abundance. There is nothing quite like eating your own produce.

Beverly and Paul, with Daniel, Gemma and of course Heidi, often came to visit us. Anne had gone with Kevin to Belfast, where he was on a social worker's course at Belfast Polytechnic, and had a rented house just outside Belfast. We had intended to visit them, but the outside toilet was a real put off. When Kevin qualified he secured a job as a social worker in a large hospital in Kings Lynne and they found a house there.

When our new granddaughter Rachel was only a few months old Sarah resumed work teaching. I began walking to work and Barbara would drive to Cirencester to look after Rachel until they returned home. Barbara was quite happy to do this until she had a nightmare drive back to Cheltenham in fog. Stephen was also concerned and after this they used to bring her to us early on the Monday morning and pick her up on Friday evening. Once she was toddling, Rachel used to tell Stephen and Sarah to go home as soon as they arrived as she wanted our undivided attention.

Barbara still had to make a visit to Stoke every six months for a routine check up. Our house in Stoke was eventually sold and we were able to redeem our bridging loan. Our tennis club organized a coach trip to Wembley to see a tournament which included lots of the world's top tennis players. We saw some wonderful matches. However Boris Becker had just come on the court when Barbara began to feel ill. We managed to get her to the first aid post before she collapsed. There she was treated by the doctors who were in attendance primarily for the players, but they were happy to treat Barbara. After checking her over they could find nothing wrong and put it down to the atmosphere in the enclosed stadium, but suggested she should see her own GP when she returned to Cheltenham. When we stopped for refreshments on the way back she tucked in to a hearty meal and I was very relieved.

We purchased a motor cycle for Richard, to enable him to go to and from work, and he was very happy with it, though we wondered if we had done the right thing.

This was about the time when Margaret Thatcher decided not to allow GCHQ employees to belong to a trade union, which caused a lot of trouble throughout the workforce. We were all given £1000 and told no union membership at all could be considered. This resulted in widespread protests across the country, and our own Civil Service Union, with our old friend Jack Hart at the helm, was never off the radio or television. Mrs Thatcher prevailed and the tumult gradually subsided, but several people refused and some even left the job over this issue . Incidentally the £1000 bribe was reduced to £800 when tax was taken off.

Life was progressing quite smoothly for us when Louise asked us if it would be all right for Ian Lock to stay the night with us. This was the young man Louise had met while she was staying with Anne in Birmingham. He seemed well mannered and very presentable and Louise was obviously taken with him, so we agreed that he could stay the night, and thus another problem entered our lives. After only a few months Ian found himself a job in Cheltenham and a few months later Louise moved in with him in a basement flat, not with our approval, but there was nothing we could do about it. We were also aware that it was developing into a stormy relationship, but it was Louise's choice and our hands were tied.

They bought a car and quite a few things on hire purchase, all on Louise's credit by virtue of her job with the building society. Ian's job was going around the local stores and supermarkets selling billing heads and advertising and apparently he was very good at it according to his boss. After a short time he decided to branch out on his own and took off with all his work materials to set up business on his own in the Birmingham area. We had Louise back living with us, very chastened and in debt, which we paid off, though she did repay us later. Ian's boss decided it wasn't worth the expense of taking him to court, so he had the benefits of his boss's materials and Louise's car.

Imagine our amazement when the following year, after receiving several letters from Ian, Louise decided to move in with him again, this time in Coventry, where she succeeded in acquiring another building society position.

Anne by this time had just had her first baby, Fiona, and we drove over to Kings Lynn to see her. Of course she was beautiful. We often drove to Cleethorpes and brought Barbara's mother back with us for a break. She loved Cheltenham, and especially shopping.

Bernard and Edith came to visit us, and that was when we began to realize that Edith was not her old self. They had only just moved into their new bungalow and only three weeks later Edith died - so sad. It was round about this time that we talked to Richard about furthering his education, and because of the work he had been engaged in with the environment he thought he could be interested in a career in arboriculture. His first foray into this work was to go to Merrist Wood for a week to see if he had a head for heights. He had no problems with heights and was enrolled the following September. One of the first things the students had to view was a horror film showing the dangers of chainsaw accidents.

Surrey was quite a distance from Cheltenham, so he had to find himself some accommodation and he ended up sharing a house with some other students. As my service had included a three-year tour in Cyprus during the Eoka troubles and a tour in Hong Kong when the riots and troubles were ongoing, those times counted for time and a half for pension purposes, which meant I could retire at fifty eight and a half if I so wished, a useful option to have in reserve.

Because of an unpleasant situation which was developing at work I decided to take up this option. The hierarchy had decided that our handover time between watches would no longer count as overtime, but after a meeting with the Staff Federation it seemed to have been amicably resolved. At our next bi-monthly meeting with Ron Hood presiding and me taking the minutes, everything was minuted, but Ron extracted certain items. When I tackled him about this he took umbrage and made a ridiculous statement to me that if I pursued this matter he would mark down any past or present recommendations in my annual reports on staff. He went on to remind me who had made my transfer to Cheltenham possible. This was the last straw as far as I was concerned, and I requested an interview with the Director of GCHQ. The very next day I was summoned to Oakley, But instead of seeing the Director I was ushered into the office of the head of my division, one of his second in commands. I repeated my story, which I think he already knew. I also said I would like to take a polygraph test on my allegations. I was hurriedly assured that it would not be necessary and that they believed me and that any of my recommendations in annual reports would be considered as valid.

This was the end of the road in the relationship between Ron and myself. He did however call me into his office a few days later to say "All right Jim, you've won." I no longer took minutes and he didn't speak to me again other than operationally in the set room.

As I was about to retire I thought it might be a good idea to look for another job to occupy me part time, and decided that I would volunteer for the Citizens' Advice Bureau. I thought I would be accepted with alacrity, but

I had to have an interview with about eight people including the manager all sitting at around table, just like a promotion board. I received a letter a few days later saying they would be happy to accept me and suggesting I should attend in my spare time to get some experience of the routine. By virtue of being a shift worker I was able to go in once or twice a week to see what the routine was like.

I had only been there a few weeks when I was asked if I would go to the Tewkesbury office, which was only open two days a week, and update their files, as new legislation on various things was about to come into force. The CAB office was a small room in the market, and I had to see someone there to obtain the keys. It was made even more difficult because I didn't know the layout and where certain files were kept. I did succeed in my task, but I began to wonder what I had taken on.

We both attended the church at Warden Hill, and if I was on duty Barbara would go on her own. The churchwarden was non other than Brian Blacklock, the same person who as a young I Corps corporal had been caught play wrestling with Ken Spring in the set room in Cyprus by his CO, Major Bickerstaff, on our first tour of Cyprus. He soon had me enrolled as a sidesperson whenever I was off duty on a Sunday. We truly felt we had integrated into a good way of life there. This was however about to change!

At the start of 1988 my retirement date had been set for May and we were beginning to look forward to it.

Our allotment was still providing practically all we required and I was doing my CAB work once or twice a week. Then out of the blue Barbara and I had the same thoughts - that it would be good to return to Staffordshire! On reflection it seemed a crazy idea to leave an area like Cheltenham where life was good and return to Stoke, find a new home and move, with all the trauma that could involve. But as we considered the pros and cons we thought it would be good to be near Bev and Paul again. We would also be there to give a bit of support to Bernard, now on his own, and instead of having the long journey bringing Barbara's mother to and from Cheltenham the journey would be almost halved. So we decided to put our house on the market while we went over to Staffordshire to look for properties that might be suitable for us.

The house went on the market on the Friday we went looking, and when we returned on the Monday our next door neighbour said that on the Sunday there had been a queue of about 50 people waiting to view and the 'For Sale' notice hadn't even gone up! That same day the agent rang us to say he had already sold the house, so it seemed the die was cast. We had to find ourselves a suitable property fairly quickly.

We looked at quite a few properties and finally decided on a large four-bedroomed house in Bromsberrow Way on Meir Park, the site of the old airfield, which was now growing into a large estate. The previous owners, who had built the house themselves, had dogs and cats which had been allowed to roam the house upstairs and downstairs and consequently the rooms were all pervaded by a strong smell, but Barbara recognized its potential and she was right as usual. After we had taken up all the carpets and paid the council to take them away, the walls were all washed down with strong disinfectant and at last the smell had almost gone. Paul had begged us not to buy the house because of the smell, but after it was re decorated, new carpets had been put down and our furniture was in situ he agreed that it was a wise buy.

We resumed attending St Andrew's church in Weston Coyney, which was now a very active and lively church, well attended every Sunday, and we had only been back a few months when Joyce the curate's wife asked Barbara if she would help to run the mums' and toddlers' group which took place on Monday and Tuesday afternoons. Of course she agreed, and within a few weeks she was running the Tuesday session with me and another lady assisting.

I had contacted the local branch of the CAB to see if they needed any volunteers and they were only too happy to accept my services. Working at this branch in the middle of a recession really opened my eyes to how poor and needy so many of the people in the area were. Jobs were at a premium and so many miners and pottery workers were either being made redundant or laid off. It was not unusual for people to queue outside before we opened with plastic bags full of outstanding bills etc, and we often had to spend half a day or more dealing with just one client. Debts were usually our main concern, but there was a myriad of reasons why people needed our help. We often wrote to charities on behalf of clients, and because I had composed a number of successful requests I found myself being asked to undertake this task on many occasions.

Living behind us in a specially adapted bungalow were a couple called Bill and Lily who were handicapped, and they had acquired a Schnauzer puppy called Ben and I often used to take him for a walk or a run. They had a son Kevin who had learning difficulties but worked for Remploy after an accident at a previous employer, and he had been awarded damages. Only a few months afterwards Lily died and Bill said that if anything happened to him he wanted us to take Ben, so when he died a few months later we felt honour bound to give Ben a home.

The night Bill was taken into hospital Kevin brought him to us just after midnight. We thought he was going with his father to hospital but no, he just went back to bed, and Ben became our dog. He was a lovely little dog, no trouble to anyone, and was good with the children, so he soon became a member of the family.

Louise and Ian had bought a small house in Coventry through the building society where Louise was working, and she had really made it look special. When Ian was offered a job as a salesman in Lancaster they decided to sell and move on. First they lived in

Lancaster for about a year, but then they bought a house in Galgate, a village just outside Lancaster. By this time Ian had given up his salesman job and opened a shop selling phones, radios and electronic stuff, and he seemed to be doing very well. Unfortunately he then decided to open another shop, and during the recession firms which owed him money defaulted. As a result he lost both shops, and so ended his first business venture.

It was while they were at Galgate that Jasmine was born and we often came over to stay with them. I have fond memories of walking down to the canal with Jasmine on the carrier on my back and Solo, their Golden Retriever, on his lead. When we reached the canal Solo liked to dive in and uproot water lilies, and it was always difficult to coax him back to the side.

We often went for days out to the Lake District, which was only a few miles away. Barbara's mother came to stay with Louise and she loved it when Ian took us on a guided tour around the Lake District.

We were very much involved with our church and were now part of a house group run by our friends Terry and Yvonne Bagguley, which met once a week at their house in Caverswall.

Barbara had been having problems with her hips, so the consultant decided that she needed both replacing as soon as possible. He said that because she wasn't carrying any extra weight he thought he could manage to replace them both at the same time, but said not to worry if she woke up and he had only done one because he would not take any risks. When she came round he was at her bedside and told her he'd managed both, so we were very pleased.

Six weeks later we were in Cyprus staying with our friends Les and Ina Dowsett, who had a rented apartment there. Cyprus had changed so much since we had left almost thirty years previously, and we were very impressed with Paphos, which was now a well-planned pleasing holiday resort instead of a sparsely-populated sleepy little backwater. There was now a fine road which went all the way up to Troodos and a frequent bus service which could take you relatively cheaply to anywhere on the island. We had a wonderful holiday with Les and Ina and the three weeks went in a flash and we were on the plane heading for home.

We had by this time moved the venue of our house group to our house, as we had a large front room which we called the 'games room' as we had a miniature snooker table in there (it was no longer played on so it was consigned to the rafters of our garage). Our numbers seemed to gradually increase until we sometimes had fifteen or sixteen people every week. I usually did the prayers and Terry took us through the particular bible reading we were studying. It was amazing, because every member of our group seemed to have a need for one thing or another and we all helped each other in whatever way we could.

We also had a routine with Bernard whereby we usually met on a Friday evening at Beverly's playing

Chase the Ace and contract whist with Daniel and Gemma, and of course Beverly - not Paul, as if he was there he was usually busy in his massive garden. Later on Bernard began to see a lady called Elsie who had been a neighbour of ours when we lived in Orchard Rise. One day we had a message from Ian to say that Louise, who was due to have her third child, had been taken into hospital in Blackpool. It was touch and go at times and mother and baby were in danger, but thanks to the doctors and lots of prayer she began to recover and Emily was born safely, and was of course another beautiful baby.

We visited Louise and the children at Poulton as often as we could as we were concerned about them and usually stocked them up with groceries before we left. Money was short there and Ian was obviously depressed at his situation. Fortunately Louise had become a regular member of the local United Reformed Church and used to attend with all three children, including baby Emily, every Sunday, and consequently had made some good friends there. This was to be a great help in the troubles and tribulations which were to come for her.

We then had to visit Chesterfield to survey yet another beautiful little baby girl, Catherine, a sister for Fiona. When we visited Poulton we often attended the church where Louise worshipped and came to know her pastor, Peter Meak, and his wife and another couple of good friends to Louise, Rose and Sam Tomkins. We realized that Louise was getting into debt, and though we paid a lot of the bills I advised her to go to her local Citizens' Advice office. They were extremely helpful as I knew they would be.

We discovered that Ian had taken out a loan on their house in Poulton even though it was in Louise's name, about £19,000, and it looked as though they could lose the house. It was during this horrendous time that Ian began ill-treating Louise and she couldn't believe it when he did it one day while she was holding Emily. The first we knew about this was when Peter and Jane Davis, also church friends, rang us from the solicitor's office telling us what was happening and asking us to come over, as the solicitor was applying to the court for an injunction to be heard by a judge the following day.

When we drew up outside the house Ian came out and said "What are you doing here?" He obviously thought we were behind the injunction and refused to believe we were not. He then left. Louise looked terrible. She brought us up to date with her side of the story. We wanted her to come back that evening with the children to our house, but she was adamant that she couldn't leave the house with Ian in it as she wouldn't be able to sell it. So we decided that we would take the children back to Stoke with us and I would return the next morning and accompany her to the Judge's chambers to see if we could get the injunction.

I returned the next morning, and though I was told I had to remain silent the judge did allow me to ask a couple of pertinent questions. After listening to Louise he granted the injunction and Ian was ordered to leave the house and not come anywhere in the vicinity as from Friday midnight.

So began one of the worst weeks of my life. When Ian had the injunction served upon him he started a barrage of questions and abuse at us both, blaming Barbara and myself and her church friends at Poulton for the situation. I had to stay by Louise's side whenever possible because he was constantly badgering and threatening her with all sorts of dire consequences if she didn't relent and let him stay in the house. Louise looked ghastly, and we ate out sometimes just to get away from it all.

Arrangements had to be made to change all the locks, as Ian had keys. We knew someone in the area and had a good relationship with this tradesman, who arranged to come and change the locks on the Saturday morning. Barbara had been alone looking after Jasmine, Alex and Emily for almost a week, so I decided to return home on the Friday evening as church friends had volunteered to keep looking in on Louise and make sure Ian was not trying to get in the house. As I was leaving Poulton I stopped at the phone box and explained the situation to Barbara, saying I was on my way home.

My journey home from Poulton to Stoke was the most memorable journey of my life. When I left the weather was overcast with light rain, but as I joined the M6 and started heading south the skies darkened and it began to rain quite heavily. There was heavy traffic, including lots of heavy goods vehicles, and I cut my speed down accordingly. Then the skies turned black and the rain became absolutely torrential, worse than any tropical downpour I had encountered in Cyprus or Hong Kong. My windscreen wipers were on their fastest speed and making no impression, and I was driving into a black void with no visibility whatsoever. I expected one of those lorries to plough into me at any moment.

Strangely enough I felt no fear. I just thought "This is the end, and there is so much I have to do in life". Then I said "Help me Lord", and immediately a bright light shone in front of me, illuminating the middle lane of the motorway. I could see clearly ahead and the rain eased dramatically.

For the rest of my journey home I was in a state of euphoria at the realization that God had responded to my prayer. I could hardly wait to tell everyone about it. During the next few months there were several "God incidents" relating to Louise's situation, of which more later. She placed her house on the market and we were looking for a suitable property in our area. The building society were pressing Louise for the £19,000 loan Ian had secured on their house, and I happened to see a case in *The Guardian* of a similar incident where a partner had taken out a loan in similar circumstances and the court had decided that £10,000 was the maximum any building society should advance in such circumstances. When I pointed this out to Louise's solicitor he took the matter up and the debt was reduced to £10,000, but she needed that amount to allow her to sell the property. Fortunately her friends Rose and Sam loaned her the money, so she was able to go ahead with the sale - friends indeed!

Louise decided to return to Poulton with the children as she thought the house would sell better if it was occupied, and Jasmine was missing school. There was now a new pastor at her church called Norman Vivian, and he and his wife Chris were also looking after Louise's interests, which was a relief to us as we were so far away. The previous pastor, Peter Meak, had now moved to Derbyshire. A friend of the new pastor had told him that they had a policy which was about to mature and they wanted a good cause to donate the money to, and Norman told them about Louise and her circumstances. Shortly after this the Vivians arranged for Louise and Jasmine to go for the weekend to a church conference at Swanwick, and while she was there Jasmine managed to get lost in the conference centre and her name was given out over the tannoy system. The couple who wanted to donate their nest egg were actually at the conference, but had only decided to go at the last minute, and when they heard the call that Jasmine Lock was lost they knew why the Lord had prompted them to attend. They met and chatted to Louise and decided there and then that Louise was the one they wanted to help and arranged for the money to be given to her in a few weeks' time. Here comes another God incident, because the amount they gave her was the exact amount needed to settle the amount owed to the building society.

We had been looking for a house for Louise and so far we hadn't been successful. But when Louise came over one weekend she spotted a house which was for sale just a few hundred yards from our church, St Andrews in Weston Coyney. it was an ex-council house, built and on the market for £43,000. Louise liked it and thought she could be happy there, so we were awaiting the building society's valuation before going ahead. When the valuation was announced it was £5000 less than the advertised price, so it looked as if it was out of the question, but at the last moment he decided in view of Louise's circumstances that she could have it for that amount, and we all breathed a sigh of relief. Louise had already sold her house, so it was just a matter of arranging for a furniture van to bring her belongings to Weston Coyney.

Paul and I went over to assist with the move and bring Louise back with us. The children were already at our house being looked after by Gemma and her friend Emma, while Barbara and Beverly went over to Hall Drive to help to get the house ready for occupation. It was a close-run thing, but somehow the furniture men managed to load every item into the van and set off following Paul, Louise and myself in our car. It was late at night by the time we had some semblance of order in the new house and we locked up and went to our house, calling at the fish-and-chip shop on the way. Gemma and Emma had worked miracles with the children; they were all fed, bathed and tucked up in bed fast asleep, something we have never forgotten, as they were only about fifteen at the time.

There were quite a few teething troubles when they first moved, in but we managed to enrol Jasmine, Alex and Emily at St Peter's church school even though Emily was only four. Louise was determined to get a job and come off benefits, and she commenced an Open University course with a view to becoming a social worker. She was receiving nothing from Ian for the children and times were hard for her. Our friends in our church house group were very supportive, especially Terry and Yvonne as well as Mike and Geraldine. Louise worked hard at her OU course and eventually, with the help of a recommend from our vicar, Neil Jefferyes, was accepted for a degree course at Staffordshire University. During this time Ian had moved into the area and was quite a problem at times, of which more later.

CHAPTER 12

TESTING TIMES

As the new millennium dawned, little did we know what trials and tribulations were in store for our family. We were already aware that Anne had been diagnosed with cancer. Fortunately it seemed to be responding well to the drug Tamoxifen, and we went over to Chesterfield to see her whenever we could manage it. We also looked after Fiona and Catherine when they went away on weekends to "Marriage Encounter", a weekend organised by the Church of England with the aim of improving new and old marriages. Both Anne and Kevin were part of the counselling team and went to various venues all over the country. By this time they had sold their house and were looking to buy another suitable house in Chesterfield.

In the interim they were living in a rented house just off the main road. When we stayed there we were appalled by its condition. It was very dusty, and they were for the most part living out of boxes. Anne was in no condition to do anything other than basic cleaning. She had a hospital appointment at Nottingham and

Kevin dropped her off there and then went on to work. We were there to see to the children when they came home from school.

It was about noon when the phone went and Barbara answered. Through her tears, Anne was asking us to come, as she had just been told that the cancer had spread and the prognosis was bad. We set off straight away and when we reached the hospital Anne was very distressed, so we asked to see the consultant and explained that we had just come over from Stoke and told him what the situation was at their house. He was emphatic that Anne needed cosseting and that she should move into our area so we could do this. He went on to say that the worst scenario was that she might only last six months.

We drove back to Chesterfield feeling very down, but trying not to show it for the sake of Fiona and Catherine. Barbara busied herself preparing the evening meal before Kevin arrived home from work. He had become disenchanted with his work at Chesterfield and was now working at Lincoln. He became very tearful and said "Why, why does it always happen to me? I've already lost one wife and now I'm going to lose another, I shall have to marry again you know!" These remarks were made to us his, wife's parents, the same day that we had received the bad news about our daughter!

He did however agree that we could go ahead and look for a suitable house in our area, as they had already sold their house and were in a position to buy. Anne came home a couple of days later and we took Fiona with us to enable her to start at a new school, Sandon High, which was quite near where we lived, so we began to look around for a house which might suit them. There were several possibilities, but we thought it was up to them to decide.

I contacted Kevin's manager at Lincoln and she was amazed to hear the news about Anne. He had not mentioned it to any of his colleagues and had never asked for any of the time off or compassionate leave which would have been available to him. She agreed to facilitate any move to a new job on public interest terms.

A few weeks later, with their furniture in store, they came to live with us in Bromsberrow Way, and we were able to try to make things easy for Anne. Catherine was given a place at St Peter's church school, where Jasmine, Alex and Emily attended. Kevin found a job with Social Services in Stafford and they settled in a four-bedroomed house only about ten minutes' walk from us.

Anne had to see her consultant at the Queen Elizabeth hospital in Nottingham every four weeks and I usually went with her, but after doing this for a few months Anne decided it wasn't fair that I should always have to take her and that Kevin ought to take a turn. I suggested that I would take her one month and Kevin the next, and he agreed to this arrangement. When the time came for Kevin to take her he had managed to arrange ambulance-type transport, and Beverly went with her every month from then on. Beverly also came to the house as often as she could to try and keep the house clean, because unfortunately Anne had not brought the girls up to help with household chores and such jobs were not Kevin's forte.

When Louise began her University course I used to transport her in the morning to university. It was often heavy traffic at that time, but she usually made her own way home. When she was a few months into her course she went out one evening to a night club with friends from her course and met Gilbert, whom we came to know as Gil, a Londoner of West Indian background. It seemed that they had made a hit with each other, because a few months later Beverly came round to see us and said "I'm afraid I've some bad news for you, Louise is pregnant and she dare not tell you so she asked me to."

We were shocked, but not really surprised, and said prayers that we would be able to handle the situation. Unfortunately Ian had just moved into the area, as not unnaturally he wanted to be somewhere near his children. He had endeared himself to them by buying them a Golden Retriever puppy which they called Cassie. He caused a lot of problems over the Christmas period and I had to go with Louise to see a solicitor for a restraining order.

When I was at Louise's one day, Barbara was helping Louise with some decorating and Beverly and Anne were also there helping. There was a banging on the front door, and when we opened it we found it was Ian, who practically knocked us both over as he burst through the door. Fortunately Anne was watching from the stairs and immediately dialled 999 while Ian proceeded to verbally abuse us all, but especially Louise. He said some terrible things. He had obviously discovered that Louise was pregnant and was blaming us and the church for coming between them.

We don't know what Anne said on her 999 call but in the space of three or four minutes there were three police cars outside. Ian then became relatively calm and denied bursting in, but the police were having none of it and pointed out that he shouldn't have been in the vicinity of the house in any case in view of the court order. They escorted him to his car and ordered him to move out of the area.

The next few months were difficult ones for us all, but by pulling together as a family we were getting by. During this time Anne had lots of ups and downs but she rarely complained. On several occasions we were told that she only had a few days or even a few weeks at the most, but we were convinced that it was combined prayer from so many people that enabled her to improve, if only temporarily.

One day she collapsed in the doctor's surgery and they called an ambulance and took her to North Staffs hospital. The consultant oncologist said her cancer was so far advanced that it was doubtful if she could last the weekend. We called Stephen and Richard and they both came over on the Saturday morning.

Anne had been attending the local Macmillan Hospice one day a week for respite, and she begged me to try to have her admitted because she had so much faith in the doctors there. I contacted the hospice and they said they would make her a priority and try to admit her as soon as possible. She was admitted the following Tuesday and immediately began to improve, praise the Lord! Over the next few months she had quite a few ups and downs, but it always seemed that Dr Wicks, a lady doctor at Macmillan, could bring about an improvement and allow her to return home.

Barbara and I celebrated our Golden Wedding with a lot of family and relations at Caverswall Village Hall. The catering, which was magnificent, was provided by our House group friends Jean Rhead and Jackie Oakes, and of course Alan Rhead. There was also lots of help from other church and house group friends and it was an occasion we will always remember.

We had noticed at our Golden Wedding that Stephen wasn't his usual self. We also knew that he had always wanted to go and teach abroad but Sarah was loath to leave her parents, who lived just a few miles away in Birdlip, the area where she was brought up and where most of her relations lived. Stephen had the offer of a job in Spain, with one for Sarah at the same school. Rachael was just about to begin teacher training at Cheltenham and she could have lived in at the college and enjoyed holidays in Spain. Stephen thought this was the ideal situation and the time to make the move, but

Sarah was adamant she didn't want to go, so Stephen took a teaching job in Ireland and stayed for almost two years.

This led to their marriage breakdown and a divorce. Though such things were anathema to us, it was happening all around us. The divorce was as amicable as a divorce could be, and as Stephen considered he was the cause of the divorce he made things as easy as possible for Sarah. Shortly afterwards he was offered a job in Cyprus, which he gratefully accepted, and so he returned to the land of his birth.

Anne continued to have her ups and downs, but she enjoyed being in the same locality as her sisters and ourselves. She had her own little runabout car and often took Beverly or Louise shopping with her while the children were at school. She became a fairly regular member of our congregation at St Andrews, where she made a lot of friends, often attending our house group. Kevin continued with his many strange habits. The family would arrive at our house for Sunday lunch and he would excuse himself and go up to the bathroom and proceed to wash his hair while we were all waiting to begin our meal. Anne must have despaired of him at times. In the meantime Louise's pregnancy was continuing and Gil had moved in with Louise. We hoped her baby would be born in the summer vacation from university, and that she could continue her course, as we had agreed to look after the baby.

Lydia arrived on the 16th of September, which

coincided with Anne having a bad spell. She was re-admitted to the hospice, but we managed to get permission for Louise to come over from the maternity unit to see her sister just before Lydia was born. Our life continued at a hectic pace for a considerable time after this. Somehow Dr Wicks worked her magic once again and Anne recovered enough to be allowed home once more. The next cloud on the horizon was that Kevin had applied for and been offered a job in the court in Belfast as a social worker with the responsibility of deciding whether children in care should be able to return to their parents or vice versa (no comment!) When Anne told us about this we were flabbergasted, in view of her condition, and advised her that she should not agree to the sale of their house.

One day he took Fiona and Catherine up to the Park Hall country park in Weston Coyney and offered them all manner of things they would be able to have if they agreed to a move to Belfast, and of course after several hours of his incessant haranguing they reluctantly agreed. We pointed out that such a move was against all her doctor's advice and Kevin's rejoinder was that in any case the Northern Ireland hospice was far superior to ours at Stoke.

By this time we were well into our daily routine of going round to Louise each weekday, and Barbara would attend to Lydia while I transported Louise to University. Then I returned and took Cassie for a run in a nearby green field area while Barbara was either washing up or tidying up the house. Finally we would return to home with Lydia. She was yet again another beautiful baby. She loved her routine and came on in leaps and bounds, and would often stay overnight with us if it worked out better that way.

The children were all doing well at St Peter's school. Jasmine was now Head Girl and she and Catherine were in the same class. Fiona had expressed a desire to change schools and had left Sandon High for Blythe Bridge High. She was really a bright intelligent girl, but she was in constant conflict with her father, because she thought he wasn't treating her mother the way he should when she was so ill. Having said that, Fiona did little or nothing to alleviate her mother's plight by helping out whenever she could. As a young woman she was perfectly capable of taking a lot of the load, but because Anne had always done everything for Kevin and the girls she probably didn't even think of helping with food and cleaning.

Things came to a head one Sunday afternoon when Fiona and her friend Natalie ran across from their house and burst into our house very distressed, saying that there had been an argument over which property they were going to buy in Ireland. They had been looking through the estate agents' brochures and Anne was very upset about Kevin's choice of house. We walked back with the girls as quickly as possible and Kevin greeted us with words to the effect that it was all a fuss about nothing. He then went on to say that Anne could choose which ever property she liked and he wouldn't mind - it was her choice!

How wrong that turned out to be. One night in November they called in to have a last meal with us and say goodbye, as they had the car all loaded up and were off to catch the overnight ferry to Ireland. We all were feeling down and depressed and Anne looked terrible, but it was up to Anne to make a stand, and she didn't. Needless to say the house was not the one of her choice and was completely unsuitable for someone in Anne's condition. Within a few weeks Anne was back in hospital again. Fortunately she had two good and staunch friends near where they were living in Carrickfergus, Roy and Jeanette Crowe, who were instrumental in finding Anne a place in the local hospice.

Whenever we rang up Kevin would say that Anne was fine, but Jeanette would tell us the truth. Anne soon endeared herself to most of the hospice staff and as we were to find out, they really were a wonderful bunch of people.

Our morning routine involved me taking Louise to university while leaving Barbara to tend to Lydia and tidy up the house until I returned and took Cassie for a run. This particular morning I was running on the green with Cassie, throwing her ball and trying to beat her to it, when I discovered I couldn't run uphill and felt I had none of my usual energy. I went to see my GP, who gave me a thorough examination. He said it looked like angina, but he was convinced that my heart was as sound as a bell. Just to be on the safe side he made me a hospital appointment to go on the treadmill, which would definitely show if it was Angina. The following week I was on the treadmill only a couple of minutes when I said enough. The graphs showed that I was urgently in need of a bypass operation, but I was informed that the waiting list was at least a year. I didn't like jumping the system, but I couldn't afford to be out of action, so I called on my Civil Service Benenden Healthcare and they arranged for me to see a consultant, Mr Obed, very quickly. He had a pretty full list but said he hoped he could fit me in before long.

I received a call to go for my pre-op assessment in mid March, then a few days later I was told my op would be on Friday 26th, but then I had a phone call from the ward asking me to come that evening, Tuesday the 23rd. This set a few alarm bells ringing, but Paul took me down about 9 pm and I was settled in put on a nebuliser straight away as Mr Obed had been unhappy about my breathing and wanted it improving before he operated.

Some urgent cases came in while I was waiting, so they apologised and told me my turn would come on Sunday. This was Barbara's birthday, so she spent the whole of her birthday at the hospital and surprisingly enough was able to watch me most of the time and converse with the specialist nurse who was assigned solely to me while I was in the High Dependency Unit. It seemed the nurse had tried several times to take away my breathing attachment and make me breathe on my own, but each time I resisted. It was about 11 pm then and Barbara had been there all day, so my nurse asked her to ring about midnight and she'd let her know how I was at that time. When she rang she was told that all was well and I was now breathing on my own, marking the end of a memorable birthday!

The day after the op I was moved into the intensive care area and Mr Obed came to see me. He told me he had hoped to perform my op without putting me on the breathing machine, but when I asked him if he had managed this he said no, it had got tricky so he had had to put me on the machine. The next day I was moved into the cardiac ward and quite a lot of family and friends visited me. I seemed to be making a good recovery. The yardstick for being discharged was to have your stitches removed and to be able to walk around a certain route within the hospital, including a flight of stairs, and I think I accomplished this by my fifth day, so all that remained was for them to say my stitches could be removed.

On the Friday night I had a minor catastrophe when I fell out of bed. Although I was right by the nurses' station and they looked through the ward door window at the sleeping patients quite often, they obviously couldn't see me lying below my bed. After about an hour I struggled to my feet and managed to climb back into bed. I was worried that I might have messed up some of the stitches in my legs where they had taken the veins for my bypass, but all was well.

A few days later, when I had my stitches removed, the nurse told me that the tests showed that when I had been admitted I had been recovering from flu, so I am amazed that they admitted me. Bev, Paul and Barbara came to take me home and I was very pleased to be home again. Doctors, nurses and the ancillary staff were all outstanding in their attitude and work ethic, creating a lovely atmosphere.

One evening in early February we were having one of our weekly house group meetings when Beverly phoned us from the maternity unit to ask us all to pray, because Gemma was in great pain and the midwife and doctor were undecided what to do, as it was proving a very difficult birth. Needless to say we did some ardent praying and later we had a call thanking us for our prayers and to let us know that Gemma had to have a Caesarian but all was well, and she and Terry now had a lovely baby girl, who they were going to name Eve.

The next morning we had a letter from Jim, one of the nurses at the hospice, writing on Anne's behalf to ask us if we could go over to Belfast and stay a few days. He told us that the previous evening there had been an altercation which had led to Kevin storming out of the hospice, leaving Fiona and Catherine there, and the hospice had let them sleep there for the night. We rang Jim and said we would try and get a flight the next day and he promised that one of the hospice staff would meet us. We found it very difficult to get a flight at short notice, but eventually we managed to get a British

Airways flight from Manchester to Belfast City Airport, which meant we had to be at Manchester at 5 am to check in. Fortunately our good friend Alan Rhead stepped in and picked us up from our house at 4 am and duly deposited us at the airport with plenty of time to spare.

The previous evening we drove to the hospital to see Gemma and our first great grandchild Eve, yet another lovely baby, and we were able to take a few photographs with us to give to Anne. The weather that night was atrocious, with torrential rain and a howling gale, and we were soaked just getting from the hospital car park. The weather didn't improve for our flight, which was extremely bumpy, and lots of people were using their sick bags, including Barbara. After we had checked in at the airport and retrieved our luggage, a young lady approached us. She had guessed that we were Anne's parents and said she would take us to the hospice or to our hotel first to freshen up. Unfortunately Barbara was feeling wretched and was sick in the car, which was a nice saloon belonging to her mother. We apologised profusely and said we had better be dropped off at our hotel first to give Barbara time to recover and to tell Anne we would be over to see her later on.

It is very rare for Barbara to give in to sickness, but that night she felt so terrible she just had to lie on her bed. She told me I must tell Anne how sorry she was and that she would be over to see her the next day. It was still wet and windy, but I had a good idea where the hospice was and had been given directions by the hotel reception. I fancied a walk to clear my head, and about half an hour later I was entering the hospice. Needless to say Anne looked terrible, and she was constantly apologising for us having to come over to Belfast instead of taking our advice and remaining near us with friends and family.

Kevin had apparently calmed down now and the girls were back at home with him. Anne told me that the hospice had arranged a Sunday lunch for us and the family in a private room in the hospice and Kevin would be coming along with the girls. When I returned to the hotel Barbara was slightly better but was unable to leave her bed for long without feeling sick. To top it all there was a Valentine's Night ball at the hotel and we seemed to be immediately above the function room. It was 1 am before it ended.

Barbara felt much better the next morning and we arrived at the hospice about ten. Anne had so much to tell us and said she had written down lots of the things she wanted done when she had gone. She had also given copies of her wishes to the hospice, so there should be no misunderstanding. Anne said she would like us to accompany her to the hospice chapel, where we met one of the hospice chaplains, a lady whom we came to know quite well in the next few weeks.

When time came for Sunday lunch, which was set out for us in a private room, it seemed an age before Kevin arrived with the girls. His trait for being late was one which we were well used to, but was annoying just the same. We were served a beautiful traditional Sunday lunch, though Anne of course was not up to eating very much. Catherine seemed very subdued, but Fiona was still firing on all cylinders and was dying to tell us about the circumstances which had led to them having to spend the night at the hospice the previous week, when Kevin had stormed off and left them. Anne had already told us her version of the event, but Fiona of course embellished the story.

During the week that followed we met all the doctors and most of the staff. We were told what we already knew - that Anne had only a few weeks left, but that they would do everything they knew to make her comfortable and pain free during the time she had remaining.

Those next few weeks were a bit of a blur. We travelled to Ireland and back several times and during that time Beverly, Louise and Richard all came to see Anne in the hospice and quite a bit of reminiscing went on between them. On our second visit Kevin wanted us to go to the Sunday morning service at his church, so we agreed. Several people came up to say hello and asked us if we were enjoying our holiday in Ireland, and were quite shocked when we told them we were there to visit our daughter, who was terminally ill in the hospice. Beverly accompanied us on our second visit and we stayed together in a quaint bed-and-breakfast place where you had to go next door for your breakfast, but it was clean and the hospitality was good, and it was within walking distance of the hospice.

It was during these last few weeks of her life that Anne had painstakingly written out her wishes for when she passed away. She wanted her service at St Andrews, her choice of hymns, and to be buried in Caverswall. She also stipulated that Catherine should come over to stay with us on all the major school holidays. She thought Fiona could make her own decisions because she was now eighteen. Unfortunately Kevin found this list of her wishes in her bible at the hospice and took it away, saying she lacked faith that she would get better. After this, in her weakened state, she rewrote all her wishes and gave a copy to the hospice so that there would be no ambiguity about what she wanted.

Shortly after this Kevin arranged for the pastor of his church, Cecil, his wife, Elizabeth, his assistant and one or two leading members of his church to come to the hospice and pray for a complete recovery around her bedside. We knew that prayer had brought Anne back from the brink several times during the last few years but we were now resigned to the fact that she couldn't last much longer. The third time we returned to Ireland we had previously had a phone call from the hospice saying they knew how expensive it must be for us in bed and breakfast and suggested that we might like to stay in the new children's hospice a couple of miles away. This included rooms where parents could stay with their children while they were patients, or just for respite purposes.

This was a wonderful offer and the accommodation was first class. We had a communal kitchen and it made those last few weeks so much easier. We were able to get a bus from there to the hospice and back there every night. Most evenings Kevin dropped the girls off at the hospice and Catherine would usually sit by her mother's bed and do her homework. Often we would take them both out for a meal at some nearby eating place. Fiona decided to return to Stoke, probably in response to the pull of a much older boyfriend she had acquired called Adam. Less than two weeks later she borrowed money from Gil and returned to Ireland with her friend Natalie, perhaps because she had misgivings about leaving her mother, but she negated any misgivings by returning to the UK on the Saturday before her mother died.

Anne was now eating little or nothing, so Catherine and I walked out to try and find something she might fancy and returned with a small tray of custards we had found in the local Iceland shop. We gave Anne one to try and she ate every morsel and said how she had enjoyed it, so we put the other three cartons in the fridge and hoped she might eat the others later. On the Saturday we knew the end was near, so we arranged to stay at the hospice. Barbara was going to stay with Anne that night and I was going to stay with her on the Sunday night. Anne was weak but very lucid, and constantly reproached herself for agreeing to go to Ireland even though we assured her it didn't matter.

When Sunday dawned Kevin made a brief

appearance to drop Catherine off and then went on to his church. I believe he was supposed to be preaching that day, but he didn't return until early evening. Later that afternoon Barbara and Catherine were trying to make Anne more comfortable by sitting her up further in her bed, but she was obviously becoming very distressed and it seemed she couldn't breathe. She gasped to us to call Jim, who came straight away and she said to him "Help me!". he called the doctor, who said that he wanted her to understand that if he gave her the injection that would help her she would no longer be able to talk to any of us. She nodded, but she was obviously so frightened of not being able to breathe and was almost choking. He explained to us that this would ease things for her, but she only had a few hours left.

All we wanted was for Anne to be out of her distress, and a few minutes afterwards she appeared to be much more peaceful. Roy and Jeanette then arrived, and a few minutes later Deidre, another old friend, appeared. She was very distressed as she didn't realize that Anne was almost at the end.

It was another hour before Kevin made an appearance. He said he had been busy ringing people up. Catherine, Barbara and I sat around Anne's bed talking to her, because for all we knew she could still hear us and we reassured her that all her wishes would be carried out, that Catherine would come and stay with us every school holiday until she had completed her GCEs and also that her funeral would be exactly as she had wanted it to be with a service at St Andrew's and burial in Caverswall. We told her she could now "go to Jesus, as everything will be taken care of just as you wish".

About a couple of hours later the nurse said she had gone. Of course, although we knew it was inevitable, we were all very distressed and tried to comfort each other. The lady hospice chaplain then arrived, a very pleasant lady who had already formed a good relationship with Anne and was aware of Anne's wishes. She had confirmed with Kevin that he would be adhering to all Anne's. Barbara was still trying to comfort Catherine, and they stood together sobbing with their arms around each other.

When Kevin returned from seeing Anne in the chapel of rest he made an amazing statement. He said: "This morning I was married and in debt. Now I am no longer married and I have plenty of money!" We were all flabbergasted. Was he in shock, or did he mean it?

We returned to the children's hospice in the early hours and pondered over his amazing statement. Eventually we dropped off to sleep. Early next morning we had a visitor; it was Elizabeth, the assistant pastor at Kevin's church. She said she was so sorry but when she and Cecil and other senior members of the church had visited the hospice to pray for Anne's healing, they had not realized that her condition was terminal and had so little time left. They said Kevin had misled them all about how serious her condition was at that time.

We finished making our phone calls to friends and

relations to tell them the sad news, and made arrangements to return home the next day. We visited the hospice on Monday morning and thanked as many people as possible for all the care and love they had lavished on Anne and indeed on all of us, as they had been truly wonderful. The days leading up to Anne's funeral were a bit of a blur, but we were absolutely inundated with phone calls, sympathy cards and letters of condolence. The ladies of our church insisted on doing the catering and we hired the village hall, as we knew there would be an awful lot of people from all over the country who would be attending as well as our own friends and relations.

Needless to say the church was packed, and so many people wanted to come up and say how Anne had touched their lives. I must admit we thought one or two went on a little too long, but it was a wonderful service. There was a touching tribute from Roy and Jeanette, who asked me to read it out, but it was far too emotional for me that day and our friend Terry Bagguley read it out to the congregation. Our vicar, Steve Osbourne, took the service and I'm sure he allowed us quite a lot of leeway, as it wasn't quite an orthodox Church of England funeral service and it went on for quite a while.

Catherine eventually returned to Ireland to complete her exams, and in spite of all the turmoil she had suffered she managed to obtain good GCEs and Kevin allowed her to come to us each holiday. During the summer she decided she would like to take a course in child development at Blythe Bridge High, which was the equivalent of two A levels, and it was further decided that she should live with Beverly and Paul during the week and come to us on the Friday until she returned to school on the Monday morning when I dropped her off at school, which was a relatively short distance for her to walk home to Bev's house. We continued this arrangement for the next two years, but now Catherine usually went to visit her father and I became very familiar with the run to the East Midlands Airport. during the school holidays.

My brother Tom was not very well when he attended Anne's funeral. We knew he had been diagnosed with terminal cancer and probably hadn't a lot of time left, but you would never have thought so from his attitude to life and he was the life and soul of his hospital ward when he was admitted a few months later. I suspect he was too much of a joker for some of his fellow patients, but that was the way he was, and most people enjoyed his wit and repartee.

We had also suspected that Tom's wife Irene was not well. She too was diagnosed with cancer and entered a hospice while Tom was in hospital. We were informed that Tom only had a few days left. We went to see him in hospital, but it seemed too late, as he was on a life support machine and a mere shadow of his former self. Barbara and I talked to him as if he could hear all we were saying. As we said our goodbyes to him I said to him "You are not going to say 'wait for me' Jim." This was a phrase he always used when we were evacuated and I was running home at lunchtime. At this he stuck his arm up in the air and we knew he had been listening to us. Shortly after this they switched off his life support and he was pronounced dead.

Later that evening his daughter Lesley visited her mum Irene in the hospice and Irene said "Your dad has been to see me and told me everything is going to be all right" so of course they didn't tell her that Tom had already passed away. Because they knew Irene had only a few days left, Tom's funeral was held up for a couple of days and they then had a joint service. This was a sad yet joyous affair, with many of Tom's ex colleagues in the Fire Service attending. Many people had stories to tell about Tom and his exploits in the Fire Service, including one who said Tom had grabbed his wrists when he was falling from the top of a burning building. He had said to Tom "I've had it, you'll have to let me go". At this Tom said "If you go can I have your watch?" With that he promptly hauled him up.

We later travelled with Mark and Lesley to the cemetery at Grimsby to have the ashes buried. Many of Tom and Irene's friends and relatives who hadn't been able to attend their funeral were crowded into the little chapel in the cemetery and had another farewell service, which I did my best to conduct. We even had a few hymns with Peter Munnings playing the organ. It was quite a memorable little service. It revived memories of Chris, Thora's son, such a handsome young man, who had died of a brain tumour only a few years previously, and of course my sister Val, who had died of cancer while Kevin and Anne were living with us in Bromsberrow Way.

Forgive me if there seem to be so many tales of death and cancer in this narrative, but I'm afraid that is how life is, as we all know only too well. There was a lovely celebration however when Rachel, Stephen and Sarah's daughter, married her fiancé Dan Perring. The reception was at the Barcelo hotel in Cheltenham and most of us stayed at the hotel. Catherine and Emily came with us and we had a wonderful weekend. Stephen and Jose came from Shanghai, where he was teaching, and brought Jacob and Jessica with them. They behaved impeccably, but fell asleep on chairs later on in the evening. Stephen gave a brilliant speech and a good time was had by all.

I think the time has come for me to close this narrative after giving you a brief synopsis of the how things are in the Ryan family at the moment, in May 2012. In July Fiona will be receiving her nursing degree and has already started work at the University Hospital here in Stoke. Catherine has moved in with her partner Carl here in Stoke, in a joint ownership house, and they are hoping to get married in the not too distant future. Louise and Gil are still soldiering on in a house which sometimes contains Jasmine and boyfriend Joe, Alex and his girlfriend Jess, Emily and occasionally her boyfriend, another Joe, and of course our beloved Lydia, who will be nine in September and living in that household thinks she is a teenager already.

Jasmine will also be receiving her degree in July, and she hopes to be able to obtain a position teaching drama, but she is so versatile that we are sure she will succeed in whatever job she takes. After a sustained period of what we can only call 'messing about', Alex is taking a law degree, a long and arduous course. It remains to be seen whether he will complete it, but he is a clever lad and should succeed in anything he really turns his mind to.

As for Emily, she is due to begin a university course in September, a three-year degree course in Social Work. She is another one like her mother, Louise, with lots of empathy, which can sometimes be a great asset in that job but can sometimes be a hindrance.

After sojourns in Cyprus, Spain and China, Stephen is now living back in Cirencester. He has just had his sixtieth birthday and he and Jose now have her two children, another Jasmine and Jeremy, along with Jacob, Jessica and the recent arrival Josh. Jeremy and Jasmine are now seventeen and sixteen. It looks as though Stephen will have to carry on working for a considerable time yet, but they are a lovely family!

Richard is now in business as an arboriculturist in Hampshire. Luke is about to start a course at Merrist Wood in Surrey, but his will be a two-year course while his father did a three-year one. Whether he will go into business helping Richard we don't know yet.

Samantha, who has a great voice, is forecast to achieve As in her GCSEs. We have seen her in several productions in Haslemere, along with her sister Rebecca, a superb dancer, who is currently in the chorus of the West End show "Billy Elliot", so it is possible that she may have a promising career in this field - and she is only thirteen years old. Transporting her to London three days a week must put quite a strain on Richard and Alison, but they obviously think it is worth it.

Paul has now retired from the police and does a part-time job as a delivery driver for Tesco, while Bev still works for Tesco at weekends, as she has done for the past seventeen years. Daniel, our eldest grandchild, has a very good job working for Vodafone and has worked in India and Cairo. He had recently taken up a new post with them, which should offer excellent prospects for further advancement in the company. He will be 35 in August, but is as yet unmarried, though his latest girlfriend, Kate, seems a very nice girl.

Gemma, his sister, is married to Terry and they have two lovely little girls, Eve and Phoebe. Gemma works for Npower, thanks to Bev helping out with the looking after the girls. Needless to say she dotes on them.

Barbara and I were blessed this time last year when we celebrated our diamond wedding. We had a celebration at the North Staffs Hotel here in Stoke, attended by friends and family from many different places as well as church friends from here at St

Andrews. It was a wonderful evening and we even had the pleasure of the company of our latest great-granddaughter Lexi, who was as good as gold at less than six weeks old. Rachel and Dan stayed with us that night and she continued her good behaviour - not a single cry all night. On the Sunday we renewed our wedding vows in church to end a very memorable weekend.

Incidentally most of the organization for this event was carried out by our granddaughter Jasmine, with some assistance from her boyfriend Joe, and they made a superb job of it. My sister Thora and her husband Peter are now living in Grimsby, as is her daughter Tina and their grandson Sam.

Their other daughter Lisa is currently residing in China with her husband Soren - they are missionaries. I feel I must give you a brief account of how they met. About ten years or so ago Lisa was in an unhappy partnership and had a daughter, Abigail. Lisa was a senior sister in a mental hospital when she felt that the Lord wanted her to go to Israel, and the call was so strong she felt compelled to obey it. Off she went with Abigail and found her way to the Baptist Church in Jerusalem. The minister, Pastor John, took them in, and it was there she met Soren, who was always on the door welcoming people in. He was a Dane who had also felt a strong calling to work for the Lord. When they contemplated marriage he warned Lisa that he had no money and that he really wanted to be a missionary in China. He told

Lisa that if she agreed to marry him that was all she had to look forward to. They were married in Jerusalem and Thora and Peter went out to their wedding. Later they went to Denmark to meet Soren's parents and with sponsorship, I believe, from the Danish church, they set off to Katmandu in Nepal. They stayed for a while and set up a shelter for the street boys before returning to Denmark, where Soren worked as an electrician until they had sufficient money to go to China.

For some unknown reason they went to the province of Hunan in the north west of China. Soren then had the difficult task of learning Mandarin to enable him to communicate with the local people. Lisa and Soren now work under the auspices of the Vineyard church and have done amazing work with the street girls, rescuing them from prostitution. They have set up a small jewellery factory and are currently selling their products in various countries. Every six months or so Soren flies back to Katmandu to oversee the hostel for the street boys. Usa has also been working in Shanghai on a similar mission. They now have two more children, Israel and Nativia, and Abigail is studying at the University in Copenhagen.

One more amazing coincidence was that Soren found in the local graveyard the grave of his mother's aunt, who was also a missionary and had died there, the place where Soren had been drawn to for so many years. Soren was completely unaware that his great aunt had been a missionary in China. The Lord moves in mysterious ways!

Though we no longer run a house group, we remain firm friends with all the ex-members, particularly Michael and Geraldine Emery, Terry and Yvonne Bagguley, Jean and Alan Rhead, Jacquie Oakes, Ruth and Nigel Macdonald, Bob and Carol Yeomans, among so many church friends. Our vicar, Steve Osbourne, is currently having a hard time healthwise, but he can always be relied upon, as can our dear friends Mary and Bert Poole.

My brother Terry and his wife Wendy are still living near Grimsby. They are a close-knit family and we see them when we can. This was relatively easy when Barbara's sister Jean was alive, but unfortunately she died early this year, almost a year after her second husband Norman, who had been her carer, passed away in sad circumstances. As we always made several visits a year to see them it was relatively easy to see my side of the family at the same time.

As I rapidly approach my 86th year I feel it would be tempting providence to prolong this narrative any longer, as the Lord may well consider that Barbara and I have had our share of blessings.

Last November we made a trip to Bexhill-on-Sea for the golden wedding of Barbara's sister Norma and her husband Royston. It was a truly joyous occasion, with a sub-tropical weekend of wonderful weather. We travelled with Gil, Louise and Lydia, and on the journey home we called in to Liphook in Hampshire and had a pub lunch with Richard and Alison and family to crown a truly memorable weekend; the last recollection I shall record in these memoirs, and one of the happiest.